GW00643210

FROM
NIGHT FLAK
TO HIJACK

FROM NIGHT FLAK TO HIJACK

IT'S A SMALL WORLD

CAPTAIN REGINALD LEVY DFC

EDITED BY

ALEX L. SCHIPHORST

The History Press

First published 2015

The History Press
The Mill, Brimscombe Port
Stroud, Gloucestershire, GL5 2QG
www.thehistorypress.co.uk

© Captain Reginald Levy DFC, Edited by Alex L. Schiphorst, 2015

The right of Captain Reginald Levy DFC to be identified as the Author
of this work has been asserted in accordance with the
Copyright, Designs and Patents Act 1988.

All rights reserved. No part of this book may be reprinted
or reproduced or utilised in any form or by any electronic,
mechanical or other means, now known or hereafter invented,
including photocopying and recording, or in any information
storage or retrieval system, without the permission in writing
from the Publishers.

British Library Cataloguing in Publication Data.
A catalogue record for this book is available from the British Library.

ISBN 978 0 7509 6104 2

Typesetting and origination by The History Press
Printed in Great Britain

Contents

MY STORY

This narrative was started in New York, in September 1982, when I was there on a shopping trip after I had retired. It is an attempt to leave, primarily for my grandchildren, a record of times that have thankfully in many ways changed out of all recognition.

I have not stressed the hardship and privation that we endured, particularly during the war years, nor have I been able to pay sufficient tribute to the courage and support of my wife, Dora.

I hope that none of you who read this will ever have to go through the trials and tribulations of raising small children in one small room, sharing a kitchen and bathroom with the landlady and her family, often with only an outside toilet, no heating, very short of money and at one's wits' end trying to scrape a meal for nothing.

I had a very glamorous life, but it was not so glamorous at the beginning and no words that I can put here will ever tell you how much I owe to Dora.

Time plays funny tricks with memory. If I were asked what regrets I have I would reply, 'Oh if only I had kept a diary.' That is the only advice I give to you. Put it down on paper and take care of it.

CHAPTER ONE

I was born in Portsmouth on 8 May 1922. At a very early age, certainly before I was two, we moved to Liverpool where we lived for a while in the house of my father's mother.

My father, Cyril, who was Jewish, had met my mother in Edinburgh, while she was visiting her elder brothers. My father was in Edinburgh on business for his father. My mother was sixteen and certainly not Jewish but it was love at first sight and they were married in Edinburgh after she had converted to Judaism.

I was born when she was seventeen. My father was twenty-one when he married and I was the same age when I married and so was my eldest son, Peter.

The house in Liverpool was a lovely Edwardian one in the then fashionable quarter of Bedford Street, just off Abercrombie Square, to which we had our own key to enjoy the beautiful gardens in privacy. The house, No 76, was a child's paradise having dozens of rooms in which to play 'Hide and Seek'. There was a real 'Upstairs, Downstairs' with a huge kitchen, scullery, larder, and servants' quarters. Upstairs were a big billiard room, cloakrooms, parlour, dining room, and lounge.

My paternal grandfather, Louis, was a successful businessman although he once turned down the offer of financing another

Liverpool man who came to him with the idea of opening one or two tea shops. 'It will never catch on,' said my grandfather, so Joe Lyons went on to do very well with someone else!

Living with us at Bedford Street was the second youngest of my father's family, my Auntie Muriel, who was a pioneer of radio. She was already famous as 'Auntie Muriel' of the *Children's Hour* broadcast every day at 5.15 p.m. She was a prolific writer of children's stories and had her own page in the *Liverpool Echo*. She was a scriptwriter for the *Toytown* series and played the part of Larry the Lamb in many of the *Toytown* episodes and partnered Doris Hare ('Aunty Doris') in radio skits.

Also living with us at Bedford Street was the youngest brother, my Uncle Stuart who eventually became a very successful film producer and partnered Nat Cohen in Anglo-Amalgamated Films Ltd, which became famous for the *Carry On* series.

My father was given the job of managing the 'Scala' cinema on Argyle Street in nearby Birkenhead. His Uncle Alf was a Liverpool councillor and owned the cinema together with the Liverpool 'Scala' and 'Futurist' on Lime Street, Liverpool.

We were, by now, living in another big house at 42 Hamilton Square, Birkenhead, which my mother promptly opened as a café/restaurant called Nan's Café. Even living in Birkenhead, I attended my father's old school, the Liverpool Institute, later to become the school of Paul McCartney amongst other famous old boys.

There was a Preparatory section of the Liverpool Institute in which I was enrolled and I used to take the ferry to Liverpool. This was an economy measure as the fare was only a penny as opposed to threepence on the much faster Underground. I was given the fare for the tram from the Pier Head to school but would very often walk, if I was early enough, and pocket the money with a gentleman's agreement from my parents. The Mersey Tunnel was not to open for another three years and I was to benefit from a school holiday to watch King George V and Queen Mary open it in 1934. Not that it would have helped me had it been open as it was only for cars.

Around this time, my father was offered the 'Plaza' Cinema, in Manchester Square, Blackpool. So we moved to a semi-detached house at 29 Horncliffe Road, South Shore and I started at the Blackpool Grammar School. These were happy days. I had a brand new bicycle, a Royal Enfield costing £3.19s on which I used to cycle the not inconsiderable distance to school every day, even coming home for lunch.

I, like most boys, was fascinated with aeroplanes. Even in 1935 people would run out of the house if one were heard overhead. I remember seeing the Graf Zeppelin flying over Blackpool Tower on its way to Barrow-in-Furness where the Naval Yards were only too visible from the skies.

My heroes were Sir Alan Cobham and Captain Barnard whose flying circuses toured Britain. I was a horrified witness to the disaster when the passenger-carrying formation flight from Captain Barnard's Circus collided over Central Station and plunged into the town. There were few survivors and yet, thirty or more years later at a dinner party at our house in Brussels, I would recall the event only to hear the amazed comment from one of my greatest friends, Gordon Burch, an Air Traffic Controller with Eurocontrol, that his father had given him the 7/6d fare to be a passenger on the flight and that he had seen the whole incident and had been in the one aircraft that had managed to land safely.

My own experience with aeroplanes began when I was given a Warneford stick model aeroplane which actually flew. My father and I took it down on the sands, wound up the elastic then hand launched it. It soared up to about 20ft, turned and flew, beautifully, out to sea, never to be seen again. Then came the splendid Frog models; an ingenious and well-made monoplane which came in a winder box with instructions to lubricate the elastic with banana oil which could be purchased at an expensive shilling extra. How lovingly that was applied and how well the Frog flew.

Aeroplanes were always well-featured in the so-called Penny Dreadful comics that actually cost twopence. At least one came out every day and there were always free gifts including catapult-launched gliders which actually flew very well and could be made to 'loop the loop'.

As I remember, there was the *Adventure* on Monday, the *Wizard* on Tuesday, the *Gem* on Wednesday, the *Rover* and the *Champion* on Thursday. Saturday brought my favourite, the *Magnet* and also, years ahead of its time, *Modern Boy*. The *Hotspur* with all its different types of school stories came later but soon caught up with its many rivals. Even then there was 'flak' from people who said that the stories were too lurid and encouraged violence. There was no television to blame in those days. Also, reading too much would 'strain' your eyes but despite this I was and am blessed with wonderful eyesight and am still an avid reader. I am grateful to the wonderful free library service which I used all the time as a boy and I must have read every Percy F. Westerman novel ever published.

I left school at fifteen years of age. English, particularly elocution, and French were the only subjects I was any good at. Maths were terrible and I loathed them, and Science. I hated school, mainly because of the rampant anti-Semitism that reigned in that era, particularly in Liverpool. I was small for my age and was bullied, particularly in Liverpool.

I went on to find a variety of jobs including a grocery assistant at 'Blowers' at Abingdon Street Market, darkroom assistant at 'Valette Studios' in Bank Hey Street, and general factotum at a photographic developers, Hepworth's D&P Studios in Catherine Street. On my first day, I walked into a very dark room so switched the lights on. About sixty puzzled customers were later told that their films 'hadn't come out'. Despite the inauspicious start I enjoyed working there and learned the whole procedure of developing, printing, enlarging etc. which I have never forgotten.

I had always had a good singing voice and was one of the 'Sisters and the Cousins and the Aunts' in *H.M.S. Pinafore*, complete with crinoline and bonnet, at the Liverpool Institute, which boasted a full-size stage and auditorium in the school hall. One day, when about 14 and before my voice had broken, I entered for *Opportunity Knocks*, then called simply, *Hughie Green and his Gang* and run by the child prodigy who was then about seventeen. He was starring at Blackpool's famous old music hall, Feldman's Theatre. I sang 'Marta, Rambling Rose of the Wildwood', the signature tune of Arthur Tracy, the 'Street Singer', a famous radio and music hall star of that time. To my amazement I won my heat and had to come back for the Final on the Saturday night. The judging was by audience applause and I was thrilled to hear the noise that acclaimed my effort. I won the first prize of £5 which bought me a new bike and I was convinced that my future was on the stage. The strange thing was that Hughie Green also went on to become a pilot during the war that was so close. He was a ferry pilot bringing much needed aircraft from the US to Britain. I never met him again but would have loved to have done so to recall those days.

I was a very keen supporter of Blackpool Football Club, and loved playing in goal, but was at Blackpool Grammar, which was a rugby school and I loathed rugby. A typical Saturday then would be to play football for my local club, 'Streamline Taxis', at Stanley Park in the morning, then stand in the Boys' enclosure at Bloomfield Road to cheer on Blackpool. In the evening I would either be at the newly opened 'Marina Ice Drome' at the Pleasure Beach or be playing table-tennis for my club 'Blackpool Jewish'. I was quite good at this and was selected by the Lancashire Association to be trained for a season by the visiting World Champion, Victor Barna. He would put a sixpence on his side of the table and it was yours if you could hit it with a half volley return from one of his famous 'Barna flicks', a devastating backhand smash. With all this physical exercise I was always being told, 'you will overstrain yourself' but I wish I was as fit today as I was then.

Blackpool FC was managed by the great old Bolton and England inside-forward, Joe Smith. Clubs kept their managers for years then and Joe managed Blackpool from before the war until he was past seventy. I had the pleasure of flying him and the team back to

Manchester in the Fifties when I had joined Sabena. I introduced three of our children to him and the team, including the famous Stanley Matthews.

It was my pleasure and privilege, many years later, to meet up with Stanley Matthews, by then Sir Stanley, in South Africa where he went every year to coach underprivileged black footballers, and we became good friends. By coincidence, he was a Corporal in my father's office when my father had been stationed as an RAF Signals Officer in Blackpool during the war. My wife Dora and I went to a great dinner in honour of Stan in Johannesburg and it was wonderful to meet up with Scottish international centre-forward, little Jackie Mudie and the South African English international left-winger, Bill Perry, who scored the winning goal (from Matthew's copybook pass, of course) in the famous 'Matthews Final' of 1953. We also met Stan Mortensen several times during the war, as he was also in the RAF and was always good to me in providing excellent seats wherever they were playing.

Around 1936 the 'Plaza' was sold and my parents went into the boarding house business, buying or more probably renting 164 N. Promenade, which they named the 'Avalon'. It had about twelve bedrooms and was in a good position opposite the Hotel Metropole. As it was also next to a sweetshop and the 'Princess' Cinema, I was in my element, particularly as we had free tickets to the cinema due to Dad's association with the trade and the fact that we used to put up a poster in the hall showing what was on next door. It was a very good cinema and showed 'first run' films and I can remember the hullabaloo that went on when *Gone with the Wind* was shown there just before war broke out.

In the summer holidays I would get various jobs along the 'Golden Mile', though it wasn't called that then. It was just 'Luna Park' or Central Promenade. A lucrative job was acting as a 'stooge' for the operator of the fruit machines that were scattered along there. The fruit machines were arranged in a circle with the man in charge on a stand in the centre and when business was slack he would catch my eye and I would play the machines and he would ensure that I kept on winning until a crowd gathered around and I would walk away.

Among the many attractions all along the Central Promenade, the Rector of Stiffkey, in his barrel, and Dr Walford Brodie with his genuine American Electric Chair were popular, while Pablo's was *the* ice cream parlour and deservedly so. At the end of the season – and the day was never publicised – he would give away all his remaining stock. Somehow the word would spread around through a magic grapevine and schoolchildren from all over Blackpool could be seen running and cycling to the little back street behind the Winter Gardens where Joe Pablo would be sitting on the running board of his Rolls-Royce reading the *Daily Worker*.

About this time, Gracie Fields was making *Sing As We Go* in Blackpool and I was one of the lucky extras paid £2 per day to run behind a lorry, supposedly carrying Gracie waving back to us. In fact there was only a camera on board with the Director, Basil Dean, shouting, 'Come on, you buggers, wave, earn your bloody money.' I met Gracie when she was appearing at the Grand Theatre. I asked her, politely, for her autograph. 'Here you are, luv,' she said, and gave me sixpence for 'talking so lovely'.

CHAPTER TWO

When Neville Chamberlain made the sombre announcement on Sunday, 3 September 1939, that 'this country is now at war with Germany', I was seventeen and four months.

I had been working for some time as the office boy to a well-known firm of chartered accountants, Ivan G. Aspinall. God knows how I survived as my maths were still non-existent. Ivan G. was a distinguished looking gentleman, the double of Walter Connolly, an American film star of that time. Ivan was also a Director of Waller and Hartley's, the toffee makers, and it was always a pleasure to take documents up to the factory, behind Devonshire Square, where the factory girls would make a great fuss of me and load me with Milady toffees despite the rationing.

Conscription was now in full swing. The 'call up' age was twenty and you could be put into any of the Services, later even sent down the mines as a 'Bevin Boy'. You could, however, volunteer for flying duties in the RAF from the age of eighteen. This I did, causing such a row between my father and mother that he promptly followed suit and volunteered for the RAF even though he was over age. He was accepted, commissioned and became a Signals Officer for some time at Blackpool and later in the Middle East in Palestine and Egypt.

He was present at the famous Yalta Conference between Roosevelt, Churchill and Stalin.

I made my first ever visit to London to be interviewed by a Group Captain for flying duties. He tried to persuade me to become a Navigator (the RAF was already looking ahead even in 1940) but I was completely set on becoming a pilot and would have nothing else. In the end he gave in but warned me that I would have to wait a long time before I was actually called up. In the event I was called up four weeks later, enlisted as AC2 R. Levy 1380172 and sent to Cardington in Bedfordshire for my 'jabs' and kitting out. I was then sent to Bicester in Oxfordshire as an AC2 awaiting training and given 'ground duties', which were mainly latrine cleaning. There were about six of us and we arrived late at night but it was like daylight outside as it was the night that the Germans bombed Coventry.

Bicester was a bomber station of Bristol Blenheims and I became friendly with one of the pilots, also from Blackpool, Sergeant Hoggard. He told me that he was flying up to Squires Gate, the Blackpool RAF station, and would take me with him if I wanted. Did I! I was so naïve I didn't even get permission but just got into the cockpit of the old Avro 504 biplane and off we went. This was my first flight ever, some time around November 1940 and it was wonderful. I just had time for a quick tram ride to the Avalon to find it full of airmen as it had been 'commandeered' by the RAF. My mother was far from pleased with this and complained bitterly to the authorities that it was not 'proper' that she and my sister should be alone in a big house with so many 'licentious' airmen. The authorities agreed with her, removed the airmen and filled the Avalon with some thirty WAAFs as the Womens' Royal Air Force was then known. I wasn't grumbling but my mother was livid, as the airmen used to do all the heavy odd jobs and repairs around the place. The WAAFs though stayed until the end of the war.

I arrived back at Bicester only to find myself on a charge or 'fizzer' as it was known. 'Absent without leave' was the accusation but an understanding Flight Lieutenant dismissed it, then gave me six days 'jankers', which consisted of cleaning out the Sergeants' Mess latrines. I took great pleasure in using those latrines two years later when I visited Bicester as a fully fledged Sergeant Pilot.

Towards the end of December 1940 I found myself posted to Stratford-upon-Avon, which was a receiving centre for would-be pilots. I was billeted at the Shakespeare Hotel, which was very comfortable albeit I shared a double room with eleven others. After a couple of weeks of marching up and down Stratford and passing Anne Hathaway's cottage ten times a day I was posted to start my training proper at No 6 ITW (Initial Training Wing) Aberystwyth. This time I was billeted in the Marine Hotel, right on the freezing promenade. At Aberystwyth we had extensive courses in maths – still my bête noire – navigation, Morse and Aldis signalling, rifle and clay pigeon shooting, meteorology, aircraft recognition and of course hours and hours of 'square bashing'. We would have a big breakfast at six then meet on the promenade for half an hour of PT followed by a run up and down 'Constitution Hill', the huge mountain, or so it seemed, that lay at the end of the promenade.

We were also given extensive medical and dental check-ups. I remember the aged Welsh dentist (at least forty!) saying to me, 'I am too old to fly but I will make sure that you have your own teeth all of your life.'

At the end of six weeks and well into a freezing February we were 'passed out' as LAC (Leading Aircraftsman) u/t (under training) and were paid the princely sum of 6s 6d per day. It really was a lot of money as all our food and accommodation was paid for.

Because of the very severe winter of 1941, the British Flying Schools had ground to a halt so there was nowhere for us to go. We would breakfast at seven, report for PT and roll call at nine and then be dismissed for the day. The majority of us were aged between eighteen and nineteen so were already hungry again. We would go to one of the several cafés where a breakfast of two poached eggs on toast, chips, bacon and sausage could be had for tenpence. Rationing seemed to have bypassed North Wales although it must have come later.

Our ample leisure time was well catered for as the London University for Women had been evacuated to Aberystwyth. We were given leave and leave again and I spent more time in the Blackpool Tower Ballroom than on the parade ground.

Eventually, towards the end of March we were taken to a school hall in Aberystwyth and told that we were no longer to consider ourselves as being part of the RAF. It was explained to us (us being 'B' Flight) that we were being sent to an unnamed country that was 'neutral' and were being trained there, and that they, the neutral country, could not accept belligerents in uniform. Accordingly we were given £20 clothing allowance to buy 'civvies' suitable for a hot climate and sent off on a short overseas leave. We were issued railway warrants and told to report to Wilmslow, near Manchester, in a week's time. At Wilmslow we were issued with the heaviest grey flannel double-breasted jacket and trousers that had ever been made. To cap these bizarre items we were issued with old-fashioned pith helmet 'topees' complete with ear pockets for inserting radio ear pieces whilst flying. They had obviously lain in some storehouse since the 1920s when they would have been issued to the intrepid pilots of such aircraft as Wapitis, and Harts for use in the Middle East. With these in our kitbags, which must have weighed 55lb, we struggled along the road to the railway station where a train was waiting to take us on the long journey up to Greenock, near Glasgow.

Arriving there, one cold morning in May 1941, we found a large ship waiting at the dockside. Due to the wartime restrictions there was no name on the bow but, on boarding, we found out that she was the White Star liner, *Britannic*.

As an eight-year-old I had gone down to the Pier Head in Liverpool to watch the *Britannic* set out on her maiden voyage. I little knew then that eleven years later I, with 400 other cadets and a complement of 2,400 Air Force, Army and Navy personnel, would be standing on her decks waiting to start the biggest adventure of my life up to then.

We left Greenock escorted by the famous battleship *Rodney* and four destroyers. The size of the escort for one troopship was astonishing but the cargo was precious. On board was all that was necessary for setting up the pilot training scheme in the United States, to be called the Arnold Scheme, after its founder, General 'Hap' Arnold. This plan, of which we were the forerunners, was to train some 6,000 pilots for the RAF.

We were only two days out into the Atlantic when the *Rodney* and three of the destroyers left us. We cadets were pretty good at Aldis and as one destroyer left he signalled, 'Bismarck out. Knows your course and speed. Make full speed. Good luck.'

Full speed on the *Britannic* was about 28 knots and the Atlantic was quite rough. There were many of us, especially those in the crowded quarters of the bow and stern, who would not have minded too much if the *Bismarck* had caught up with us.

Then we heard of the dreadful loss of the *Hood* with only a handful of survivors and the news that our escort, *Rodney*, had finished off the *Bismarck* after she had been crippled by the gallant attacks from the old 'Stringbags' as the Fairey Swordfish torpedo-carrying biplanes were called.

We docked at Halifax, Nova Scotia, towards the end of May 1941. We were marched straight on to a waiting train, and we stayed on that train for nearly two days and nights before being disembarked on to a platform that stated this was the Manning Pool of Toronto. A huge figure of a man with the rank of Flight Sergeant in the RCAF stood before us. 'Get fell in, you horrible lot!' he screamed. We formed into a sweating, humid, weary, grey-flannelled blob. We were told to 'forward march' and were marched in to a large hall where tables were groaning with all the foods that we had forgotten existed. Steaks, chops, eggs, ham, bacon, butter; everything was there. The RSM's face broke into a thousand lines, wrinkles and cracks, which was the nearest he could get to a smile. From then on we were given the freedom of Toronto. We had now been issued RAF uniforms again to wear until we went on to the USA. We were the first RAF to be seen there and the sight of our uniform was sufficient to open up the doors of cinemas, restaurants and pubs. It was physically impossible to pay for anything. One day a friend and I decided to hitchhike to Niagara Falls. A car pulled up; the driver, a middle-aged man, asked us where we wanted to go and, on learning, told us to get in. He returned home where his wife and two very pretty daughters made up a picnic and we all drove over a hundred miles to see the Falls.

Another wonderful evening was when we were all invited to a dance where the great Louis Armstrong was playing. No one danced but we all stood in front of the orchestra and applauded; just like in the movies! It all had to end of course and after two wonderful weeks in Toronto we entrained for the long journey to our destination, Albany, Georgia.

CHAPTER THREE

Albany was a very small southern town and in 1942, still, at heart, part of the Confederacy that had seceded from the Union. The first thing that we learned was that 'damyankee' was just one word and not two. The accent, especially that of the girls, completely charmed us. The phone in the lounge mess would ring and we would very often hear, 'Are y'all a British boooy? Would y'all just tolk?' They were completely disbelieving when we told them that it was they who had the accent.

We learned how to fly and we learned the hard way. General Arnold had made it quite clear that we would follow the very tough itinerary prescribed for the US Army Air Corps, and that standards would not be relaxed despite the crying need for pilots in the UK. We got the full peacetime training, and very much later in my career, I said, over and over again, that I am alive because of that training and I am eternally grateful for it.

Of the 500 or so cadets who started training at the Southeast Training Center as it was known, only 120 of the class of 42A (the first class to graduate in 1942) were awarded the coveted silver wings. Many of those who were 'washed out' were sent to Canada to continue their training and were flying operationally in England long before we returned.

The school, run by civilian Instructors, but with army officers as Check Pilots and responsible for discipline, was based on the West Point system of Upperclassmen and the 'honour system'.

We, as the first class of British 'caydets' had an American class (41F) over us to administer discipline and the 'hazing' that was the way of life. There were many rigmaroles and set phrases to learn. At meals an Upperclassman would tell an unfortunate Lowerclassman. 'Take a square meal, Mister' and the poor underdog would have to bring his food to his mouth and insert it at right angles throughout the meal whilst sitting on the obligatory front 6in of the chair, which was all that we were allowed throughout our Lowerclassmen days.

Room inspection, always carried out by the Upperclass, involved the running of white silk gloves over cupboards, beds and floor. One speck of dust and a 'gig' was the result. A nickel (5 cents) would be thrown on your stretched-out blanket and it had to ripple. The sheet had to have just 6½in showing and this was measured carefully. So many 'gigs' and our only free time off camp from Saturday noon until Sunday 6 p.m. was curtailed by hours of marching in full dress uniform, sword and pack in a blazing Georgia sun and 100 per cent humidity.

There were several 're-mustered other trades'. Hard bitten corporals and sergeants who found the hazing very hard to take. To be told to, 'Take a brace, Mister' by some green college boy and made to stand with your chin and stomach tucked in was more than some of these veterans of the bombing of airfields such as Biggin Hill could take. 'Get stuffed' and 'Belt up' were some of the milder replies but they didn't see much of Albany during our six weeks of being the Lowerclass. The 'Special Relationship' wore a bit thin at times. There was a patriotic song at that time which began 'Off we go, into the wild blue yonder' and finished 'nothing will stop the Army Air Corps', to which the RAF lads would add 'except the weather', with the ensuing often bloody result.

The Commanding Officer was a West Pointer with absolutely no sense of humour. We nicknamed him the 'Boy Scout' because of the wide brimmed hat he wore. He never understood the British and despaired of us ever winning the war.

The compensation for the really tough going was the hospitality we received during our precious few free hours, from the citizens of Albany who took us, sometimes quite literally, to the bosom of the Deep South. We all tasted the fabulous Southern hospitality. I still have the memory of lush, warm evenings with the croaking of bullfrogs, the incessant noise of the crickets, the scent of magnolia blossom and the creaking of rocking chairs on Southern porches to remind me of the adolescence I spent there.

CHAPTER FOUR

Our day began at 5 a.m. with calisthenics, then the room had to be cleaned and left spotless. We were billeted two to a room with our own shower. Fabulous luxury compared to our RAF billets. The school had its own resident dietician, a new word to us. 'Miz' Tickner saw that we had the most fabulous meals I can ever remember eating in my entire life. We were bronzed from the sun, supremely fit and ready for anything.

Flying training always took place in the early morning before the relentless sun could bake the landing surface so hard that you would float for miles when trying to land, cushioned by the warm air rising off the ground.

The aircraft that we first flew in was the Stearman PT-17, made by Boeing and a wonderfully aerobatic aeroplane. It was a sturdy biplane but we were not allowed the luxury of any instruments as we were being taught to fly 'by the seat of your pants'. No airspeed indicator or altimeter. You quickly learned to judge your speed by the different sound of the airstream whistling through the struts and wires that held the wings together and estimated your height from the dwindling trees and figures beneath you.

My first Instructor was a very small man, the size of a jockey who had come to Darr Aero Tech, as the school was called, straight from Hollywood where he had been a stunt pilot featuring in such films as *Hell's Angels* and *The Dawn Patrol*. He was called Gunn and rejoiced in the nickname 'Kinky'. Although we had all passed our ground training at ITWs, mainly in seaside towns such as Torquay, Babbacombe, Newquay and Aberystwyth, few, if any of us had ever been near an aeroplane, let alone flown one. Kinky Gunn's initiation for his bunch of three pupils was to take us up – one by one – and throw that Stearman all over the sky until we couldn't tell the horizon from the sky or the ground. If you survived that without losing the fantastic breakfast you had just had then the battle of teaching you had begun. It started with some basic rules. 'There are old pilots and there are bold pilots,' he would say, 'but there are no old, bold pilots.' To the end of my long career I could never line up on a runway, after being cleared for take-off by Air Traffic Control, without a long hard look at the approach to check whether there was an aeroplane coming in to land. Pretty basic you might think but we had no radio at Darr, just a man who gave you a green light or a red and was human and so, fallible.

One of Kinky's favourite tricks was to 'buzz' the (out of bounds!) red light district of Albany on one of the very early training sessions. 'That'll shake them out of their beds,' he would yell over the slipstream as the wheels of our plane would scrape the roof. He must have been a good teacher, though, because we three were the very first pupils to solo after some seven hours of 'dual'.

I had made what I thought was rather a bumpy landing when the figure in the cockpit in front of me disappeared and there was Kinky, standing on the wing beside me. 'OK Reg,' he said, giving it the hard 'G' that was the American pronunciation of my name. 'Take her up and give me a nice landing,' and he was gone. I suspect that his heart was beating as loudly as mine. With the now lighter aircraft, I was airborne before I knew it. It was 28 June 1941 and I was nineteeen years and forty days old.

The thrill of that first time of being alone in an aeroplane and master of it, albeit a very timid and quivering master, remains with me to this day: forty-one years and 25,097 flying hours later. The tales of our adventures and misadventures were related that week over the ubiquitous Cokes. All flying schools in the US were dry and we were only allowed out at the weekend if we hadn't collected the dreaded 'walks'. The tales that we recounted were part of our relaxation and we would gather in the comfortable lounge after we had completed our homework from the extremely thorough ground courses we were being given.

One of our chaps, Ted Headington, later tragically killed at Advanced Flying School, had been sent for his first solo, and his Instructor, as was the custom, was standing in the centre of the field watching his pupil. As Ted was approaching he encountered a strong thermal current which turned him upside down at about 500ft. Ted continued the 'roll' and made a perfect landing to find his Instructor apoplectic with rage at Ted's disregard for safety in doing aerobatics and gave him enough 'gigs' to keep him at Darr for the rest of his time there.

As we became more proficient and as our confidence grew we were introduced to the thrill of aerobatics. Slow rolls, loops, lazy eights and spins (which I hated) were all taken in our stride although, even in those days, I began to feel the urge to fly big aeroplanes with lots of engines.

Like all American colleges, Darr Aero Tech encouraged their pupils to produce a class magazine. Ours was called *PEE TEE* (Primary Training) and a position on its editorial staff carried the privilege of being allowed into Albany, occasionally, to liaise with the printer and to find advertising from the many willing shopkeepers who loaded us with samples of their goods including a very nice record player. I had always been a very keen photographer and loved writing so I was appointed one of the editors. The magazine boasted the usual photographs of each class member with a brief biography, which make interesting reading today. I still have a copy of the original issue. The photographs were reminiscent of the Hollywood films in which my Instructor,

Kinky Gunn, had figured. Cloth helmets with goggles worn on the forehead and skilfully re-touched. Not that we had many wrinkles at that age!

Our sorties into Albany always took us to the only hotel, the Gordon. It had a downstairs lounge called the Clubroom where we were introduced to a lethal drink called a Zombie … strictly only two to a customer! Mint juleps were also very much in fashion but we were not heavy drinkers and Cokes were always the drink most in demand. After all we were only a few miles from where they were invented. There was a piano and one of our bunch, Joe Payne, used to astound the American cadets with his wonderful rendering of 'Honky Tonk Blues'.

The drugstore on the corner was another American institution that we loved and Lee's, in Albany, was our favourite. The pretty daughter of the Lee family who owned the store was the main attraction, but she broke many hearts by marrying a popular aerodynamics Instructor, 'CsubL' Clark, so called for his love of the phrase CsubL in explanation of the equation of Lift. We were introduced to banana splits, the like of which I have never tasted since and in the little restaurant next door, we were served sizzling T-bone steaks that really did sizzle as they were served on an iron platter at the special price of $2 to British cadets … $2.50 to everyone else.

The nearby Radium Springs, was our favourite swimming place with its restaurant and weekly 'Georgia Peach' competition. It was also noted for the iciest water that I have ever encountered in the world, including Alaska.

We were, by now, Upperclassmen ourselves to the new class of 42B, also British cadets but we were not able to bring ourselves to treat them as we had been treated by the American Upperclassmen and after a few half-hearted (and derisively greeted) efforts we gave up and settled down to completing our course of Primary training and proceeding to the next stage … Basic.

CHAPTER FIVE

Basic training was later cut out altogether and replaced by a much shorter course of just two stages, Primary and Advanced. As we were still doing the full peacetime training, we were given a wonderful two weeks leave in Florida at the expense of the US Government. There we first met the wonderful USO Servicemen's entertainment organisation. During that time I had the privilege of dancing with the beautiful Rita Hayworth; the orchestra was playing 'Amapola', and as I took that beautiful woman around the floor, I would not have changed places with anyone in the world. We were, however, soon Greyhound bussed to Macon, Georgia, to the Cochran Field Basic Training School, which was now under the US Army's control. There were no civilian Instructors, but rather fierce-looking Second and First Lieutenants (pronounced lootenant) with weird and exotic names. We also renewed acquaintance with our previous tormentors of Class 41H who had preceded us there.

Basic meant the Vultee BT-13A, a huge, or so it seemed to our Stearman-oriented eyes, underpowered, fixed undercarriage monoplane. I remember it as a brute of an aeroplane, heavy on the controls and very difficult in the aerobatics, which were always such an important part of the American training. The hours began to pile up and suddenly we were 'veterans' with over 100 hours.

At that time, our more unfortunate colleagues in England were flying against the enemy with only thirty or forty hours. At Cochran Field we were introduced to the pleasant practice of sending two cadets up together to practise their skills without the eagle eye of the Army Air Corps Officer on you all the time, and these flights were very much appreciated.

Towards the end of our Basic course the rumours spread that our Advanced and final training would take place back at our beloved Albany. Not at Darr Aero Tech but at the large military field named, in the American tradition of calling their airfields after Air Corps personnel, Turner Field. I never did find out who Lieutenant Turner was.

So now it was Turner Field and our first encounter with a 'real' aeroplane. The AT6 (Advanced Trainer) was already in use all over the world. It was, and still is, better known as the Harvard and was absolutely identifiable from a distance by its characteristic 'buzz' or high pitched drone caused, I was told by the knowledgeable, by the effect of its propeller tips nearing the speed of sound as they rotated. The Harvard had a retractable undercarriage (one more thing for us to remember!) and even looked like a fighting warplane. Its main disadvantage was a tail wheel which was partially steerable by the rudder pedals. If one was not extremely careful on landing, the whole aeroplane would suddenly make a complete 360 degrees turn which was very disconcerting, to say the least, was violently disliked by our officer Instructors and was a certainty to earn at least an hour's 'walking' at the weekend.

Georgia, from the air, was predominantly red from the characteristic colour of the red earth or clay, but there were plenty of good fields around that we used as practice grounds for forced landings. Your Instructor would suddenly cut the engine when you were at about 6,000ft and not expecting it, and woe betide you if you had to use the engine again before you put the aeroplane down in one of those fields. The fields had another use, however. It was fairly common to arrange with the current girlfriend to rendezvous at one of them and we would land and then take them for a 'spin' as we called it. The penalty for being caught was instant expulsion from the course, which only made the whole thing more savoury. A certain Irish corporal had made a date with his girlfriend at one of these fields but, unfortunately, got so excited about it that he forgot to put his wheels down and slid along on the belly of the aircraft in front of the startled girl who thought that he had done it to show off. His reflexes were fantastic, however. He grabbed the microphone and called up 'Mayday, Mayday,' the international call sign for an emergency. 'This is Army plane 100,' he said. 'My engine has cut and I am going to try and force land in ...' naming the field where he was sitting. Back came the reply from Turner Tower, as our home base was called. 'Keep a cool head, boy, and do not, repeat, do not put your wheels down.' This was standard practice in a real emergency to avoid tipping over if you landed on rough ground or in one of the many swamps. It also kept the landing distance shorter and only bent an easily replaceable propeller. Paddy actually got a 'green' endorsement in his logbook for outstanding airmanship. I don't know what his girlfriend gave him!

Another story that went into the 'line book' as it was called in the RAF (shooting a line was boasting of a personal feat) was when the Tower was trying to contact a plane with one of the cadets in it. 'Army plane five zero zero, this is Turner Tower. Are you receiving me?', was repeated several times without success. Eventually the Tower came up with 'Army plane five zero zero, is that you over the field? If you are receiving me waggle your wings.' Back came the reply in that clipped British accent that the Americans tried, vainly, to imitate. 'Turner Tower, this is Army plane five zero zero, if you are receiving me waggle your Tower.' That earned him a couple of hours 'walking'.

Another time the Tower was called by a British voice that said, 'Turner Tower, this is Army plane 100. I am out of petrol. What shall I do?' There was a flurry of words then one of the Instructors was hurriedly summoned to the microphone. 'OK Army plane 100.

Don't panic. Keep cool and calm. Put the nose in a gentle glide and look around. Try to find one of the emergency fields. What is your height and position?' The cool British voice sounded rather puzzled. 'I'm sitting here on the tarmac waiting for the petrol truck, Sir.' The 'Sir' didn't stop him from 'walking' most of the next weekend.

The hazing and the strict discipline that we had endured for all of 1941 were relaxed during the last few weeks of our course. We were all more at ease with ourselves in the air and could actually look forward to receiving the coveted silver wings. We even mixed with the class of 41H during our more frequent sorties in to Albany and actually learned the ingredients of the awesome Zombie served at the Cadet Clubroom at the Gordon Hotel: one third dark rum, two thirds white rum, a little apricot brandy, pineapple juice, papaya juice, lime juice, sugar. Shake well then serve with a splash of dark rum on top. Lethal!

We were to meet quite a few of the Americans in the pubs of Lincolnshire when they came over with the 'Mighty Eighth' Air Force in 1942–43.

December 7th 1941 was a Sunday. It was a bright sunny morning, and normally, we would have been lazing around, but this morning was special. The RAF was joining forces with the US Army Air Corps at the local football stadium. We were giving the Americans a demonstration of RAF drill which, although not up to Guards' standard, was still pretty good. The crisp, quick marching contrasted strongly with the more informal, and to us, sloppier style of the Americans and we were warmly applauded by the large crowd gathered there in the stadium.

We were standing there side by side with our American classmates with the Stars and Stripes and Union Jack fluttering together in the breeze when the PA system came alive. An emotional voice broke the news that the Japanese had attacked Pearl Harbor and consequently we were all in the war together.

The next few days, to us war-hardened veterans, bordered on panic. We were all confined to camp, and sirens would go off at all sorts of odd occasions. Security became almost paranoiac and heaven help you if you hadn't got the right password when challenged, as you frequently were. Gradually, however, things got back to normal and RAF uniforms miraculously appeared and were issued anew to us.

On 3 January 1942 we filed into the camp theatre to receive from the major general commanding the Southeast Training Centre, General Walter R. Weaver, the hard-earned solid silver wings of the US Army Air Corps. We proudly wore them on the right breast of our tunics with the RAF wings (issued to us by Stores) in their proper position on the left. Later, in the UK we were forbidden to wear the US wings – an order conveniently ignored by most of us.

We celebrated our new status as fully qualified pilots with a gigantic party on the airfield. Dates for the evening ball were presented with orchids and gardenias in true American movie style and we danced the night away to 'Amapola', 'You are my Sunshine', 'The Hut Sut Song', 'Frenesi', 'Elmer's Tune' and 'Green Eyes'. We finished, of course, with 'Off we go, into the wild blue yonder' with its traditional and provocative ending; but there were no Upperclassmen there to retaliate. The evening before the ball we had celebrated with some drinks with our Instructors. My very good and kind Instructor, Lieutenant Millar, handed me the keys of his car when the beer ran low and told me to go and get a couple of cases. 'But I can't drive,' I said. I was nineteen years old, could fly an aeroplane but had never driven a car.

Then it was a sad farewell to the still so peaceful South and back to face the harsh realities of wartime Britain.

CHAPTER SIX

We were soon shipped out of Georgia. I now had the rank of
Sergeant Pilot. Those lucky enough to be given commissions were
kept in the States to become Instructors. The US could never
understand the British method of non-commissioned pilots and
neither could I.

We travelled by train to Moncton in New Brunswick, Canada,
where we stayed a week or so before setting sail from Halifax, Nova
Scotia, in an old Dutch tramp ship, the *Vollendam*. It had already been
torpedoed and all but cut in half but had managed to reach port
where it was 'put together again'. One of our escorting destroyers
disappeared in front of our eyes the second day out, blown up by
a torpedo without a single survivor, but that was the only incident
and we landed back in Glasgow on a damp dismal day around
19 February 1942 where a train was waiting to take us the entire
length of England to Bournemouth where we had to wait until
April before passing to our various Operational Training Units or,
as in my case, a conversion course on to twin-engine aircraft.

The waiting in Bournemouth was not too hard as I was billeted in
a lovely block of flats that had been requisitioned for 'the duration'
as the phrase went. The block was called Bath Hill Court and we

were only two to a self-contained apartment earning 13*s* 6*d* per day with all our food and accommodation paid for.

We were also given a lot of leave and I returned to Blackpool to show off my stripes and wings to the thousands of new entries to the RAF who were doing their 'square-bashing' there.

The Avalon was still full of WAAFs, much to my mother's disgust and I did not endear myself to her by refusing to be paraded in front of all her Bridge Club cronies. My father, now a Flying Officer, was home on embarkation leave before being posted to Egypt. Eventually the good times had to come to an end and I was posted to Brize Norton in Oxfordshire for multi-engine training. Brize Norton was a small grass aerodrome and the aeroplane used for training was the appropriately named Oxford. It was a very versatile aircraft, not too easy to handle but an excellent training machine.

On the first day there I was introduced to my Instructor, Sergeant Holloway, also from Blackpool. 'How many hours have you got?' he said. 'Two hundred,' I replied. 'Oh well, I've got thirty-five so let's get stuck in,' he said. At the risk of being repetitious I must reiterate that I soon found out that the training I had received in the US was superb, probably the best available in the world at that time, and future courses and aeroplanes held few problems for me. True, we had to learn how to navigate as there were no Water Towers with town names on them. Even flying by 'Bradshaw' (reading the names on station platforms) was out, as all these, together with road signs, had been painted out for the duration in order to bamboozle possible German paratroops.

In July 1942 I was posted to No 17 OTU at Upwood, near Huntingdon, for Operational Training on Blenheims. Upwood was in 2 Group of Bomber Command and 2 Group were the specialists in low-level daytime attacks on shipping and special targets.

I soon found out that the Blenheim was a very awkward aeroplane to fly and even getting in and out of one was a nightmare. You had to climb up onto the wing and then lower yourself into the cockpit. This, in full flying gear of Irving jacket and flying boots together with parachute, was a feat in itself. The cockpit layout was a hideous mixture of sharp edges, knobs and levers with no logic or cohesion about them at all. After take-off you reached behind you with your left hand to change the pitch on your two-pitch propellers. Next to these levers were two identical ones that were the fuel shut-off valves to your engines! Enough said!

The Blenheim had been developed from a private venture 'Britain First' monoplane. Unfortunately, by 1942 it was outdated and outclassed by the German fighters which easily overtook its top speed of about 180mph (in a dive and with a following wind!). Casualties on the Blenheim squadrons were extremely high but once again, as I was to find throughout my career, my luck intervened.

We were sitting out at dispersal playing cards whilst waiting our turn to fly one sunny day, when there was a burst of machine-gun fire and a Junkers 88 flashed across the airfield at nought feet. We all dived under the table then burst out laughing as we saw that we had all grabbed our cards and money as well. The German had hit our crew room at the other side of the airfield killing three airmen. Later in the day the most fantastic airplane that I had ever seen also flashed across the airfield even lower than nought feet and much, much faster than the Junkers. Luckily we could see the roundels of the RAF and we realised that this was the new and already talked about Mosquito. It disappeared into cloud after performing an upward roll with one engine feathered and I knew that there would be no other aeroplane for me.

Thanks to finishing towards the top of my Operational Training at Upwood I was rewarded by a posting to 105 Squadron of 2 Group. They were based at Horsham St Faith, near Norwich and were commanded by the redoubtable Wing Commander 'Hughie' Edwards VC, DSO, DFC.

It was the first RAF Squadron to be equipped and to go into action with the Mark IV unarmed, light bomber version of the Mosquito. It was capable of carrying four 500lb bombs – the same bomb load as the American B-17 Flying Fortress, a four-engine aircraft with a seventeen-man crew. The Mosquito, made from wood by de Havilland with little or no government support, was developed from the Comet, the winner of the pre-war London to Melbourne air race, and was one of the finest aeroplanes to come out of the war and was certainly the most versatile.

The first squadron to have the privilege of operating on 'Mossies' was the 105. They had only just received them when I joined them in September 1942 and had suffered grievous losses with the outdated Blenheims with which they had been operating.

The forceful 'Digger' Kyle was the Station Commander. He was later to become Sir Wallace Kyle. 'Hughie' was also to be knighted and became Governor General of Tasmania.

My Flight Commander was Squadron Leader Roy Ralston who, with his Navigator, fellow Blackpudlian, Sid Clayton, was amongst the many already famous personalities on the squadron. One of their most talked about exploits had been the bombing of the entrance of a tunnel in France just after a troop train had entered it and then dropping another one on the other side, neatly sealing it in. Sid Clayton made the incredible number of 100 sorties as a Navigator and then persuaded the RAF to send him to train as a pilot in Canada and came back to make yet another forty-five trips, on 'Mossies', of course.

I had already 'crewed' up with my Navigator, a Southport lad of my own age, Les Hogan, and we were thrown straight into the fray. After a few 'circuits and bumps' in the 'Mossie', no dual instruction – you just read the pilot's notes and off you went! I found that I was now flying a wonderful aeroplane as different as chalk from cheese from anything that I had flown previously. We were sent on comparatively uneventful low-level daylight sorties against targets in Belgium and Holland. It was wonderful to roar over the enemy coastline at nought feet and see the German gunners lounging in their sandbagged emplacements. There would always be a desultory burst of light flak after you had passed so as to explain to their higher ups that they had not been caught napping. On another occasion

I was the third Mosquito of three bombing the railway yards at Courtrai and saw the bomb from the machine in front of me bounce over my wing and then explode just behind me.

By now the squadron had moved to the larger aerodrome of Marham near King's Lynn and I had met the WAAF Flight Sergeant (Discip!) who was to become my wife. From the moment I met her I knew that she was the girl for me and I courted Dora Shawcross assiduously even though she was engaged to an Air Gunner at another RAF station. We were both members of the Sergeants' Mess of course and romantically shared the chamber pot filled with beer which was traditionally passed around at Christmas and other festive occasions. Breakfast was served until 8.30 a.m. and was rarely worth getting up for in those days of rationing, but when real eggs, not the awful dried variety, were on the menu, word would quickly and magically spread around and tousle-headed, unshaven aircrew would rush in at 8.29 a.m. with battledress tops over pyjamas to partake in the luxury of a real egg.

On 30 October 1942 I was sent, with another Mosquito piloted by Flight Lieutenant Bill Blessing, an Australian, to attack Leeuwarden Aerodrome in Holland. Leeuwarden was a German night fighter base and the plan was to fly over the Dutch coast, then turn and attack the airfield on the way out. Somewhere in the mist and poor visibility over the North Sea I lost Bill so attacked the airfield on my own. We dropped our bombs from about 50ft but got well and truly plastered by the ground defences who were giving us everything they had. The whole nose of the aircraft disappeared, the port (left) engine was on fire and both Les and myself were wounded, myself in the left thigh and Les in the chest, although we were both completely unaware of this at the time. I 'feathered' the port engine but it was still burning furiously. We were still only at 50ft and I was having great difficulty in controlling the aircraft so I yelled at Les to press the fire extinguisher button.

He promptly pushed the wrong one and discharged the extinguishing fluid into our only good engine which coughed, spluttered and – good old Rolls-Royce Merlin – miraculously came to life again. The fire in the other engine had now gone out of its own accord.

The dashboard had gone, I had no instruments and my feet were on the rudder pedals sticking out into space as the nose had gone. To add to my troubles the rudder trim lever had also been shot away so I could not ease the strain on my left leg which had to push the pedal hard over to the left to counter the asymmetrical power of our good starboard engine.

Luckily we were already on our way to the nearby coast and we went out between two of the Frisian Islands but also straight between two small German naval vessels who began firing at us until the vessel on our port side hit the other one with a shell burst and we saw the German sailors shaking their fists at us. As we had no instruments we could not climb into the low cloud so we flew just above the surface of the North Sea. Had the Germans sent a fighter after us we would have had it, but the low cloud was our saviour and we almost made it back to our base at Marham. We were actually in the circuit and had just lowered our undercarriage when the long-suffering starboard engine gave up the ghost and we crashed into a small copse taking down thirty-one trees according to the farmer who claimed compensation for them.

I remember seeing the trees coming through the windscreen and hoping that my watch would not be broken! My foot had gone through the wooden fuselage and I could not move but Les stepped out from where the nose should have been and took my boot off. Luckily, as it was a low-level operation, I had not been wearing the thick, long flying boots so was able to withdraw my foot and we ran, despite our wounds, which were now beginning to make themselves felt. The aircraft blew up almost immediately but miraculously, we had not got a scratch on us from the actual crash. We had gone into the trees almost level and they had cushioned our fall and had gradually decreased our speed. Had the aircraft been a conventional metal one I am convinced that we would have been killed as it would have come in on us and trapped us. We collapsed in a clearing where we were found by two Land Army girls who promptly pulled my trousers off and did some hasty first aid on my now copiously bleeding thigh. The RAF ambulance was soon at the scene and the personnel could not believe their eyes when they saw two airmen whose only injuries were from the shrapnel and who had survived a complete and total crash with nothing left of the aircraft. We were taken to Ely hospital where several fragments of cannon shell were removed from my left thigh as well as a fragment of shrapnel in Les's breast pocket that had just broken the skin beneath but had not penetrated the chest.

It was Dora's birthday. We had not yet got to know each other but had spoken briefly the night before. One of the WAAFs told her that we had both been killed as everyone on the station had seen us go down with the ensuing explosion, and could not believe that anyone could have survived.

Whilst in hospital, we were visited by the Squadron Commander who commended us both and was very kind about the outcome of the Op. We had severely damaged the buildings and put the airfield out of use for a time. We were in Ely for about a week and were back on Ops six weeks later.

On New Year's Eve 1942 we were on a lone operation against the marshalling yards at Monceau in Belgium. It was late afternoon and very murky with a very low cloud base. Once again we were flying at our usual 50ft. We actually flew between two slag heaps, near the target, without seeing either of them until we were actually between them. There were some bursts of light flak; we were not hit but just after successfully dropping our four 500lb bombs on the mass of railway lines below us, there was a loud bang and the windscreen disappeared. I had felt a thud on my chest and when I looked I was covered in blood. Les cried out and I saw that he too was covered in blood but there were also feathers everywhere and we realised that we had hit a bird, later discovered to be a large crow. Luckily we always wore goggles above our helmets and we needed them as the wind was terrific inside the cockpit and it was freezing.

Once again we were speeding back over the North Sea at 50ft but this time we had our two engines but had to restrict our speed because of the windstream in the cockpit. Suddenly there was a bang and Les let out a yell; 'I've been hit in the arse' he cried. He discovered that the trailing aerial, which we had let out to radio to base, had been left out and had obviously touched the sea a few feet below and had rapidly wound out causing the handle in the cockpit to whizz round and hit him where he said it had. We were convulsed with laughter but he had quite a bruise.

This time we made it back to base but no amount of scrubbing, bathing and showering could get rid of the dead bird smell so Dora and I had to forego the traditional Sergeants' Mess New Year's Eve dance and spend it in the NAAFI instead.

Many more fortunately less eventful operations followed. Often, whilst flying low over the occupied countries of Holland, Belgium and France, we would see children waving to us and sometimes, in the dusk which was one of the favourite times of returning, we would see the three dots and the dash of the 'V' sign, obviously from pocket torches. Radar was still in its infancy but in any case, the low level at which we flew guaranteed our immunity from being seen on what few scts the Germans had. That same low flying claimed many victims, however. Many failed to return from hitting trees, telegraph poles and even other aircraft, and flying into the sea was the greatest cause of accidents as the horizon was very uncertain at that altitude.

CHAPTER SEVEN

Although the Mosquito was such a wonderful aeroplane I still had the urge to fly the really big ones with my eyes set firmly on the future. Bomber Command was now beginning its long awaited offensive on Germany so, ignoring the sound RAF advice of 'never volunteer for anything', I asked to be transferred to Heavy Bombers. After a short period flying the American Boston and having my first experience of a tricycle undercarriage, I was posted to the Heavy Conversion Unit of 4 Group Bomber Command operating from the famous battle site of Marston Moor near York. Before I got there I enjoyed the unusual experience of flying a captured German Junkers 88 which I found to be a very good machine. Although it had RAF roundels we still had an escort of three Spitfires to protect us from some trigger-happy RAF fighter pilot.

4 Group were equipped with the four-engined Handley Page Halifax. I had secretly hoped to be posted to the more well-known and glamorous Lancaster but I soon found the 'Halibag' to be a very tough, strongly built aeroplane capable of taking terrible punishment. It is true that it did not have the load-carrying ability of the Lancaster, and until the four Rolls-Royce Merlin engines of the Mark II were replaced by Bristol Hercules sixteen air-cooled engines in the Mark III, it was not capable of reaching a cruising

altitude above 18,000ft, which left it vulnerable to both fighters and heavy flak. Nevertheless it was rugged, and once the rudders had been modified to eliminate the dangerous rudder stall of the earlier marks, it was a very manoeuvrable aircraft. We had no such luxury as servo controls so throwing a Halifax around the sky took a great deal of physical strength. Nor did we have two pilots. A second pilot was a luxury that Bomber Command could not afford so a good aircraft Commander, and the pilot was always the Captain irrespective of rank, would train his Flight Engineer or Bomb Aimer to fly well enough to get an aircraft back to England where the crew could, at least, bale out.

At Marston Moor we were crewed up and so met the chaps who would share the dangers looming ahead of us. My crew was Howard Phillips, Navigator, a Welshman from Neath, Bill Fox, Flight Engineer, a Yorkshireman, Jacky Collins, Bomb Aimer from Epsom, Surrey, George 'Paddy' Graham, wireless operator from Belfast, Roy Burch, mid-upper gunner from Calgary, Canada and Tommy Walker, the rear gunner or 'Tail end Charlie' as the rear gunner was always called, a Geordie from Ashington. Roy was the eldest of the crew and was around twenty-eight. The rest of us were all within a year or two of each other and I had celebrated my twenty-first birthday the month before.

Dora and I became officially engaged very early in the year and decided to get married when I had finished my Heavy Conversion course at Marston Moor, as it was usual to get some leave before joining whichever squadron you were posted to. The course was scheduled to finish on 21 June 1943 so we decided to get married in Blackpool.

Paddy Graham was my best man, Roy Burch joined us and Dora's best friend and inseparable WAAF companion 'Jackie' Hindle was bridesmaid when we were married by the wonderfully named Registrar, Johnny Jump, on 26 June 1943. I say 'inseparable' because for the most part of our courtship, Jackie had accompanied us wherever we had gone. Not that there were many places that one could go in those dark days. We cycled or walked everywhere. There was the good old NAAFI in the evenings and of course the camp cinema, which could be the gym or NAAFI converted for the evening to show films like *The Wicked Lady* and *Target for Tonight*. The air raid warning would inevitably go in the middle of the performance and everyone would have to go to the shelters. I never did get to see the end of *Night Train to Munich*. Everyone smoked like a chimney and I once stopped the show when I stubbed out my cigarette on what I thought was the back of the seat in front of me, only to find that I was stubbing it out on a poor little WAAF's neck. Her screams effectively stopped the film.

Occasionally, ENSA, the forces entertainment organisation would send us one of their wonderful concert parties. Ralph Reader and his Gang Show were the most well-known ('We're riding along on the crest of a wave') but I well remember Gordon Harker, the famous cockney actor and film star, coming back to the Mess after one of the shows. Written on the ceiling, just under a cross beam were the words, 'Pinky Wood peed in the fireplace from here.' 'Anything Pinky Wood can do, Gordon Arker can do,' he said and straightaway proved it.

The pubs, or more usually *the* pub, were always a long walk from the necessarily isolated camp. They were always short of beer and we were always short of money but we were young, we were alive and lived for the moment and morale was high, so the ever present Jackie was always very welcome.

We went back to the Avalon for our wartime-rationed wedding reception and then made our way to Blackpool railway station to take the train to Southport, where we planned on spending a few days of our honeymoon with one of Dora's aunties who lived there. Unfortunately we had to change at Preston and as was so often the case then, the train to Southport never turned up so we found a little boarding house next to the station and spent our wedding night listening to the stentorian Lancashire-accented voice coming over the station loudspeakers. 'The train standing at platform one is the delayed London Carlisle express …' rang in our ears all night with different destinations, cancellations and, occasionally, arrivals. We eventually got to Southport the next afternoon and were made very welcome by Dora's aunt, who must have felt very sorry for the bedraggled and tired honeymooners who were standing on her doorstep. The honeymoon passed all too quickly and my posting came through.

CHAPTER EIGHT

I received a railway warrant telling me to proceed to Heck in Yorkshire. The ticket seller at Blackpool refused to believe that there was such a place and thought that I was having him on but it did, and still does, exist. It was a small train halt not far from Snaith, near Goole, which is where my new squadron, No 51 of 4 Group, was based.

I was put into C Flight which was, unusually, commanded by a Squadron Leader who was not a pilot. Charles Porter was an Observer and one of the finest and bravest men I was ever to meet and I met many. He would put himself on operations with each and every pilot in his flight, replacing the normal Bomb Aimer for that one flight. I was still a Sergeant but when Squadron Leader Porter flew with me, I was the skipper and my word was law. He seemed old enough to be my father but was probably around thirty years old. It says volumes for his assessment of ability – and luck – that he survived the mandatory tour of thirty operations despite having to fly with all and sundry. He survived the war and was a popular figure at the annual 51 Squadron reunions until, sadly, he died around 1992. Strangely enough when he had finished his tour he was replaced by another Squadron Leader Observer; a very different character to Charlie, called Simmonds, who was an ex-Guards Officer re-mustered to the RAF.

My first trip on the Halifax was as second pilot. This, to gain experience, was an expensive practice that was soon discontinued by Bomber Command as two valuable pilots were lost if the machine was shot down. My skipper was Flight Lieutenant Bill Irwin and the target was Hamburg on the night of 24 July 1943.

On that raid a new device was to be tested on the German defences. It consisted of thin metallic strips which were to be released in their thousands from each aircraft as it flew over the target. Each strip, as it floated down, would give an echo on the German radar similar to that of an aircraft and, it was hoped, would swamp the German defences. Although the British had known of this device for a considerable time it had not been used in case the Germans used it against us. However, with the mounting losses of Bomber Command – a loss of thirty to forty aircraft, each containing at least seven aircrew on every raid, was not uncommon – the powers that be decided to unleash 'Window', as the strips were code-named, over Germany. It was my job, as the spare man on board, to drop the bundles of Window down the flare chute as we flew over Hamburg. It certainly worked well that night. We heard from our Intelligence that it had caused complete chaos in the German night fighter defence. Pilots were being ordered to sectors to intercept the hundreds of British planes reported there and were being virtually accused of cowardice when no sightings were made. The use of Window in the next few months certainly saved hundreds of British lives but the Germans brought in all their fighter planes, including day fighters, and illuminated the target area with thousands of searchlights, silhouetting the bombers above them. This was called Operation Wilde Sau and was very successful. Window though had served its purpose well and was to play a huge part in the D-Day landings when about thirty Lancasters, dropping Window and doubling back upon themselves repeatedly, convinced the Germans that a large naval force was approaching the German-held coast.

The raid on Hamburg that night was to take its place in history as the first where great fires were started; giving birth to the terrible 'fire storms' that literally sucked the oxygen from all around. The devastation and death toll was terrible. I take no pride in taking part in this attack, just a deep sadness that it was found to be necessary.

I had found an elderly couple in the nearby village of Pollington who were willing to let their spare bedroom so Dora, by now pregnant, joined me. The accommodation was spartan, to say the least. There was only an outside non-flushing toilet so many night-time visits with a bucket of water were necessary. Mrs Bent always had a large piece of bacon hanging from the old-fashioned kitchen ceiling. They killed a pig once a year and then salted it down. The result was the saltiest bacon you have ever tasted in your life.

Mr Bent had no teeth and used to say, as he supped his porridge, 'I like owt wi' a spoon'. They were hardy Yorkshire folks and kindly in their own way but any sort of accommodation was at a premium and at least we were together; but it must have been a terrible time for Dora to be left alone in such cheerless surroundings, not knowing whether she would ever see me again when I left her to go on the many operations that followed.

During the day of an operation we would take our aircraft up on an air test to give all the equipment on board a thorough workout. On one occasion I asked Bill, my Yorkshire Flight Engineer, to feather one of the engines so that I could practise some three-engine flying. A rotating propeller, without power, causes enormous drag on the aircraft so the blades of the propeller of the 'dead' engine are turned, electrically, so that the leading edge is presented to the airstream. This is called 'feathering' as in rowing when the blades of the oars are turned in similar fashion so that they do not cause drag in the water. We always carried out air tests at an altitude of 5,000ft or more and it was just as well. When Bill pressed the button of the Port Outer engine (the engines were numbered from 1 to 4 looking from the tail towards the nose so Port Outer was No 1) bingo, all four engines promptly feathered themselves and of course, stopped. Bill, the unflappable Yorkshireman, said 'Bloody quiet up here,' leaned forward and pressed the same button and all four engines unfeathered themselves. We found later that a drop of solder from some electrical work above had neatly fused all four circuits together.

On another air test, much later, we were just about to touch down so I tried to close the throttles but the Port Outer throttle (again!) stuck halfway open and would not close. We were racing along the runway towards the 50ft drop at the end where, with typical RAF planning, the bomb dump was situated. I could see startled airmen running away from the huge aircraft hurtling towards them and the brakes could do nothing against the power of the still roaring engine, so I did the only thing possible and pulled up the undercarriage. The cockpit was immediately filled with sawdust from the disintegrating wooden propellers. The Halifax was still sliding along on its belly but Bill had his screwdriver out and was unscrewing a little clock which had been attached to the dashboard to help us on our bombing run saying, 'No other bugger's having this.' We stopped about 20ft short of the end of the runway and it was later found that the linkage to the throttle had broken and jammed the control.

Only a few weeks before I got to Snaith, the bomb dump had actually blown up, killing over fifty people, but it was still there after we had slid to a halt a few feet before the drop. The only time I ever saw Bill lose his calm was on yet another air test when we were at about 6,000ft and saw a jeep drop down from above us and slide under our nose. True it was going down at a large rate of knots but we had been to Betty's Bar in York the night before and I think Bill was just about ready to sign the pledge that day. We found out later that experiments were already being made in dropping equipment in preparation for the invasion that was still a long way ahead of us. The unfortunate jeep's parachute had, evidently, not opened.

The Wireless Operator had his position directly underneath the pilot's rudder pedals in the nose of the Halifax. The toilet, a chemical seat called the Elsan, was way back in the tail and virtually impossible to reach for the pilot who was encumbered with a seat-type parachute so a bottle was always carried for emergencies.

The predictable result of using it was Paddy's usually unshaven face appearing on the step up to the cockpit, breathing fire, saying in his broad Irish brogue, 'All over me log again, skipper.'

The Navigator and Bomb Aimer shared a bench forward of the Wireless Operator in the plastic nose. There had once been mounted a small machine gun but it was removed from all Halifax aircraft as it was useless – frontal attacks at night were virtually unknown. Phil, our Navigator, was a highly volatile Welshman and one night, over Germany on the way to the target, a coloured flare went down ahead of us. As these were dropped by the preceding aircraft of the Pathfinder Force they had a certain significance so I asked Phil whether it was a turning point on our route. Back came the reply, 'What do you think I am? the Encyclopaedia Britannica?' There was silence then Jacky the Bomb Aimer came up on the intercom. 'Skipper, Phil's unplugged his intercom and has stopped working.' I put in 'George', the somewhat dodgy automatic pilot, got out of my seat and sat down next to the Navigator. He took a startled look at me, hurriedly plugged in his intercom, took up his pencil and got back to work.

Many of our trips were of very long duration; Berlin took from seven-and-a-half or even more than eight hours. You could count on five hours as being the shortest, (to the Ruhr). Munich and Nuremberg took about eight-and-a-half hours. However, on the infamous flight it took over nine hours – we lost ninety-four aircraft due to strong headwinds. Continuous 'weaving' for 90 per cent of these trips was a very hard and tiring task as the Halifax was not power assisted on the controls and was a very heavy aircraft to fly manually and there was no second pilot to give you a respite. The temptation to engage the automatic pilot and take a rest from the hard physical work was great, but I resisted it from the beginning (I always thought 'George' was the cause of many casualties), and even 'Corkscrewed' the Halifax all the time over enemy territory which was virtually the entire trip. The 'Corkscrew' was a prescribed manoeuvre which consisted of continually throwing the aircraft around the sky, diving and climbing, at the same time as turning from side to side, losing up to 2,000ft and turning 25 to 30 degrees right or left then climbing and turning again and repeating the procedure trying not to maintain a pattern. It wasn't easy for the crew and especially the Navigator, but it was done to avoid, and I am sure that it did a lot to get us through, the favourite German night fighter attack where the fighter flew, unseen, under the blind spot of an unsuspecting four-engine bomber then pulled the trigger of the upward firing guns mounted on the top of the fighter's fuselage. *Schräge Musik* was the German codename for it. This, without fail, got the central fuel tank and the resulting explosion could be seen for many miles away and invariably caused panic.

The ops mounted up. We were operating nearly every two or three nights and we had many close shaves. On 8 October 1943 we were briefed to attack Hanover. Taken all round this was one of the most dangerous and yet successful trips that we did because from the time we crossed the Dutch coast on the way in until we crossed it again going out, we were constantly harried and followed by fighters, searchlights and flak. We saw many combats and many aircraft going down in flames.

Just after releasing our bombs over Hanover there was a terrific crash and the whole aircraft shuddered. We thought that we had been hit by flak. I managed to control the aircraft and sent the Flight Engineer back to investigate and called out to him, as an afterthought, 'put your parachute on'. It was just as well that I did because he nearly fell through the hole caused by a 2,000lb bomb from an aircraft above which had gone through our roof and out through the floor just aft of the mid-upper turret, leaving its outline, still horizontal, showing that the aircraft could only have been a few feet above us. It was quite commonplace to find unexploded incendiaries, which were dropped in sticks or 'clusters', sticking out of the wings with the business end embedded in the petrol tanks. Collisions of course, occurred often, and it was quite normal to find yourself battling to control the aircraft to counter the effects of another aircraft's slipstream.

One night over Munich a burst of flak under the tail put the aircraft into an inverted dive. It was the most horrible feeling looking up and seeing Munich blazing and coming down towards us. Some several thousand feet later, after wrestling with the controls and all my instruments, I was able to get it straight and level by rolling it out, but the inverted G-forces in the pull-out nearly forced the rear gunner out of his turret. That same gunner, Tommy Walker, saved us all with his excellent marksmanship when a Messerschmitt 110 night fighter attacked us over Mannheim. The German got in one burst which hit the fuselage shattering the Perspex of the mid-upper turret. I had insisted that the mid-upper gunner replace the armoured plating which he had removed before the flight to improve his vision and which was common practice amongst gunners. Luckily for him that I had, as a cannon shell exploded right on the plating. We had immediately gone into a very tight turn and we could clearly see the fighter and Tommy's bullets striking home when there was a burst of flame from it and he went into a screaming dive and we saw the flash on the ground as he exploded there.

I joined 51 Squadron as the Bomber Command assault on Germany was gathering momentum. The losses were horrific. Over 50,000 young aircrew lost their lives from that one branch of the RAF. I was extremely fortunate.

There was always a huge gasp when the curtain was drawn at briefing and we saw the red ribbon of our track that night, finishing at Berlin. It was very heavily defended and was a long way into Germany entailing a round trip of over eight hours. I took part in six raids on what we called 'the big city'.

The tactics of Bomber Command, by now, were to put as many aircraft over the target as possible in the shortest possible time to swamp the defences. Collisions accounted for many casualties of course. On the night of 28 January 1944 I was in one of the very last aircraft to attack Berlin. We were now flying the Halifax Mark III with radial Hercules engines and had reached the dizzy altitude of 22,000ft. It was as light as day over the city with the cloud below reflecting the glare of the fires and the searchlights. We were amazed to see a Messerschmitt 109 line up on our port wing but just out of effective range of our guns. He flew across the target with me, as we bombed, then the pilot pointed forward to his guns, shrugged his shoulders to indicate that he had no more ammunition, then half rolled on to his back and dived away. Then we were 'coned' by three powerful searchlights but managed to get away from them by some very violent evasive action.

I had been a Flight Sergeant for a long time but was, at last, commissioned and made my first operational trip as an officer to Peenemünde. This op was to become famous after the war as, unknown to us at the time, Peenemünde was where the secret V-1s and V-2s were being developed. Despite the loss of over forty aircraft I only remember the trip as very quiet and unusually, for us, made in bright moonlight.

We had been posted to Burn, near Selby, to form a new squadron at the end of the year. The new squadron was No 578 and was the only Halifax squadron to have the holder of a VC amongst its members. Cyril Barton was awarded the medal posthumously when he stayed in his crippled Halifax after ordering his crew to bale out so that he could avoid crashing on a nearby village. He was a colleague of mine but was just starting his operations as I finished. He was exactly the same age as me.

Dora had gone to her parents in St Helens and on that afternoon of 28 January 1944 I was sitting in the Officers' Mess at Snaith after attending briefing with my crew and being told that, once again, the target for that night was Berlin, when I was summoned to the phone and a WAAF from Signals told me the wonderful news that my son Peter had been born. On the day of an op the Station was cut off completely. No outgoing phone calls were allowed and everyone was confined to the camp, so there was no way that I could contact Dora. I had to tell someone and luckily Phil, who had also been commissioned with me, was in the Mess so I told him. In no time at all the whole of the Mess was around me, shaking my hand and congratulating me. The ensuing trip to Berlin and back was the longest and most frightening operation that I had ever been on, but there was an added bonus to a wonderful day when our squadron commander, the charismatic Wing Commander Wilkerson, came out to the dispersal to greet me as I got out of the Halifax, personally congratulated me on the birth of Peter and told me that I had done my last operation and I was to be 'screened' from further operations. I had been on operations from October 1942 until 28 January 1944.

So I went to St Helens the next day, as a 'sprog' (raw or new) Pilot Officer to see Dora and our new son, Peter Howard. He was not exactly a prepossessing sight. His eye had been slightly damaged during the birth, he had slight jaundice so was very yellow and his lips were covered with Gentian violet from a dressing Dora had on her but he was our first child and so the most beautiful baby in the world.

Roy Burch, our Canadian mid-upper gunner, had come with me to see Dora and the baby. He returned to the squadron and foolishly, volunteered to do a couple more ops. Alas, he was reported missing, believed killed, on the second one. He was the only member of my crew not to survive the war.

CHAPTER NINE

During the months that followed, many important events took place. Dora's paternal grandmother, 'Frosty' as she was called by the entire family (but not to her face), purchased a tiny little house in Blackpool and rented it to us. The address was No 2 Ferndale Avenue, South Shore. It really was tiny but it was our first real accommodation.

I had been sent on a course to gain an Instructor's certificate, at Lulsgate Bottom near Weston-super-Mare. One May morning, I opened one of the Mess newspapers and saw that I had been awarded the Distinguished Flying Cross (DFC) for my operational tour. Due to strain and ill health King George had given up the practice of investing honours personally so my DFC came through the letter box many months later and the enclosed letter of apology from the King still bears Peter's tooth marks where he tried to eat it when he found it one day.

At the end of the course and passing out with the requisite Instructor's rating I was posted back to 4 Group to the Heavy Conversion Unit at Marston Moor. There I was entrusted with the task of converting sprog pilots to the beaten up old Halifaxes that were all that Bomber Command could spare for the necessary training of crews about to be sent to the squadrons reeling under the dreadful losses that they were taking. Here I renewed my acquaintanceship with one of the great characters of the RAF. Arthur Caygill was a fellow member of 51 Squadron and also a fellow Blackpudlian and schoolmate. He was always known as 'the Baron' and had finished his operations with the squadron just as I was finishing mine. Arthur was a couple of years older than I and was in the sixth form at Blackpool Grammar School when he was expelled. He was notorious for a series of escapades but the last one was when he looked out of the classroom window and saw a busload of girls from our sister school waiting for the driver. He climbed out of the window and took them for a round trip of the surrounding Fylde. They probably had a better time than they would have done otherwise. Trouble was it was the first time he had ever driven anything in his life. He had an old Austin 7 at Snaith. It was the custom to fly low and 'beat up' the airfield on returning from the last trip of an operational tour, but when Arthur did so his aircraft was seen to literally jump 50ft higher as he went over the Control Tower and saw his Austin 7 perched there on the balcony where his ground crew had manhandled it with some valuable help from the engineers' crane.

We were both made Flight Commanders of different flights at Marston Moor and as such were given motorbikes for our personal transport. We organised a series of motocross races around the airfield with the finishing lap up the steps of the Officers' Mess, round the anteroom finishing at the bar.

I had by now purchased my very first car. It was a BSA three-wheeler that I bought from one of the 'erks', as the lower ranks were called, on the Maintenance Flight for £5, which was a fair amount in those days. It was an open-topped car that had seen better days but it was soon put into better shape by our good lads from Maintenance who even 'won' the Perspex nose from a beaten up Halifax and attached it to the car so that I had a convertible saloon when I pulled the Perspex over me. Trouble was the exhaust was non-existent and when I drove over the Pennines to see Dora and proudly pulled up outside our little house in Blackpool the noise was so loud that the neighbours came running out. I persuaded her to come for a ride with me and she did so but stuffed little Peter's ears with cotton wool. We set off proudly but it broke down in the centre of Blackpool and we all had to get the tram back. Once, later on when the car was running comparatively well, we went for a run out taking Nell, our little dog. The Perspex top had gone by now so we had attached Nell to one of the hood supports with her lead. We had just set off from traffic lights when we were stopped by shouts and arm waving from pedestrians. Nell had jumped out at the lights and was running like mad on her lead still attached to the car. Luckily she had not come to any harm, probably because the old BSA could not go fast enough.

One day the Baron suggested that we should go and visit the nearby Tadcaster brewery of Sam Smith and Sons. Petrol was very strictly rationed, of course, but the problem was solved by the Baron who produced about 3 gallons of MT Petrol (MT was the Motor Transport section of the RAF). The MT petrol was always coloured red so that it could easily be identified. The Directors of Samuel Smith warmly welcomed the two Flight Lieutenants with wings and DFCs emblazoned on their chest, although their transport got some funny looks, but would not hear of us sampling the light ale for which the brewery was famous. No, out came the malt whisky and it was two rather fragile figures that staggered to the waiting BSA a few hours later. We managed to get it started, there was no self-starter so it always had to be hand-cranked, and wound our way through country lanes in the general direction of Marston Moor. Then the engine began sputtering and we realised that we were running out of petrol. The Baron, as always, had a solution. The petrol tank was placed in front of the dashboard underneath the bonnet and gravity fed the carburettor. There was no pump. So by opening the bonnet which folded to the side then lying along the windscreen with his legs on the offside, the Baron could get his mouth over the tank filler opening and by blowing hard, put enough pressure into the tank to feed the last remaining drops to the engine. It worked and we were weaving our way along when we heard the sound of a bell, a gong to be precise. All police cars 'gonged' you in those days. A disbelieving policeman pulled his Wolseley in front of us and nearly collapsed with laughter when the Baron with all the dignity of a country squire got off the bonnet and said, 'Is there something wrong, Officer?' His dignity was rather marred by the circle of red around his mouth from the petrol. The nearly hysterical policeman went to his car, got out a can of petrol, poured it into ours, then said, 'Now bugger off and for God's sake don't tell anyone you've seen me.'

England in 1943 was a veritable island aircraft carrier. I always maintained that at an altitude of 5,000ft, anywhere from Newcastle down to Cambridge along the East coast, you could cut all your engines and make a dead stick landing on an aerodrome.

The RAF magazine, called *Tee Emm* for Training Manual, carried a monthly award of 'The Most Highly Derogatory Order of the Irremovable Digit'. This was given for the worst incident, or 'black' of the month. I was the recipient one month. No. 4 Group, to which I belonged, had three Heavy Conversion Units; Riccall, Rufforth and Marston Moor. They were all very close to each other. Our job as Instructors was to take crews as they came to us, probably already with a certain amount of time on aircraft such as Oxfords and convert them to Halifaxes prior to their postings to operational squadrons. We had also to try and make sure that they were beginning to interact as crews as it was very unlikely that they had ever flown together before. After some satisfactory daylight circuits and bumps they had to do a few night landings. The procedure was that the Instructor went up and watched his pupil do a night landing and then, if it was satisfactory, got out and let his pupil do four or five more on his own with his crew that were already on board. I watched with approval one night as my pupil took off and landed perfectly. 'OK,' I said, 'taxi to the Control Tower, I'll get out and you can do four more by yourself.' When I got inside the Control Tower I didn't recognise any of the personnel. We had taken off from Marston Moor but landed at Rufforth. Not only that but my pupil had taken off again and had finished his landings successfully at Marston Moor. When I telephoned Marston Moor and asked for transport I was told by the OC Flying to 'bloody well walk back'.

The Station Commander of an RAF station always had a Tiger Moth at his disposal for communicating with other RAF stations. The *Tee Emm* award was given to Group Captain X (who was never named, happily) for landing in his Tiger Moth at an airfield and studiously avoiding all conversation until he had the chance to see DROs (Daily Routine Orders) on the notice board to find out where he was. Next month *Tee Emm* acknowledged receipt from four Group Captains asking them how the hell they had found out!

The system of 'screened' operational pilots being used as Instructors was not entirely successful. A fine operational pilot did not always make a good teacher so Bomber Command decided to open an Instructor's school where the pilots, fresh from their ops, would undergo an extensive course on how to become a successful Instructor. I had always taken a keen interest in this aspect of flying and had come out towards the top of my Instructor's course so I was very pleased when my old CO, Wing Commander Wilkerson, called me and asked me to join him at Finningley, near Doncaster, to help set up the new Bomber Command Instructors' School (BCIS). The aircraft to be used were Lancasters, Mosquitos and Wellingtons. I had, of course, flown the Mosquito but had to learn how to handle the 'Lanc'. I soon developed an affinity with what was a marvellous aircraft. 'Limit' flying was a wonderful experience for me. We taught prospective Instructors, all battle hardened, but somewhat doubting veterans, how to fly the Lancaster to its absolute limit including landings with two engines actually feathered on the port side, which was the worst side to lose an engine on the Lanc due to the direction of gyroscopic, rotational effect of the propellers. Tragically, before he was able to take command of BCIS, Wing Commander Wilkerson, or 'Wilkie' as everyone called him, was killed whilst flying as a passenger in a Baltimore. He was one of the most popular figures in the RAF and a splendid leader.

Finningely was a magnificent 'peacetime' station. 'Peacetime' meant that it was purpose-built before the war and had solid permanent buildings. The Officers' Mess was beautifully furnished and the RAF was trying to get back to some semblance of dignified living even though the war was still raging.

Dora and Peter had joined me at nearby Kirk Sandall, by coincidence the Yorkshire home of the St Helens glassmaking firm of Pilkington where her father had worked for most of his life. Her Uncle Joe and Auntie Polly lived there and managed to find us a small house opposite them. We were only there a very short time before we had to find rooms once again. There followed a series of adventures with landladies such as Edith, our first one in Kirk Sandall, whose favourite expression was, 'Her! She's had yards!' referring to some innocent looking woman sitting in our local, which was completely built from Pilkington glass and was called, appropriately enough, the Glasshouse. She had a vocabulary that would put any seaman to shame and all that with a very loud, broad, Yorkshire accent. One night we were all sitting in the Glasshouse when Edith nodded towards a very quiet elderly lady sitting a few tables away. ''Er!' she almost shouted, 'She's 'ad yards.' The number of Edith's acquaintances who ''ad yards' must have added up to a lot of miles. We moved to the front room of a semi-detached house in Doncaster where our landlady turned out to be a nymphomaniac. She was a well-educated woman with three children. Her husband was in the Army and she used to confide in Dora. She told her one night that she had been out with a man and it was the first time she had been 'paid for it'. Later she told her that the same man one night later had been short of money but had given her a pound of streaky bacon instead! True, bacon was severely rationed and this remained a lifetime joke between Dora and I. A 'Tiger' sandwich was another well-known word between us. I once told Dora that if she put some mustard on a slice of bread and made a sandwich of it she would think that it was a real ham sandwich.

Jokes apart, life in a single room, sharing a small kitchen with a two ring stove and bringing up a fifteen-month-old baby was not funny. I, of course, was having a good lunch in the Mess and then coming home in the evening and to this day I don't know how Dora managed to feed the three of us on the bare rations that we had. Dora was pregnant again and expecting the baby in June so life was very hard on her at that time but we had many a laugh together.

The BSA had been replaced by a motorbike and sidecar. The bike was the most magnificent machine: a 1929 Henderson, an American make, of 1301cc. It had four cylinders in line and even had running boards on which to rest your feet. Wherever I stopped, a crowd would gather to admire the beast. Once, on the Great North Road, now the A1, with one of our landladies on the pillion, a terrified Dora and little Peter in the sidecar, we were doing 90mph with the throttle only half open. I had paid £35 for it.

On 6 June 1945, the first anniversary of D-Day, Dora gave birth to our eldest daughter, Linda. There were no beds to be had at hospitals in Doncaster so Dora had gone to nearby Lindrick Park Golf Club which had been pressed into service as a wartime maternity home. Linda was born in the clubhouse, which was the ward. I used to fly fairly low over the course whilst Dora was still there nursing the baby and fire off 'Very' cartridges to let her know that I was in the plane.

One of my most vivid memories of Doncaster is the veritable 'pea soup' fog that used to occur regularly. There was very little coal to be had but what there was, was certainly not the smokeless variety. There were times when you literally could not see your hand in front of your face. This did not stop one of the most popular Saturday night Officers' Mess events called 'Hare and Hound'. Doncaster had more pubs to the square mile than most other towns in England. An area in the town was made the 'hunting ground' and the two hares would set off from the Mess. Given half an hour's start they would be followed by the hounds. The rules were simple. You had to have a pint in each pub that you visited. If you spotted the hounds you had to buy them a drink and have one with them, then give them ten minutes start after they had left. The winner was the one with the most hares' signatures and the prize was the traditional chamber pot full of beer, which had to be consumed back in the Mess. There was no breathalyser in those days; come to that there were very few cars. We would all pile onto the station bus, which usually left town at about 10 p.m. As the pubs usually closed at 10.30 p.m. you were faced with a walk of several miles when, as often as not, you missed the bus.

The categorisation of all Flying Instructors was carried out by the Examining Flight of the prestigious Empire Flying School (EFS) based at Hullavington, near Chippenham, in Wiltshire. I was very pleased when I received the coveted A1 Instructors category from them on their first visit to Finningley. I was even more pleased when I was asked to join their staff as a 'Tutor' on their newly formed All Weather Instrument flying course. No longer an Instructor but a Tutor whose task it was to take three or four pupils through the six months' course of advanced flying and theory. The pupils came from all over the world and included members of many different air forces. They were usually of very high rank. One of my first pupils was the grandson or nephew, I forget which, of Charles Kingsford Smith, the famous Australian pioneer of aviation. We had the choice of any aircraft in service to fly including captured German aircraft. I soon availed myself of this wonderful opportunity and flew the incomparable Spitfire for the first time. Our Chief Flying Instructor (CFI) was a tough Lieutenant Colonel of the Royal South African Air Force called, after his famous Boer *Voortrekker* grandfather, Piet Retief.

Much later, on 6 May 1947, he called me over to his office one day and said, 'Reg, I want you to take a Lancaster over to Little Rissington this afternoon. They are having a VE Day air display and have asked us to show them a Lanc. Nothing showy. Just a few circuits and, perhaps a three-engine landing.' Little Rissington was the important base for the Central Flying School and a very short flight from Hullavington. I picked up one of our Lancs and got a Flight Engineer from the 'pool' that we had and I noticed I had a Flight Lieutenant Jones as second pilot. I thought that we would show them what a Lanc could do so I called up their Flying Control and got permission to come up from behind the hangars and sweep over the crowd at a 'fairly low altitude' and then pull up in front of them to about 2,000ft and execute a couple of very steep turns (60 degrees of bank) in both directions within the perimeter of the airfield then dive down over the spectators, disappear and come back and make a landing with both port engines feathered. I tried to forget the CFI's instructions of 'nothing too showy'. I went back to Hullavington and landed. I could see the imposing figure of Lieutenant Colonel Retief waiting for me at the dispersal and groaned inwardly. 'I have just had the CO of Little Rissy on the blower,' were his opening words. 'I thought that I told you, nothing showy.' Then he started smiling. 'The CO was raving about the performance. Evidently you stole the show and he wants you to have dinner with him tonight.' We had a very fine evening.

CHAPTER TEN

I had been selected for a permanent peacetime commission in the RAF and things were looking very rosy when along came the terrible winter of 1947. Dora was pregnant again and we were living in a farm cottage at Halt which was, literally, a train halt on the line between Calne and Chippenham. The cottage was owned by a Margaret Rutherford-like character called Mrs Bod. She was an eccentric, lovely old lady with a heart of gold. She was a widow and lived in the cottage and let out the farmland around it to a local farmer.

By now we possessed a little Austin Ruby saloon and I was teaching Dora to drive. We used to take our little dog in the car over our own level crossing (no gates, just a wooden platform with 'Halt' on the signboard) and then I would get out and take the dog, which Peter had named 'James', for a walk. One day, Dora abandoned me and proudly drove back to the cottage leaving me, fuming, to walk back with the dog. When I got back to find Dora sitting smugly smiling in the car I said, 'You know I always leave it facing the other way.' She reversed, put her foot on the accelerator instead of the brake and shot backwards into the hen house in a cloud of feathers and squawking chickens. Mrs Bod came rushing out, looked at the devastation then said, 'If it wasn't so funny I would be very angry.'

The snow started coming down late in January of that terrible Arctic winter of 1946-47, then never stopped. We were completely cut off from anywhere for over a month. The only telephone was a little way down the river which ran behind the cottage and was owned by an elderly man who was a recluse. When I went to phone Hullavington to tell them that we were still alive, he couldn't even find the phone, which was buried under hundreds of books and covered in dust.

I used to go shooting pigeons with him. He would stand there with the shotgun shaking like an aspen tree, fire it, still shaking, and down would come at least two pigeons. Mrs Bod used to go out every morning and blow a hunting horn and when he answered with a toot on his she would know that he was alright.

On a Sunday Mrs Bod would invite our two children to tea. She would say that she was the Lady of the Manor and they would be Lord Peter and Lady Linda. Her chickens were her personal friends and each had their own name and were called collectively, her Cubbadees. She would bring their food out, scattering it, and calling 'Cubbadees, Cubbadees …'

The terrible winter ground remorselessly on. There was no way of getting to the aerodrome and in any case flying was impossible. As soon as the field was cleared, down would come the snow again. The temperature plummeted. We were boiling snow for water and living on what scraps the farm could produce. There was no gas or electricity in the cottage and the only heating was from a wood burning stove in the big kitchen.

Every morning Dora would go downstairs and try and light this stove. One morning I heard the most God Almighty bang and I rushed down to find Dora there with a charcoal-covered face and nearly in tears. She had got fed up with trying to light the rather awkward stove with newspaper and shavings so had primed it with some paraffin from our oil lamp. The top of the stove had blown off and when Mrs Bod came down she said, 'It's happened. I heard a little explosion this morning and I always knew that the cold would do that to the pipes.' How we kept our faces straight I will never know.

We shivered under our woollen blankets which were covered with ice in the morning from our own frozen breath. The only contact with the outside world was with the accumulator-driven radio owned by Mrs Bod. She would only allow the news to be heard on the lowest possible volume to conserve the lead-acid filled batteries. One night Dora and I were sitting gloomily reading by the light of our paraffin lamp when in swept Mrs Bod. 'My, aren't we looking cosy?' she boomed and turned the lamp down a few notches.

Another night, when the snow had stopped for a few hours, I attempted to take Dora to the cinema in Chippenham. We had only gone about a hundred yards when the car slid backwards into one of the huge snowdrifts and down into a hidden ditch. I was standing there cursing when out came Mrs Bod, swinging a lantern and holding a spade, looking for all the world like a large member of the Seven Dwarfs. 'My, aren't we having fun,' she boomed before pitching in and digging us out. We never did get to the cinema.

The bitter cold went on into April and Dora was expecting the baby in May. Eventually the coldest winter of the century gave way to one of the hottest Mays ever experienced and little Roy was born in Chippenham Nursing Home on 30 May. Tragically he was only to live a week. It was the first real setback of our lives, which had been so fortunate until then.

My position and such interesting work as Tutor at the Empire Flying School was the pinnacle of my RAF career. I was secure with my permanent commission but it was all to change drastically. Civil aviation was just starting up again and British European Airways (a separate branch of BOAC, later all joined together as British Airways) wished to start a Check Flight, composed of First Class Instructors, to train and check their Captains who had very little experience of the new, and very much feared concept of All Weather Instrument flying. It was to be based at what is now the Atomic Research Station at Aldermaston, near Reading.

BEA had received Air Ministry approval to recruit directly from the Empire Flying School and I was amongst those chosen to start their Civil Aviation career right at the top as a Check Captain in the newly formed Check Flight under the command of an old friend, Neil Green, from the examining flight of the EFS.

Demobilisation from the RAF included the resignation of my precious peacetime commission. I was told to report for demobilisation at the RAF station of Kirkham, a few miles from my home in Blackpool.

I was demobilised on 26 June 1947. I had flown six years with the RAF with a total of 1,527 hours and twenty-five minutes. I had been given the substantive rank of Flight Lieutenant.

We were lucky enough to find furnished lodgings near Reading at Tilehurst in an old rectory. The demob centre was at Kirkham, near Blackpool and we started on the long journey south (there were no motorways) in our latest car, a Riley Kestrel with fabric body. We had no less than eight punctures on the journey to Reading. New tyres were unobtainable. When you had a puncture you took the wheel to the nearest garage where it had to be repaired on the spot. Once, when Dora was still pregnant, we broke down with a faulty distributor and finished the journey with her standing on the running board holding the distributor head firmly on despite the electric shocks. Every journey those days, even to the shops, was an adventure and cars ran bound together with string, adhesive tape and hope. There weren't even any nylons to stand in for a broken fan belt.

We had been warned that the old rectory which we had rented in Tilehurst Road was reputed to be haunted by a little old lady who had been seen roaming around the house. We never saw her but there were certainly mysterious sounds at night and things had a funny habit of being found in different places to where we had left them. The two children would wake crying in the middle of the night whereas they had always been very sound sleepers before. I woke one night to the very loud sound of racing hooves coming from the meadow beside our room. It was a bright moonlit night and I went to the window. The sound was still there but everything was calm and there was not an animal to be seen. The most puzzling phenomenon was the disappearance of the fairy that we had placed on the top of the Christmas tree in December 1947. One night it was there and the next morning she had gone, never to be found again.

The job at Aldermaston was to give visiting BEA Captains some dual instruction on DC3s (the ubiquitous Dakota) and the new Vickers Viking using what was called two-stage amber. This involved placing amber panels all around the inside of the cockpit windows so that the Instructor could still see outside and then placing a pair of blue goggles on the pilot which enabled him to see the brightly lit instrument panel but turned the orange panels into an impenetrable black.

The BEA Captains came to Aldermaston for two days. The first day was all instrument practice followed the next day by a comprehensive check on their flying including all emergency procedures. The job was very interesting and the majority of the Captains who came to us were 100 per cent enthusiastic. They saw the need for the different approach to instrument flying that was necessary with all the new aids to landing and flying control that were coming in, and performed accordingly. Unfortunately, it wasn't very popular with some of the older, pre-war Captains, some of whom had never been checked by anyone in their lives. They had been brought up on the old 'seat of the pants' system and resented the possible idea that their flying was not all that was now required of them, but with the growing necessity of all weather flying, the accent on instrument flying was more and more important.

After about nine months of intense flying and taking a keen interest in my job, the lives of everyone at the Check Flight were drastically changed. Churchill and his Tory Government had been ousted by Labour and they decided that poverty stricken Britain could not afford to let our hard-hit currency go abroad except on essential business and so its citizens were not allowed to leave the country with more than £5 in cash. This was, in effect, the same as putting a travel ban on Europe. BEA panicked and declared ninety-three of its pilots redundant. The 'Old Boys' were all-powerful and only agreed that it would be done on a basis of 'last in, first out' so Check Flight no longer existed and I was out of a job in a flooded market. As proof of BEA's panic, in less than six months they were writing to the sacked pilots offering them their jobs back, but not to Check Flight.

The Old Brigade had won.

CHAPTER ELEVEN

When the BEA Check Flight was no more, we were given three months' pay in lieu of notice and were let loose on a very overcrowded market. Luckily – and notice how many times in my life that word comes up – there were people in the Air Ministry who felt very badly about the treatment that we had received. I, with one or two others of the late Check Flight were contacted and were put in touch with the newly emerging international sector of Air India. I sent them my CV and was offered an immediate job as Senior Instructor based in Bombay, as it was then called. My job would be to train embryo Captains in flying the DC3s which the US Air Force had left all over India – and all over the world in fact – and also to train them on the first British civil airliner to emerge after the war, the Vickers Viking or 'Wickers Wiking' as the Indians fondly called it. The fact that I had already flown the prototype had a lot to do with my successful application. At that time I remember being astonished at the plush seating – or so it seemed to me after years of flying warplanes – and the proper toilet in place of the old Elsan.

Another Check Flight Pilot, Jack Eshelby, had been taken on with me and we were promised free passage and good accommodation for our families. We had to fly out there first, our families would join us later, and we left the UK in May 1948. This was just after the partition of India.

I had been a keen supporter of Blackpool Football Club since boyhood and had been lucky enough to form a very good friendship with several of the team that made Blackpool one of the strongest in the country during the regionalised league football in wartime Britain, due to Blackpool being the main centre of initial training for the RAF and thus able to call on many of the PT Instructors, amongst whom were some of the biggest names in football. As mentioned earlier, Stanley Matthews had been a Corporal in my father's signal centre and Stanley Mortensen, England's centre-forward, had been injured in a flying accident and was also in Blackpool. They and others were always very kind when I met them whilst on leave. Blackpool had reached the Final of the FA Cup that year and they had actually sent me two stand tickets for the Final – this was absolutely miraculous – but it was Dora and her brother-in-law who went to Wembley as I was on a brand new Lockheed Constellation on my way to Bombay. In the event Blackpool lost to Manchester United by four goals to two in what has come to be regarded as one of the finest footballing finals ever.

India was exciting. Apart from my training in the US and Canada I had never been out of England before. India was exotic and completely different. I got on well with the Indian pilots and it wasn't very long before Dora and our two children came out to join me. The lovely bungalow that Air India had promised us was for two families and we shared it with Jack Eshelby and his family. The bungalow was white marble, spacious and was practically on the beach at Juhu, which was a tiny fishing village near Santa Cruz, Bombay's airport. It looked wonderfully romantic but we were soon to be sadly disillusioned.

Our dining room overlooked the romantic beach complete with coconut palms but when the tide went out, miles of smelly mud flats were revealed. Worse was to come as these mud flats served as the communal toilets for the local villagers. First the men would come out and perform their toilets and ablutions and then it was the turn of the women. They each carried the obligatory Player's cigarette tin filled with water to use instead of the toilet paper used by Europeans. All this was performed under our dining room window. We had just about resigned ourselves to this aspect of our lives when along came the saga of the pi–dogs.

We had been pestered by these wretched half-wild packs of dogs rummaging around the dustbins, so called in the local police to do something about it. This they certainly did! I came back from the airport one day and could smell a horrible odour from over half a mile away. Our hysterical wives explained that the police had been and had put down meat which had been laced with strychnine. The pi-dogs had scoffed it and had promptly died a terrible death. The waiting kite hawks had swooped down to scavenge and had suffered the same fate. Then came the vultures… The resulting carnage was indescribable. I went post-haste to the police and, to give them their due, they immediately called the sanitary services.

We were introduced to something which had never entered our lives before – servants. We had a butler who would only touch my things but not anything of Dora's, a cook who would cook but not prepare food, an 'Ayah' for the children, who considered herself above all the other servants. There was a food preparer who also cleaned the rooms but not the bathroom or toilet, which were left to a poor little 'untouchable'.

Thomas, the cook, would come to Dora every morning with a sheet of paper for the day's menu. After wartime rationing our imagination would run riot, especially the desserts, but day after day the prescribed dessert would not be served with all sorts of excuses from Thomas. Always would 'crème caramel' take its place until we found out that it was the only sweet that he knew how to prepare. To this day the sight of crème caramel reminds me instantly of India.

It was inevitable that we would move and we did. We found a boarding house in Woodhouse Road, Bombay. We had a nice big ground floor room in a big block of flats run as a 'pension' by Major

Grey, English ex-Army, and his Anglo-Indian housekeeper friend, Miss Woods. Life there was very entertaining. The children were rapidly picking up the language and were spoiled completely by the Indians who love all children. When I used to scold Peter for something, one of the servants would get between me and him saying, 'Don't beat him, Sahib. Beat me instead.'

I would often find the two children squatting outside the building, Indian fashion, with the local newspaper seller – Paperwallah – with comics spread over the pavement, reading away to their hearts' content.

There was a lift shaft running up the centre of the building and one day, entering the place, I saw what looked like a leg of lamb going up on a piece of rope. I ran up the stairs and found one of the servants pulling it up to the third floor. The explanation was that meat had to be purchased directly from the slaughterhouse at Bandra so each family sent their bearer who would get together with the others and purchase some inferior cuts and one good one. It was the good one that was doing the rounds of the apartments to be shown to the memsahib, and then the cook would get the blame for the result of cooking the inferior ones.

One day we found the evidence that there were rats in our larder so we purchased a trap. The only sort that you could buy was the cage type. A few days later I heard the door of the trap snap shut so called the bearer and gave him instructions to take the rat outside and kill it. I found him in the garden, with the trap open, shooing the rat out. 'But sahib, it could be my grandfather,' he protested. I told him what I'd do with his grandfather if I found him in our apartment again.

We had bought a lovely 1939 Packard convertible, a real Hollywood star's car. It was a lovely green with white sidewall tyres. As petrol was still very rigorously rationed we had to rely on aviation petrol, surreptitiously siphoned from the Dakotas on dispersal from the drain valves under the wing. With our two children happily waving at everyone from the open back seat we would drive, like royalty, to Breach Kandy, which, even though the British had left

India for good earlier in the year, was still exclusively a club for whites only. There we would sit on the lush lawns and have our tea and sandwiches although one had to be very careful with them as the kite hawks would swoop and snatch them out of your hand as you were putting them into your mouth. It was at Breach Kandy that I bumped into one of my old friends, Ralph Hollis, who had trained with me in the US in 1941 and whom I had not seen since. He was flying for Decca Airlines who were based at Hyderabad, which was trying to maintain its independence from the new India.

Several notorious people were supplying Hyderabad with arms, gun-running in fact. One of the pilots who was involved, an ex-Aer Lingus man, told me that he had called in at Karachi to refuel a converted Lancaster on his way to Hyderabad with 'medical supplies'. Karachi, of course, was the capital of the new state of Pakistan and was violently opposed to the breakaway state of Hyderabad. The Lancaster was so heavily loaded that it failed to get off the ground and slid along on its belly, crashing through the airfield perimeter fence. In the pilot's own words, 'The trouble was all those "medical supplies" burst loose and there we were, the three of us, sitting amongst machine guns and rifles.' They scrambled out and stopped a bus which was coming along, hopped on and made their way to Karachi docks and were on a ship bound for England less than two hours after crashing their plane. I met up with the same chap over a year later when we were both flying on the Berlin Airlift. He was flying for Flight Refuelling, the same firm as I, and told me that he had qualified as a dentist on getting back to Ireland. Tragically he was killed when returning to England as a passenger in the only accident that the firm had, when the aircraft hit a hillside.

Although Air India had hired two of us as Instructors we found that not enough of the Indian pilots were sufficiently experienced to fly the routes and we were often pressed into service. The chief of Air India was a dynamic character called J.R.D. Tata. He was already one of the richest men in India through his textile mills and other concerns when he started Air India before the war. He taught

79

himself to fly and was the holder of the first Indian commercial pilot's licence.

Flying in India was different, to say the least. One of the first pupils I had was a very young chap who had only flown single-engine aircraft and had to be converted on to twins. His taxiing in the Dakota was very erratic and rough but we eventually lined up on the runway and I told him to take off. He took his feet off the brakes, opened up one throttle only and spun the aircraft round 360 degrees. 'Ooh yes, I forgot we've got two engines,' he said. He then confessed that his father had 'bought' his commercial licence for his birthday present!

Another day, coming in to land at Santa Cruz, we hit a buzzard whilst on the final approach. The authorities that designed the airport had overlooked the fact that there was a meat packing factory on the approach to the main runway and the resulting buzzards, kite hawks and even vultures were a constant menace. This one broke the main leg of the extended undercarriage so I retracted the other one, circled for about two hours to burn up fuel and then made a wheels-up landing on the grass beside the runway. It was safer to do this than land on the one good wheel. Luckily it was during the monsoon season and we slid along for about 100 yards closely pursued by what I thought was the fire engine but turned out to be a truck loaded with 'coolies' who jumped on to our aircraft, ignored the two pilots climbing out, and proceeded to paint out the Air India logo with whitewash before the newspaper reporters could photograph it!

The 'bread and butter' route in India was Bombay-Calcutta and Air India possessed the sole right to operate this line. The line concessions were renewed yearly by the Directorate of General Aviation (DGA) in Delhi. 'JRD', as Mr Tata was always known, phoned me one evening to tell me that I was to take him to Delhi the next day for the annual meeting for renewal of the routes. I asked him if we were 'night stopping' and he told me that we would be returning the same day. When we were going out to the plane I was amazed to see a large number of suitcases being loaded on to it. I said to JRD, 'I thought we were only staying in Delhi for the day?' He put his arm around me and gently said, 'You really don't know India, do you Reg?' The suitcases were full of rupees, of course, and the company with the most suitcases came back with the best routes. We came back with the Bombay-Calcutta route intact.

I was sitting in the old Dakota one morning, ready to check a Captain on the daily service to Calcutta when into the aircraft came JRD who politely requested that all twenty-one passengers, a full load, get off, which they did without demur. He then breezed into the cockpit and said, 'We're off to Poona to the races. You've just got time to bring your wives along as hostesses,' and off we went to Poona.

Another time I was assigned to take the assassin of Mahatma Gandhi to Delhi for his trial but I was not to appear on any photographs. The First Officer, duly promoted to Captain for the occasion, was the only one who appeared in the newspapers.

The stewardesses in India were all from very good families, generally beautiful but, with a few exceptions, not very worldly. As in all airlines new stewardesses were the subject of intensive leg pulling. One gag was for the First Officer to hide amongst the luggage which, on the Dakota, was always stowed behind the cockpit adjacent to a small cargo door on the left side near the nose. After take-off the Captain would call the poor girl to the cockpit and ask her to send the First Officer up. When she replied that she didn't think that the First Officer was in the back the Captain would tell her, in no uncertain terms, that it was her job to make sure that all the crew as well as the passengers were on board and now he would have to fly all the way to Calcutta on his own and it was all her fault. At the destination the First Officer would quickly go out through the small luggage door, run round to the main door as the stewardess was opening it and collapse into her arms saying, 'It was a hell of a run but I made it.'

On another occasion the stewardess came into the cockpit to take the two plastic cups from the pilots. Unlike modern pressurised aircraft the side windows of the Dakota's cockpit could be opened and she leant across the Captain to open his window to throw the empty cups out. He knocked her arm away and shouted, 'Don't ever do that. Can't you see that the other window is open? If you had opened mine there would have been a terrible vacuum and we would all have been sucked out of the aeroplane.' Later on, the Captain put the aircraft on the automatic pilot, opened both the windows, pressed the stewardess call button then he and the First Officer hid amongst the suitcases in the baggage compartment. The poor girl came up to an empty cockpit with both windows open and the Dakota flying serenely along all by itself.

Another favourite was the toilet flush. Remember this was India where only 'untouchables' cleaned toilets. On her first flight the stewardess would be asked by the Captain whether she had been briefed on flushing the toilet. Horrified, she would answer, 'No.' The Captain would gravely point to a large lever near the side of the seat. 'Whenever a passenger comes out of the toilet you must come up here and pump this lever twenty times to flush the toilet,' he would tell her and the unlucky girl would come up every five minutes or so and pump away at what was merely a hydraulic pump lever used for emergencies in the hydraulic system.

Juhu had its own aerodrome in those days. A tiny runway about 500 yards long accommodated the Piper Cubs from the flying club there. You can imagine the surprise when an enormous new Constellation actually succeeded in landing on the minuscule runway. Unfortunately, Santa Cruz's main runway and Juhu's only landing strip were in line and the unfortunate, but brilliant, pilot had actually lined up on Santa Cruz but had landed at Juhu. The whole aeroplane had to be dismantled and taken by road to Santa Cruz where it was put together again as the runway at Juhu was much too short for it to take off again even without passengers.

My contract with Air India was nearing its end and I was approached by one of the many companies that had sprung up in the newly independent India. The Americans had left DC3s and C47s all over India and these were seized by many presidents of banks and quite a few maharajahs. They then proceeded to form their own airlines and were always on the lookout for pilots. I eventually joined one of them who had a better reputation than the others. This time I was to really be a Captain and not an Instructor. I have exceedingly fond memories of Air India, which was a splendid company. I received nothing but kindness and consideration from such people as the incredible founder, J.R.D. Tata, Chief Instructor Biramji, and the two Gazdas amongst others far too numerous to mention.

The annual pilgrimage of devout Muslims to Mecca – The Hadj – was a lucrative source of income to the many airlines participating. Still using the old workhorse Dakota, we would fly Bombay to Aden, pick up our passengers there, then fly them on to Jedda which was the nearest we were allowed to the Holy City of Mecca. The passengers were always interesting. They would carry their possessions with them in string bags, shopping baskets and brown paper parcels. Flying along, one day, the nose of the DC3 rose alarmingly and I had to trim like mad to keep the aircraft level. The Radio Officer was sent back to investigate and found a group of the passengers huddled in the tail section cooking their meal over an open primus stove.

Once, after landing at Aden to pick up our passengers, I returned to the aeroplane after filing my flight plan, to find some forty people – all passengers – in the plane. There were people sitting on other passengers' knees and suitcases together with people in the narrow aisle between the twenty-one seats. The local agent was nearly crying with rage when I refused to take more than the authorised twenty-one people with their properly stowed baggage. 'But sahib, every Captain takes extra and we will share the money,' was his outraged plea. There was nearly rioting when I was adamant.

I flew fairly regularly from Bombay to Nairobi and quite enjoyed the different sort of life that I was now leading, but Dora was pregnant again and expecting the baby in March 1949. The heat and small apartment were beginning to get us down but accommodation on the ships sailing back to the UK was well-nigh impossible to obtain as thousands of people were leaving the country owing to the virtual state of war that had sprung up between the newly emerging countries of India and Pakistan.

On New Year's Eve 1948 we had a few people in for a drink in our apartment. One of them, by coincidence, was the Captain of the *Stratheden* that was sailing for the UK the next day. He had left his wife in our pension whilst he went on to Australia and had called to pick her up for the return voyage to the UK.

I said to him, only half-jokingly, 'I wish we were sailing with you tomorrow.' He replied, 'If you really mean that, I can fix it.' I turned everyone out, I remember we had only just wished everyone a 'Happy New 1949', and we started packing. Next morning we bought the classic tin steamer trunks, sold our beautiful Packard for the equivalent of £25 and were installed on the *Stratheden* when it sailed the evening of 1 January 1949. We had no winter clothes for the children but, luckily, the first port of call was Port Said and although we arrived there at 2 a.m., suddenly all the lights of the port came on. The shops opened up and the huge department store of Simon Aerts supplied us with the necessary clothes including two camel hair coats for the children, which were Peter and Linda's pride and joy, survived many years and were handed on until they almost became heirlooms. They were identical sizes but Peter had cut himself or had a nose bleed so his coat was always identified as the one 'with blood on the lining'.

The six weeks voyage was good fun. The food was magnificent and there were fancy-dress parties for the children who were well looked after and we made many friends. There were two Australian young women who were going to Britain as schoolteachers on an exchange scheme and it was one of those incredible coincidences that one of them should turn up at the school, in Peckham, where Peter and Linda started their English education.

CHAPTER TWELVE

Arriving back to a cold socialist Britain was a shock. There were queues for everything and housing was very hard to find. If you saw a queue outside a shop you automatically joined it without even knowing what it was for. Rationing was still in force for virtually everything including coal and there was absolutely no kind of luxury to be had. Dora's sister, Margie, put us up in her small flat in Peckham for a while and we were very, very fortunate in obtaining a nice, almost luxurious to us, ground floor flat on a council estate in Clapham in Albion Avenue, just off Wandsworth Road. There was only the 'utility' furniture to be had but we were grateful for anything and soon had the place cosy. Before we had any living room furniture we installed our pride and joy, an 8in Pye black and white television set. There were no colour transmissions in 1949. It was mounted on top of an old box and we were the only people in the huge block of flats to have such a thing so we had every child in the neighbourhood watching Muffin the Mule, Bill and Ben the Flower Pot Men, not forgetting Little Weed! They all squatted on the floor in front of the set in hypnotised bliss.

At the end of the war Germany and Berlin were divided into zones. The Western Zone was occupied and administered by the US, the UK and France while the Eastern Zone was occupied by the USSR. In July 1948 a new currency, the Deutsche Mark, was introduced into the Western Zone and to Western-controlled West Berlin to help combat inflation and bring back prosperity to the beaten nation. The USSR viewed this as an ominous threat and feared that it would bring the whole of Berlin including the Soviet Eastern Zone under capitalist Western influence. Stalin immediately closed down all road, rail and canal links from the Western half of Berlin to try and starve the people and therefore force the Western powers out of the city.

The Russian blockade of all routes into Berlin had resulted in the Allies, the Americans, British and French, deciding to supply the city of Berlin with all its vital necessities, food and fuel, entirely by air into the existing aerodromes of Tempelhof and, initially Gatow. The French had an unsuitable aerodrome at Tegel which in an unbelievably short time was turned into a vital part of the airlift by German labourers including thousands of women. Gatow was thus able to continue as the British civilian passenger airfield but with certain supplies being flown in there as well.

It was a daunting task especially in those early days of Instrument Flying. GCA (Ground Controlled Approach), where the aircraft was 'talked down' by a radar operator, was the only reliable means of instrument approach and had its very severe limitations requiring a final visual landing, so a minimum cloud base of 200ft was a necessity. The operation was also designed to show the Russians the tremendous air power and determination of the Western Allies.

Pilots, of course, were 'flavour of the month' and once again coincidence played a remarkable part in my career. I applied for a captaincy with Flight Refuelling. This company was founded by one of my boyhood heroes, Sir Alan Cobham, a great pre-war pioneer of aviation. The company had secured the contract for flying in all Berlin's petrol and diesel fuel. The UK base was at Tarrant Rushton, near Poole and I went down there to be interviewed by their Chief Pilot. I found him to be an old colleague from training days in the class of 42A in the States, Tommy Marks. I was engaged immediately as a Captain on the converted Lancaster bombers, called the Lancastrian, which the company was using.

I found myself very quickly in Germany, based at the RAF airfield of Wunstorf, near Hanover, but we soon moved to Fuhlsbüttel, the main airfield for Hamburg. From there we would fly three sorties in twenty-four hours to Berlin and back. We would fly, without any days off, for three weeks alternating the shifts that we flew, then take our aircraft back to Tarrant Rushton for servicing whilst we had one week's leave in the UK. Pay was generous. We were billeted in the Basler Hof Hotel in the centre of the city, which was absolutely flattened, of course, from the wartime bombing. All our accommodation and meals were paid for and we were given a daily allowance of 'scrip', BAF (British Armed Forces) money to pay our incidental expenses. Whisky and gin at the bar was 6d a tot and a bottle was 6s! Our travel was paid for all over the UK during our leave and our generous pay in the UK was on top of all the allowances.

During the sixteen hours per day that we had free, we would enjoy our rest and also the permanent sessions that would be going on in the bar and billiard room where we would play our own particular game entitled 'Bonzo'. There was an extra white ball worth ten points and large amounts of scrip would change hands on that and the permanent poker school that was always in session.

We would leave a session at the bar to fly our sorties to Berlin and return to find it still going on with different people. The barman was a monocled ex-U-boat Commander named 'Fritz', needless to say.

Once, after a session of 'high cockalorum' which consisted of a sort of rugby scrum with bodies piled one on the other until the goal of either the ceiling or the complete collapse of everyone was achieved, I found Fritz regarding the scene and watching one of our Captains, who had broken his neck in a crash but had recovered and was flying on the *Luftbrücke* as the Airlift was called. He retained muscular control but after a few drinks this would go and his head would roll, horribly, for 360 degrees around his neck. Fritz was at the bar, with his head in his hands, weeping uncontrollably.

'What's up, Fritz?' I said sympathetically. 'How did you bastards win the war?' was his tearful reply.

I found myself renewing acquaintance with many old friends including Ralph Hollis who became my First Officer for a short while before he got his own command. The flying was tough. You kept exactly three minutes behind the aircraft in front of you, whether you could see him or not, all the way to Berlin where you were taken over by the GCA for the landing, irrespective of the weather conditions. We were using Tegel aerodrome, in the French zone. The Americans were using Tempelhof and the British, Gatow. The Sunderland flying boats were landing on the big lake in Berlin. People were buying old Halifaxes, Lancasters, Yorks, anything to get an Airlift contract. For some weeks an old York was always the aircraft ahead of me on take-off from Fuhlsbüttel. Every day it seemed to take a few more yards to get airborne and, sure enough, one day it disappeared through the far fence with a loud bang amidst dense clouds of white smoke. Luckily nobody was hurt and the white smoke came from the tons of flour it was carrying.

From June 1948 until May 1949 the Allies flew 278,247 sorties and their planes delivered, roughly, a total of over 2 million tonnes of supplies including clothing, medicine, coal, building material, petrol and diesel oil. It was calculated that there was a plane landing every three minutes of the day and night, week in week out.

It was a very good feeling and the gratitude of the Berliners was made apparent every time we landed there. We had to wait a couple of hours each time while they defuelled every plane and they made it abundantly clear that the Allies were saving them from the absolutely dreaded occupation by the Russians. The action of a certain US pilot who devised the idea of dropping hundreds of tiny parachuted packets of sweets as he approached the runway was soon eagerly anticipated by the German children and they congregated in their thousands to scoop them up. He was called Gail Halvorsen but he got the nickname of the 'Candy Bomber'.

According to reports, Stalin was shaken to the core by the magnitude and the skilled performance of the Western Powers in performing the fantastic operation throughout nearly a year and in every possible sort of weather. He was shown that the Western Powers were not going to yield and re-opened up the links on 12 May 1949.

Our second son, Anthony, was born on 24 March 1949 whilst I was in Germany. He was born in the South London Hospital at Clapham and was a big, happy baby. He was completely spoiled by the many children that we had as neighbours in our flat at Spencer House in Albion Avenue SW8. Toys and other so called luxury items were still unobtainable in the UK but many things were on sale in the NAAFI shops that catered exclusively to the BAOR or the British Army of the Rhine as we were called. Few people realise how austere the UK was even seven years after the war when I joined Sabena. Everything was for export to obtain the precious foreign currencies. The meat ration, when I left for India in 1948, was the equivalent of two small lamb chops per person per week. Through the NAAFI I was able to buy some toys for our new son and also a bone china tea service, made in England but unobtainable there. Peter, later, was the lucky recipient of a real pedal model jeep also bought through the NAAFI.

Things were even tougher in Germany. Coffee, cigarettes and such banal things as cocoa replaced the German Mark as currency. They were eagerly sought after by the German crews who defuelled our planes in Berlin and we would bring back what we could when we returned from the UK every three weeks. Once, on my way to catch a tram to Waterloo station where I would get on my train to the airfield near Bournemouth, I was stopped by two policemen in a police car. It was about 11 p.m. and I was carrying a suitcase. The police politely asked me what was in it. I showed them that it was full of Bournville Cocoa and explained that I was on my way back to Germany. 'Hop in,' they said, 'we'll give you a lift' and took me all the way to Waterloo Station.

The aeroplanes that we were flying were Lancaster bombers that had their gun turrets removed and a streamlined nose fitted. The Lancastrian was, in fact, used for early passenger transport on the London–Australia route carrying some eight passengers in doubtful comfort. As we were carrying all the petrol and fuel oil to Berlin it was fitted with a huge internal tank down the centre of the fuselage behind the main spar. It was only a short flight from Hamburg, so the wing tanks were also used to carry motor fuel. A total of about 2,500 gallons of motor fuel per trip was thus carried by each aircraft. The result was a flying petrol tanker and was the main reason why we were so well paid. In actual fact, through careful selection of flying and ground personnel and insistence on a comprehensive three-weekly check of the aircraft back at Tarrant Rushton, Flight Refuelling never had a fatal accident on the actual Airlift although one was lost on a return flight to Tarrant Rushton when it flew into a hilltop in fog with the loss of six crew members. Many other lives were lost, however, but the show of strength in the air almost certainly prevented the outbreak of a Third World War and invaluable experience was gained in the controlling of large numbers of aircraft and in instrument flying.

On 17 July 1949 I made my last of 113 sorties from Hamburg to Berlin and then flew back in a Dakota to an England that was suddenly flooded with pilots all looking for jobs. My logbook (No 2) showed that I had 2,793 flying hours.

Civil aviation still had not 'taken off'. Flying was regarded as dangerous and was very expensive. I could not find any job in aviation and I had to take a succession of various poorly paid and dull jobs. I sold toilet rolls around the boarding houses of Paddington and Victoria. The only good thing that came out of it was that I learned my way around London by driving a small green van around the various hotel and boarding house districts. I had a brief job as a counter assistant in Bewlay's pipe and tobacco shop in the Strand and then salvation came in the shape of an advertisement requiring people to be trained as Air Traffic Controllers.

I went for an interview at Adastral House, in London and was lucky enough to be recognised from my Check Flight days at Aldermaston by several of the board of examiners. I was accepted for training at the school for Air Traffic Controllers (ATC) at Hurn near Bournemouth, but it would be three months before my course would start. To make ends meet I got a job as a 'Tallyman' around the Croydon area. A Tallyman was employed to collect the sixpences and even pennies from the customers of firms who sold household goods and clothes from door-to-door and on the 'never never', as Hire Purchase was called.

This was the very bottom of the barrel and I shall never forget the poverty that I saw and the stories that I was told as to why they couldn't pay the odd pennies and threepences that they owed each miserable week. Thank goodness it didn't last long because flying began to pick up a little and I had kept valid my B Licence. I was able to freelance at Croydon where various pre-war firms were starting up again using de Havilland Rapides, Oxfords and even single-engine planes like the Proctor, all of which I rapidly 'swotted' up and added to my licence. The two main firms were Olley and Morton, both very solid and well-known as pioneers. The Chief Pilot of Morton was Captain Bebb, one of the true pre-war charter pilots. These firms only employed one or two pilots on a regular basis and relied on freelance pilots during the summer and at weekends. The pay was 30s per hour and was very welcome especially as the odd trip to Le Touquet and Le Zoute enabled you to bring back a steak or two. Meat was still rationed in 1950!

It was during this period that I was having a drink in a pub in the West End and got talking to a chap who told me that the BBC were looking for someone to replace an announcer for the sports news on the World Service. He gave me the address of a Mr Lotbinière to contact. He was one of the tallest men I had ever seen, who greeted me courteously and arranged for an immediate voice test. 'Lobby', as I came to know him, told me that the job was mine on a temporary basis at the princely wage of 15 guineas per week. I was to read the sports news for the World Service at 6.45 a.m. for fifteen minutes and then, again, at 7 p.m.. As there was no public transport at 5 a.m. when I had to leave our flat in Clapham, the BBC sent a taxi for me to get to Portland Place. I had to take the more mundane tram to get me home in the evening though.

I will never forget the first time that I sat before a microphone and the red light went on and I realised that I was to speak to millions of people all over the world. It was a wonderful feeling but very frightening and I am sure that my voice quavered through those first few minutes. I thought of my Auntie Muriel and realised that I was following a little in her footsteps. It was Wimbledon Championship time and I dealt with such tongue twisters as Jaroslav Drobny and others even more difficult to pronounce. Looking back I am amazed to recall that I carried on with my freelance flying during the day, including taking such well-known jockeys as 'Scobie' Breasley to race meetings all over the country, always relying on getting back in good time for my evening broadcast. I never missed one which, considering the British weather and the fact that I was flying various pre-war planes, many of them single-engined, was pretty amazing.

Once, Captain Bebb told me that I was to take a gentleman from Croydon to Yeadon, now Leeds Airport, and that I was to carry out every request the client made. The gentleman in question looked harmless enough; in his sixties, somewhat old fashioned but impeccably dressed and extremely courteous. We took off in a DH Rapide and he seated himself just behind me. After about fifteen minutes he said, 'Captain, that's a nice looking cloud over there. Can we take a closer look, please?' That was to be the pattern during the next half hour or so then he suddenly announced that it was time for 'a spot of lunch'. There was no catering on board in those days so I had to find a civil aerodrome nearby, not an easy task then. I eventually found Anstey, near Coventry, where we landed and had a nice lunch in the clubhouse for which he paid and left a £2 tip that was more than the cost of the meal. When we landed on the grass aerodrome of Leeds I saw a beautiful old, chauffeur-driven Daimler coming out to meet us. It was bottle green with highly polished brass headlamps. The chauffeur, also in bottle green livery, opened the door of the Rapide, helped my passenger into the Daimler then came to me with a silver tray on which were two recently laundered huge white £5 notes. I protested that the payment for the flight was not to be made to me but was told, gravely, in broad Yorkshire, 'This, Captain, is your "Pourboire" and my employer thanks you for a very pleasant journey.' I have to admit, shamefully, that I have forgotten his name but not the memory of graceful living and an age of air transport that has gone forever. Ten pounds was a lot of money and together with my £6–£7 from my freelance activities, was more than the BBC was paying me for a week's broadcasting.

The DH Rapide, like all de Havilland aeroplanes, not only flew well but looked good. It was the maid of all work for the charter companies. If I remember rightly it took nine passengers and was used extensively on the Scottish Isles service by BEA as they were then known. The pilot occupied the single seat in the nose and the passengers sat behind him with no dividing door. A well-known character of a Captain, who shall be nameless, used to sit whilst the aircraft was on the ground, in one of the rear seats, dressed in a shabby old raincoat whilst the handful of passengers boarded. He would sit there, muttering, looking at his watch. 'Where's the pilot? If he's not here in five minutes then I'm going to take the flight. Right. That's it,' and would stride up to the nose, start the engines and take off with his startled passengers. The same Captain, when the new Vikings came into service, would board the plane after the passengers were all aboard, walk up the aisle to the cockpit, ostentatiously carrying a book with *How to Fly in Six Easy Lessons* emblazoned on its cover in very large letters. During the flight he would come back into the passenger cabin and search around the legs and feet of one of the passengers, usually a pretty girl, saying, 'Excuse me, but have you seen a loose page anywhere? You see, it's the landing ...'

One of the freelance pilots at Croydon, later to be a colleague on the Berlin Airlift, made a forced landing just short of the runway which was only a very small 'touchdown' piece of concrete leaving you to finish your landing run on the grass. He landed on the football field on the other side of Purley Way scattering the players who ran for their lives as he came in. When the Rapide came to a stop he stuck his head out of the side window, 'What's the score then?' he asked amiably. Needless to say he was one of the many Irish pilots who were freelancing at that time.

My ATC course was due to start and I, reluctantly, said goodbye to the BBC. It was impossible to break into the very tightly knit circle of permanently engaged staff no matter how hard I tried. For some years afterwards small cheques would keep coming in from the BBC when some of my news bulletins had been used in a programme of some sort. It had been a wonderful experience and I met some fascinating people. One of the most interesting was a lady to whom you referred any problem with pronunciation, no matter in what language. She would immediately give you the correct pronunciation without referring to the thousands of books with which she was surrounded. Many were the stories of spoonerisms made over the air including, of course, the 'Fleets all lit up with little fairy lights' when the commentator had been well and truly entertained by the Royal Navy prior to the broadcast. I was only 15 at the time but I remember listening to it with my father, both helpless with laughter. 'Lit Up' passed in to the language as a euphemism for being drunk. One, which was probably apocryphal, was of the Sports announcer who got the Royal Hunt Cup well and truly mixed up.

I had bought a second-hand motorbike. It was a 'bitsa' – bits of this and bits of that – but it went well. It was a hybrid of various British bikes. There were no Japanese bikes on the market then. I travelled down to Hurn, near Bournemouth, to start my six weeks ATC course. I would stay the week at Hurn and then travel up to Clapham on my bike for the weekend. The course was good fun and not very difficult as the airways system was only just starting up and traffic was light.

I made some good friends amongst my fellow trainees and often spoke to some of them twenty or so years later from the cockpit of a DC10 or a 747 flying over their area. One of them was an out and out cockney and became one of the most well-known characters at London Airport. It was still the era of the rather stilted 'BBC' accent where 'Daddy' became 'Deddy'. 'Nobby', as I shall call him, had a no nonsense, good old London twang that you could cut with a knife. Once, whilst on taxi control, Nobby asked a BEA aircraft that had just cleared the runway and was waiting for its terminal stand number, 'BEA, did I give you a stand?' Back came a very Oxford-accented reply, 'Not with a voice like that, old boy.'

I was successful in obtaining my preliminary watch keeping certificate and was very happy to be posted to Croydon, of all places. This meant much more time with Dora and the children and I could easily get to work on my motorbike. As a trainee I was not allowed to stand watch on my own and this turned out to be a great advantage as word got around the charter companies and soon the telephone would start ringing with requests for me to 'pop over' to Le Touquet or Deauville during my watch hours. The odd bottle of brandy and a nice steak kept my brother controllers happy and I was always assured of a speedy ATC clearance from them when I was coming back to land.

One of the charter companies had been asked to bring the body of an Englishman back from France where he had died. The aircraft was actually in the circuit when a Dove, flown by Tommy Gunn, a great Croydon character, called me up and requested a priority landing as he had trouble with one of his two engines. This I gave him and had the fire engine and the ambulance stand by the tiny runway strip leading to the grass. Unfortunately the hearse, awaiting the body, was standing next to them and I saw the Dove come over Purley Way and go up about 6ft in the air before touching down. 'Blimey, you cover everything!' was Tommy's remark as he touched down.

I enjoyed my ATC duties but the pay was very low and we were, as usual, struggling very hard to bring up our three children. I had always kept my pilot's licence valid, at considerable expense as all medicals and training flights had to be paid for by me. One day a pilot, who had just landed, came into the Control Tower where I was on duty. His name was Tom Chambers and he was the Chief Pilot for Short Brothers, the aircraft Instructors, who ran various flying schools at Rochester in Kent.

He told me that he had a contract with the Fleet Air Arm (FAA) to ferry their various fighter aircraft around the country and was looking for pilots. He offered me a job there and then, which I accepted, resigned from ATC and presented myself at Rochester. There I was interviewed by their Chief Flying Instructor, Frank Holt. He told me that they were very impressed with my Instructional qualifications (I held an A1 category and a master green card for instrument flying from my Empire Flying School and Aldermaston days) and offered me a much better job as an Instructor to the FAA pilots. The pilots came to Rochester for a three-week course to get the 'green card' necessary to obtain an Instrument Flight Rules (IFR) clearance, which was now mandatory for anyone wishing to fly around the country on the new airways system. The aircraft we used were Oxfords fitted with the two-stage amber system that I had used so extensively at Aldermaston with the Check Flight.

One of the great advantages of the job was that it was a Monday to Friday one, leaving me free to freelance at Croydon and even at London Airport, where a firm had started joyrides around London. They even paid 35s per hour to their freelance pilots and charged the passengers 10s each for a fifteen-minute trip.

The Instrument Training course at Rochester included comprehensive ground school, and each Instructor had his own subject on which to lecture the naval pilots who came in all ranks from the lowest to highest. My subject was Instruments, and Shorts sent me to Sperry, the instrument makers' factory in London for a week in order to get a solid background to my lectures. This was a bonus as I was able to have a nice easy run to Clapham each evening instead of the daily hour and a half each way to Rochester.

Our lectures took place from 9.00 a.m. until 10.00 a.m. Flying started soon after until 12.15 p.m. Lunch was served in the excellent Staff Mess and was subsidised by the company. We then flew again until 4 p.m. and that was a very pleasant day. As you only lectured once a week you didn't have to report until just before 10 a.m. unless you were lecturing.

Rochester was a tiny grass aerodrome set in a triangle on the top of the lovely named Bluebell Hill. The surrounding countryside was beautiful and as commuting from London became more and more of a chore, Dora and I began looking for a house nearby. Motorbikes are fine when the weather is good but I was arriving at work and coming home soaked to the skin as often as not. We eventually bought a semi-detached three-bedroomed house in the tiny village of Walderslade at the bottom of Bluebell Hill from another pilot at Shorts. We were so happy to move to the first house that we really owned ourselves. There was a long garden at the back where we grew vegetables to help out with still rationed England and Dora was able to indulge in her greatest wish to keep chickens. They were the best fed hens in Kent, if not England, and the smell of chicken cooking instantly takes me back to very happy days in Erin House, Victoria Road.

We had no telephone but our next door neighbour, Mrs Fortman, had and was nice about letting us use it so I was still able to continue with the freelancing at weekends, which helped so much with our finances.

I had progressed from the motorbike to a nice little Morris Minor and we had lovely times at the weekend, when I wasn't freelancing, touring the nearby countryside and the seaside resorts of Kent, including the Isle of Sheppey.

One day, in February 1952, I was driving to work when I saw my Flight Commander, Peter Harrison, flagging me down on the other side of the road. 'Go back home. Pack a few things. You've got to go to Corsica,' he said. Shorts, at that time, were making a small amphibious aircraft called the Sealand and one of them, on a delivery flight, had gone u/s with engine trouble and had landed at Ajaccio in Corsica. It was flown by Don Tanton, their Chief Company Pilot. I knew him by sight but our paths were to cross many times in later years. Apart from the odd trip across the Channel to Le Touquet, Deauville and Le Zoute I had never made a long distance flight in civil aviation. This was truly a big thing for me, picking up a Wireless Operator, a mechanic for the Sealand and lots of spare parts for the engine; we cleared customs at Croydon and set off on our first leg to Lyon. We did not have the equipment for night flying so decided to spend the night there. Our aircraft was one of the training flight Oxfords and performed faultlessly throughout the trip. At Lyon we persuaded one of the ATC officers, who spoke a tiny bit of English, to take us into the city when he had finished work and show us a reasonably inexpensive place to stay. He took us to a small pension with a restaurant. We were made very welcome as ex-RAF flyers were still extremely popular. After cleaning up we came down for our evening meal which was better than anything that we had tasted for years.

Lyon prides itself on being the gastronomic centre of France and we would have endorsed that. The patron came over and sat with us and with my halting, schoolboy French and his few words of English, we had a good conversation going helped by the numerous cognacs that he insisted were on the house. When he learned that we were going to Ajaccio the next morning, he nearly burst into tears. 'Me, Ajaccio,' he repeated, thumping his chest as he pointed to himself. It turned out that he had left Ajaccio as a small boy, about twenty years before and had never been back although he had large numbers of his family still there. The cognacs had done their work well because I managed to say, *Viens avec nous demain.* There was absolutely no reason why not. There was plenty of room aboard. The only thing was that we didn't know how long the repairs would take so we couldn't give him a return date. His wife, dressed in the regulation black bombazine, had been watching the proceedings with ever increasing disapproval. *Alors mes amis*, he said finally, 'You sleep and we see how you feel tomorrow.' His English wasn't as good as that but we understood perfectly what he meant. We came down the next morning to a gigantic breakfast. He had been out to buy bacon as he knew that bacon and eggs was our favourite breakfast. I told him that he could come, subject to signing a disclaimer relieving Shorts of all responsibility. His wife burst into tears and embraced him as though she would never see him again, which was probably what was going through her mind.

We had learnt that his name was Orsi and he asked us to give him an hour whilst he made 'certain preparations', then off we went to the aerodrome but this time in his car, together with his tearful wife and followed by three more cars full of relatives. We had told him that there was not much comfort in the Oxford but he had brought a large wicker basket on which he perched himself, behind me, with the mechanic sitting in the right-hand seat. Our Radio Officer had a canvas chair behind Mr Orsi. To a right royal farewell, except from his crying wife, we took off and set course for the south.

The Oxford hadn't the performance or the equipment to overfly the Alps so I flew all the way down the Rhône Valley and then along the coast to Nice before setting course to Ajaccio. We had completely lost radio contact with anyone so before setting course I flew up and down the main runway at Nice to let them see our registration and then headed out towards Ajaccio.

As we flew very low over the Mediterranean, there was a loud bang and I nearly jumped out of my skin. Mr Orsi had opened his wicker basket and had popped the champagne that he had brought, together with the roast chicken, foie gras, truffles and crisp baguettes. You name it, it was there. We sat there with the sun shining, the sea sparkling, having the feast of our lives. When the coast of Corsica came into sight, Mr Orsi's eyes filled with tears and I fully expected him to kiss the ground when we landed there on a lovely afternoon with the smell of mimosa all around.

Mr Orsi was very quickly on the telephone because, in no time at all there were cars all around us packed with what looked like the fiercest brigands that you could imagine. They proceeded to hug and kiss Mr Orsi and then, after explanations, it was our turn to be embraced. Mr Orsi explained that there were no longer any brigands on the island but they had been replaced by hoteliers and we were to stay at his brother-in-law's hotel and would be treated like that other well-known Corsican, Napoleon. And we were!

The repairs went very speedily, too speedily for our passenger, and we were ready to leave the very next day. That night we were regally wined and dined and I was introduced to Absinthe, the deadly drink which had long been banned in France but was still the local drink in Corsica. At breakfast next morning, the whole fish complete with glassy eye staring at me proved too much and I beat a hasty retreat to my room where I stayed until it was time to leave. Once again a huge procession of cars escorted us to the airfield where the Oxford was loaded to the brim with mimosa, tangerines and bottle after bottle of liqueurs of various sorts. Mr Orsi, now beaming from ear to ear, was carried on board by about fifty of his relatives and off we went.

There was no question of doing anything other than staying the night in Lyon. The restaurant was declared closed except to invited relatives and guests and a greatly relieved, and a little surprised, Madame Orsi smothered us with kisses and led us to the place of honour next to her husband at a table surrounded by at least ten more, where all his guests were seated. The ambiance was fantastic; Mr Orsi, beaming, kept on patting me. 'Mon Commandant' he kept saying proudly.

Moules marinières, as an hors d'oeuvre, followed by steak à la Lyonnaise, and then course after course followed. The flight back to England was a bit of an anti-climax but the mimosa and tangerines were gratefully received by the Customs at Croydon and the Staff at Rochester.

Years afterwards, and now speaking better French, I tried to find the restaurant whilst on the way down to the South of France for a holiday with the family, but Mr Orsi had gone and nobody around could help me.

I was still a member of the RAFVR (Royal Air Force Volunteer Reserve) for which I received about £85 per year but had to put in a certain number of flying hours in order to qualify. We were allowed to use one of the Tiger Moths at Rochester for this and I spent many enjoyable hours indulging in aerobatics and manoeuvres that I had not performed since my training days in Georgia some eight or nine years before. I remember, one afternoon, hanging upside down, suspended by my straps, looking up at the Thames and Medway saying to myself: 'What a silly position for the father of three children to be in' and enjoying every second of it.

Another source of extra money was 'Army Cooperation'. This entailed night flying with the good old Rapide over the East End of London and other places to help train the searchlight battalions stationed around the capital. I'm afraid that the 85mph we cruised at did not give them too much trouble. Fog was quite a problem at Rochester and once, after returning from one of those Army Co-op exercises, I could only see the lamppost at the corner of the airfield, sticking out of the thick fog that enveloped the rest of it. I was able to use this to land but could not see to taxi so had to leave my aeroplane in the middle of the field and grope my way to the Control Tower.

The airfield at Rochester drops away to the west and there is a deep valley along which the M2 now runs, just before the bridge which spans the Medway. Once, coming in to land with my Navy pupils and approaching across the valley from the west, both my engines cut out. I just had enough time to stick my nose down, dive into the valley and gain enough speed to pull up over the ridge and flop the Oxford down on to the airfield. Luckily my wheels had already been lowered for the landing. Blocked fuel lines were found to have cut off the fuel to both engines.

Whilst I was still at Rochester, my mother and father decided to make a coach tour on the Continent. Not liking sea travel they asked me if it would be possible to fly them to Dunkirk where they could meet the coach. Shorts had a single-engine Proctor which they hired out to the staff pilots, at cost. So together with Dora, off we set. I had written to the authorities at the small aerodrome of Mardyck, near Dunkirk, telling them when I would be arriving. I had not received any reply but, nevertheless, we flew off to Lympne to clear Customs and Passport control. There I discovered that I had left my briefcase with the 'ship's' papers and our passports at Rochester, so we had to go back there and collect them before presenting them at Lympne again. We had a lovely flight across the Channel. I think it was the first time that I had ever flown with Dora as my passenger and it was so nice to have her there sitting next to me as we flew to France. When we got to Dunkirk we could not raise anyone on the radio and Mardyck looked deserted. It was a grass aerodrome so I put down as near to the Control Tower as possible. There was not a soul in sight. Eventually a lone figure on a bicycle appeared on the horizon. When he got to us he made us understand that we were to wait until the local gendarmes arrived. Eventually two sinister, black gangster type Citroëns arrived and discharged four gendarmes. Nobody spoke any English. Papers were demanded. The radio licence of the aircraft which bore the Royal Seal impressed everyone.

Passports were examined and promptly taken away from us. All of this was done in a field with a howling wind and the papers were examined on the wing of the plane. The word 'taxi' kept cropping up. My mother was trying hard to dictate everything, but in English spoken a few decibels louder than usual. The man with the bicycle had left but turned up again about twenty minutes later, closely followed by yet another sinister Citroën which turned out to be a taxi. We all crowded into this and then, escorted by two Citroëns packed with gendarmes, swept into Dunkirk to the police station. There, at last, we managed to get the Chief of Police to understand that we were merely seeing my parents off on a tour and the ship carrying it was due in about two hours. Eventually, it was decided that we could stay as long as we kept the taxi driver with us, so we went to the docks where we were told that the ship was two hours late.

My father, who was always the worrying sort, wanted to sit there on the dock until the ship appeared, but my mother, as usual, had her own way and suggested that we had something to eat. All of us, taxi driver included, had a small meal together and then eventually met the ship and put my relieved father and mother on the coach.

On the way back to the airfield we passed the taxi driver's home. His wife ran out shouting that she had a message for us to fly to Lille and clear Customs there before returning to Lympne, in England. I was in a quandary. Because of my return to Rochester from Lympne and then back, I had not enough fuel to fly to Lille and then on to Lympne. We did not have enough money to buy petrol and credit cards were unheard of at that time. Taking my courage in both hands I took off and flew directly back to Lympne where I went up to the Control Tower and explained, to the best of my ability, what had happened. The Controller was most helpful. 'We can contact the Calais Control Tower direct by VHF [Very High Frequency – the usual method of communication speech over comparatively short distances] and explain,' he said. He did so and I asked him to apologise to French Customs. I shall never forget the answer that came back.

'Monsieur, you cannot apologise to French Customs.'

Weeks later I received a letter from the MCA (Ministry of Civil Aviation) asking me, most civilly, to explain 'without prejudice' why I had been to France, left two unknown people there without clearing Customs or Immigration and had then returned without completing any of the necessary clearance formalities with the 'aforesaid' Customs and, this time, Emigration. I duly replied and never heard another word from them. Months later I received a letter from the Dunkirk airfield people saying that they were sorry but their only Controller had been on *congé* (leave) but they had heard that I had been over and hoped that we had enjoyed the visit.

CHAPTER THIRTEEN

Around March 1952 an advertisement appeared in the aviation magazines *Aeroplane* and *Flight* that roused the somnolent world of British aviation. Sabena, the Belgian airline, wanted pilots. Practically everyone at Shorts applied but I did not. I was quite happy at Rochester. We had our little house and garden, the children were happy at school and had rapidly made friends. The hours were reasonable and left me free at weekends to freelance and enjoy family life. I learned later that Sabena had vacancies for thirty pilots and had received well over 1,200 applications.

A week or so went by and one day I came into work at about a quarter to ten, to find my Flight Commander, Peter Harrison, in a bad mood. 'What time do you think this is?' he said. 'I'm not lecturing this morning, Peter.' I said reasonably. 'It doesn't matter. Everyone is supposed to be here at nine whether they're flying or not,' he replied. I lost my temper. 'Why don't you install a bloody time-clock and then we can all clock-in and out?' was my reply. I stormed out and sat straight down and wrote off to Sabena applying for one of the vacancies.

I eventually got a reply from their office at London Heathrow Airport asking me to come for an interview on a weekday the following week. Having cooled down by now and being still very

unconcerned with the whole business, I wrote back to tell them that
I was working during the week and could not, in all fairness, ask
my employers for time off to apply for another job. I told them that
if they could not fit me in on a Saturday then they could forget all
about my application. I sent this off and forgot all about airline flying
of which I knew very little. A few days later, our neighbour came to
tell me that there was a phone call for me. It was a lady from Sabena
who told me that she was the London manager's secretary and that
they would interview me next Saturday morning. Even then I was
in two minds whether to go or not but, eventually, we all went up
to London where we stayed with our friends, Chris and Jim, who
were neighbours from our old block of flats in Clapham.

The interview turned out to be more like a questionnaire
conducted by me as it seemed that Sabena were desperate for pilots
and were trying to sell the company and the benefits of living in
Belgium. The big obstacle to getting the job was the huge number of
applicants for the thirty vacancies. Evidently Sabena was expanding
rapidly. They were one of the oldest aviation companies in the world
and pioneered flying to Africa between the two world wars. The
Belgian Pilots' Association was agreeable to the company recruiting
foreign pilots but insisted that they must be British, preferably with
RAF background. This was because the hardcore of Senior Captains
was all ex-RAF, most with distinguished fighter pilot careers who
still held a high regard for the UK. Many of them had British wives,
several of them ex-WAAF. The very high number of applications
was due to the fact that Sabena wanted pilots of varying experience,
some of them with very few hours, for future training, and had not
required current licences so ex-RAF pilots, who were in sedentary
jobs and had long given up any thoughts of flying again, had applied.
They also required very experienced pilots to fill the immediate
requirement and that is where I was lucky.

The interview board consisted of the London manager, Mr Stocké,
the Operations Manager Mr Stainier, and one of the handful of
British pilots who had already joined Sabena directly after the war,

Dougie Owen. I was told that I would be given four years seniority to compensate for my high number of flying hours (3,000, which was a lot in 1952) and would be paid around three times as much as any pilot in the UK was earning at that time. I would have to start as a First Officer but was promised a captaincy within two years. In BOAC First Officers were waiting up to twelve years and sometimes never attaining Captain's rank. There would be a probation period of three months and then the company would pay for the passage of Dora and the children to join me in Brussels. During this time I would be lodged in a first class hotel and all meals would be paid for by the company. There would be a ground course followed by examinations on general aviation subjects such as meteorology, radio procedure, air traffic and even aviation law, none of which should trouble me as I already held a commercial licence; 90 per cent of the applicants did not. All this was subject to passing Sabena's medical examination.

A heart-searching discussion took place between Dora and I. It must be remembered that this was long before the Common Market had even been thought about. Very little was known about Belgium by the average British citizen and what there was, was not heartening. The country was going through a difficult stage. The king, Leopold III, had been spurned by the country after the war and had been forced to abdicate. There were many calls for the country to become a republic and the British press reported fighting between the French-speaking Walloons and the Dutch-speaking Flemish from Flanders. In the end we decided to accept as the three-month probation period would give us the chance to see for ourselves what conditions were like. Dora and the children would stay with her parents in St Helens and as Sabena had promised free tickets at weekends and they had a DC3 service to Manchester, we would see each other regularly.

A letter soon arrived offering me one of the vacancies, subject to my passing their medical examination. Enclosed was a return ticket from London to Brussels. I went to London in March 1952. The aircraft was a Convair 240 and the Captain was British. By coincidence, yet again, he was Len Thorne who had been a pupil of mine when I was a Check Captain at Aldermaston. He was one of the First Officers who had been made redundant by BEA and had been fortunate in securing a job, very quickly, with Sabena.

There were about six of us, all prospective Sabena pilots on the flight and we were met in Brussels by two nice Sabena girls who showed us around the small complex at Melsbroek. One of us, David Cable, was so impressed by Lilian, one of the young women, that he stayed in Brussels that night, instead of coming back to England with the rest of us, and took her out to dinner. Nearly thirty years later, Dora and I were on a flight as passengers from Johannesburg to Brussels when we instantly recognised the stewardess as being Lilian and Dave's daughter.

The medical was a very thorough one and included blood tests, electro-cardiograph and X-rays. I was told by a nurse to *déshabillez-vous* so, when she left the room I undressed and lay on the couch. She came back in, burst out laughing and went out again. One of the doctors came in and explained, in English, that it was only necessary to undress, 'to the *ceinture*', the belt.

We had a very nice meal in the Staff Canteen which was better than most English restaurants at the time and, with the exception of Dave, we caught the plane back to London.

We had rented out our house in Walderslade and moved up to St Helens where we stayed with Dora's mother and father. This was a very popular move with the children who adored 'Queen Nana' and 'Big Dad' as they were fondly known. We eventually burned our boats and sold the house in Walderslade (for about £1,500!) as we had a lot of trouble with tenants.

I received a letter from Sabena telling me that I had passed my medical and offering me a job. I was to report on 1 May 1952 and enclosed was a ticket for me to fly, on their service, a DC3, from Manchester.

On arrival in Brussels I was met by a Sabena hostess who told me that 1 May was a public holiday and that there was nobody around, so she put me on a tram and told me to book in at the Palace Hotel in the centre of the town which was to be my home for the next three months. I had a wander around but everything was closed for the May Day holiday so I went back to the hotel where I met up with some of the other British pilots who had arrived from London, and we arranged to meet that evening for dinner. There were about six of us including Dougie Wilson, Jimmy Rice, Les Beech and Jack Veys. We had been given very nice rooms complete with bathroom en-suite and we met for drinks before going to the restaurant where we proceeded to go through the menu.

The very attentive head waiter plied us with wines and we had lobster, oysters, snails, steaks. You name it, we had it! When we were presented with the bill we airily told him that Sabena were paying for everything. He, obviously, was not happy, but there was not much he could do about it so we went to bed full of the best food that we had eaten for a very long time.

Next morning, we took the tram to Melsbroek. We had been told to report for lectures at 8.00 a.m. so we caught the 7.00 a.m. tram as it was about a forty-minute ride with numerous stops. We were introduced to the Continental habit of handshaking. On the tram, as each new round of passengers got on, they solemnly went around shaking hands with each of their fellow passengers, obviously Sabena employees. We were met at the Sabena buildings by the three young ladies who were to be our guides for the next few weeks and were told that the operations manager, Mr Stainier, who had a fearsome reputation, was waiting to see us. 'Ah, a welcome to Sabena,' we thought and were ushered into his office. There, on the desk and very evident, was last night's bill from the Palace Hotel. It wasn't even 8.00 a.m. so the hotel had wasted no time. The head waiter could well have been one of our fellow travellers on the tram with the bill in the briefcase that everyone carried. Mr Stainier began: 'When we said that we would pay for your food, we did not mean that you could have the equivalent of an à la carte wedding banquet each day. This bill represents about two months' pay for each of you.'

Then he actually started to smile which, we learned later, was unheard of. 'Just this once we will pay it. Now get off to your classes. In future you will have your lunch at the canteen and you will pay 14BF [Belgian francs] for that and your daily allowance is 40BF.' At that time there were 140BF to the Pound Sterling.

Lunch at the canteen was no hardship. You could have a big steak and chips for your 14 francs and we quickly learned to dip the magnificent Belgian chips in mayonnaise instead of ketchup. As long as you kept a small piece of meat on your plate to show that you had bought a main course you could go back for as many helpings of chips as you liked. This practice existed in the many good, cheap restaurants to be found in the Brussels department stores such as A l'Innovation, Galeries Anspach and Au Bon Marché. Half a dozen oysters with a glass of wine, bread and butter would cost 15BF at any of these places. There was a tea room over the English paper shop W.H.Smith which was very popular in Brussels. Once, Dora and I were having tea there and I went to the old-fashioned toilet upstairs. It was a unisex one with a urinal mounted on the wall and a closet to which I hied myself. When I came out, to my amazement there was a woman perched precariously on the urinal, with her knickers around her ankles. I could only mutter 'good afternoon' and hurry out.

We had been joined by other British pilots and there were about seventeen on the course, together with some Belgian trainees, mostly ex-Belgian Air Force. One of the British pilots had arrived at Melsbroek dressed in a pinstripe morning suit, bowler hat and tightly rolled umbrella. One of the porters said to him, in English, 'Are these your bags, Sir?' and our pilot pointed his umbrella at him and exclaimed in pure Oxford tones, 'How did you know I was English?'

The RAF spirit was still very much in evidence in Sabena. We made many friends and everyone spoke, and was happy to speak, English. Virtually every Belgian pilot who had escaped to England had become a fighter pilot and the *esprit de corps* and comradeship was still very much apparent. Throughout my long career – thirty years – with Sabena, I and all the other British pilots were treated exactly the same as the Belgian pilots. Promotion to bigger and better aircraft came on seniority, irrespective of nationality. We were issued work permits and, by Belgian law, could not have these repealed except for the obvious cases of serious misdemeanours. We were never asked to change our nationality, nor was language a problem. Every Belgian seemed to speak at least four languages and loved to speak English so that our poor efforts to speak French–Flemish, except for one or two notable exceptions – went unheeded. Despite this our ground course was conducted entirely in French, which led to some very lively sessions, particularly with Jack Veys, one of our number, who was the only one of us who spoke fluent French.

To celebrate the successful completion of our ground course our Chief Pilot for Europe, Peter Dils, a fighter pilot DFC, invited us to join him in a night out at the Maison des Ailes. It was a noisy, beery evening around a piano where we sang such songs as 'Bless 'em all'. We learned that most Belgians did not regard the obvious 'White Cliffs of Dover' as the song that represented wartime Britain: 'My Bonnie Lies over the Ocean' took this honour, and was sung at the least excuse. Even having a quiet drink in a pub, if someone heard you speaking English, out would come 'bring back, bring back ...'

The Maison des Ailes was the HQ of the Belgian wartime Pilots' Association and is a stone's throw from the nightclub quarter around the Porte Louise. We moved on from our party to one of the smaller bars where we were having a quiet drink with Peter Dils and another Chief Pilot, Paul Leva, who was to become a great friend. Paul had been a Spitfire pilot and one of his achievements was to down a V-1 by formatting on one and then tipping it over with his wingtip as he had used up his ammunition.

We were standing at the bar when the street door burst open and in rushed a short, well-padded man who put his fingers to his lips and dived round and under the bar. Shortly afterwards two big gendarmes dashed in, looked at us all and then dashed out again. The rotund figure emerged.

'Have they gone?' he said. 'Then the drinks are on me.' This was our introduction to Freddy. He and his brother had been in the RAF during the war and had married English girls. The brothers were now Sabena Captains. Evidently Freddy had been 'spending a penny' on the corner of the Avenue Louise when the gendarmes had seen him. I wondered what Freddy had done to deserve being chased, as this was a common sight in Belgium. Perhaps it was because the Avenue Louise was not the sort of place to do that type of thing.

A couple of years later, Freddy was driving up the Rue Neuve, the main shopping street, and was stopped by a Gendarme who pointed out that he was driving the wrong way in a very narrow one-way street. 'I always do something stupid when I'm drunk,' said Freddy.

Even up to 1967 there was no such thing as a driving licence in Belgium. Anyone could buy a car of any horsepower and take it straight out of the showroom. This, coupled with the '*Priorité de droite*' which gave traffic on the right absolute priority irrespective of the importance of the road on which you were driving, led to the mayhem which ruled the roads in Belgium. The ubiquitous tram had priority over everything and descending the Rue de la Loi, which had double tramways down the middle and was the busiest road in Brussels, was rather like the chariot race in *Ben-Hur* where it came down to survival of the fittest and bravest.

Freddy was hauled into court and, as there was no licence, was forbidden to exercise the right to control 'petrol driven machines' for six months. This embraced motor cars, lawnmowers and, alas, aeroplanes. Sabena gave him six months leave so he decided to visit his wife's parents in England. One day his father-in-law was doing the 'pools'. 'Come on Freddy,' he said, 'give me eight numbers.' Freddy did and they were all draws and they won £50,000. One of the first things that he did was to seek out the Gendarme who had arrested him and take him for a wonderful night out.

CHAPTER FOURTEEN

I had been fortunate in finding a very nice little unfurnished house to rent in a district called Evere, quite near to the aerodrome. It was small, but had three bedrooms and was near to the children's school, the shops and trams to town and to the aerodrome. A car was a long way off as we had to furnish the house from top to bottom. The Westminster Bank had long been established in Brussels and I made an appointment to see the bank manager, Mr High. He turned out to be a North countryman of the old school of bank managers. When I told him that I needed a loan of about £200 to furnish the house, he took me to a nearby bar called the Bodega and there, over a few beers we discussed everything except the loan. After about half an hour one of the bank employees came in with an envelope which Mr High gave to me and said, 'There's your money lad, and good luck.' I always had a good rapport with the bank. When Mr High retired he was replaced by another Englishman. Many times I would receive statements from the bank belonging to other customers, sometimes showing overdrafts of huge amounts. I would ring the manager and say, 'Your people have made a mess of it again.' And that would be good for a slap-up lunch where I would discreetly return the statements.

My appointment as a First Officer was confirmed and Dora, with the three children, flew out to join me in August 1952. Dora had tonsillitis and could not make the first date that had been suggested. She was still not well but was very happy with the house and furniture. I had prepared a meal, mostly cold meats and various goodies in aspic which did not go down well with the children but they loved their rooms and were very impressed by the downstairs toilet next to the front door.

In 1952 Sabena were operating with DC3 and Convair 240 on the European routes and DC4 and DC6 on the African and American lines. The Belgian Congo was the absolute bread and butter route and Sabena also operated all the Congo internal flights. The pilots employed in the Congo were on totally different contracts and had no place on the company's seniority list.

As a Senior First Officer I was placed straight away on the 'long courier sector'. In addition to our basic salary we were also paid on flying hours and long courier was definitely the highest paid sector. We flew as crews then. My Captain was a charming man called Simon Taut and I was made very welcome by the whole crew. The only snag was that, contrary to modern practice, the First Officer never touched the controls for take-off and landing and was the general factotum, making the flight plan, checking the load sheet, meteorology and staying at the controls whilst the Captain socialised with the passengers during the long and arduous flights. A typical DC4 flight from Leopoldville, as Kinshasa was known then, to Brussels would take well over eighteen hours.

We were settling down in Belgium very well. We threw the children straight in at the deep end and sent them to a French-speaking school in Evere where they were made very welcome.

The first day, Anthony, aged three, came home and said, 'They're all mad. They can talk but they don't know what they're saying.' Soon after he told us, 'We had "lait" at school today. It tasted just like milk.' In a very short time, well under three months, they were all chatting happily with their newly made friends and arguing furiously in fluent French. In fact it became mandatory that they spoke English at home as, very soon, French took over and they preferred to speak it as that was where they were learning their vocabulary. The speed at which the children picked up French was exemplified, one day, when I was sitting on the toilet which was next to the front door. The doorbell rang and little Anthony answered it. To my horror I heard him say, *Peter et Linda jouent. Maman fait les courses et mon Papa fait caca.*

Anthony came in crying one day because the Belgian kids called him 'puppy'. 'I'm not a puppy,' he sobbed. It turned out that they were calling him *petite poupée* as he was so cuddly and it was a term of endearment: 'little doll'. Peter had his friend, Jean-Claude, and Linda's best friend was called 'Toc Toc' as she was a 'bit crazy'!

We were living in Rue Jan van Ruisbroeck and there was a small general shop nearby on the Avenue Henri Conscience. The owner, Mr Leon, like everyone including the postman, spoke English and he took us under his wing, giving us good advice on what cuts of meat to buy and even how to cook them. The first joint of 'rosbif' that Dora bought barely weighed 300g but Mr Leon told her to cook it for five minutes each side as beef must be rare. To us heathens, meat had to be cooked forever, but we soon became converts and were then, in September, introduced to the national dish, moules (mussels). In those days they cost 6BF per kilo!

One day, there was a ring at the doorbell and a very nice lady introduced herself to Dora in a broad Yorkshire accent. She was Madge Dubois and lived nearby. She and her family were to become our lifelong friends. Her husband, Marcel, was an insurance broker and I am indebted to him for his kindness and help in smoothing our path through the initial difficulties of settling down in Belgium. He made sure that we were insured against all possibilities and had us in stitches with the list of things that we had to guard against. 'If the house burns down your neighbours will have to go to a hotel whilst it is being rebuilt, and you will be responsible.' Nevertheless, he gave me sound advice and I never regretted any insurance that

I took out with Marcel. Tragically, Madge was killed in a horrific car accident in the US and Marcel was badly injured.

I had made one or two trips on the European sector in order to familiarise myself with Sabena procedures. My first trip was in the 'jump seat' of a DC4 taking passengers to Frankfurt. The First Officer suddenly started waving to his right. I nearly jumped out of my seat. There was another Sabena DC4 in tight formation tucked in on our starboard with the passengers all waving at our passengers. Truly the RAF spirit still existed in 1952 in Sabena.

My own French was not improving, mainly because my entire crew took great pleasure in speaking English. Jean Brion the Radio Officer, Henri Crama the fatherly Flight Engineer, and Johnny Jonniaux the Navigator were the nicest people that you could meet and treated me with the utmost courtesy and good humour. I cannot stress enough how well received the British were at that time. We were really regarded as the true liberators of the country and the old-fashioned concept of the British 'gentleman' and 'an Englishman's word is his bond' still existed in Belgium.

I flew nearly two years as First Officer with Simon Taut and learned a lot including, for a brief spell, how to double your money. Once, in Leopoldville, the day before departure, Simon said to me, 'Bring 500 francs to the bank with you tomorrow.' That was a lot of money then and we British First Officers were always broke. One of the ways we all made ends meet was through the *carnet d'avances*. The Congolese franc was always on par with the Belgian franc so you could get an advance from Sabena in the Congo which would be changed, at par, in Brussels and would take several weeks to go through and sometimes, if you were lucky, got lost completely. When you were scheduled to go to the Congo there would always be some of the British Flight Officers waiting to see you off with their slips, duly signed from the *carnet*, for you to bring them back the money to see them out for the rest of the month. Anyway I borrowed 500BF and went with Simon to the bank where he asked for their value in 'Leopold the First' one franc pieces. These were huge coins with a hole in the middle and weighed a ton. We duly staggered back to the infamous Sabena Guest House where the crews stayed. I was mystified. Simon told me that all would be explained on the flight back. The first stop was Kano. It was already night and, for once, the runway lights were working. There had been trouble for a long time as rats liked the rubber around the cables and were eating through them. We staggered with our Leopold francs to the outside of the old terminal building, where, under the light of naphtha lamps, several Arab traders were squatting, surrounded by charm bracelets and other souvenirs. We deposited our burdens in front of them and were promptly given 1000BF each. Evidently the silver content of the coin was worth more than the coin itself and the Arabs would beat them down and make trinkets out of them. Unfortunately, the Leopold francs were so huge and unwieldy they were very soon withdrawn from circulation and our little racket came to an end.

I referred to the 'infamous' Sabena Guest House at Leopoldville. It was not the most comfortable place in the Congo but it was owned by Sabena so the crews had to stay there. There were no meal allowances but three meals a day were paid for by the company. This was very bad for health as everyone ate their three meals there. This led to weight problems in many of the crews. The cry *steak équipage* from a waiter to the kitchen would go down in the annals of Sabena history. Crews were definitely not served the best steaks. This situation went on for some years but, eventually, we were given meal allowances which enabled you to decide when and where you were going to eat and we were eventually moved to the Hotel Memling, which was infinitely better than the Guest House.

Sabena had one or two services a week to New York on DC4s. Although Simon Taut was one of the most senior Captains he had been left off the New York sector as a punishment for an incident which happened when Sabena based some crews in Hawaii to take part in ferrying military personnel to and from Korea when the war there was raging. There had been a big parade which had been interrupted by this aeroplane 'beating up' the parade ground. Unfortunately the ceremony was being broadcast and the commentator had reported, over the air, 'This aircraft is flying so low I can see the registration. It is Sabena 00 ...' Eventually, however, he served out his sentence and we were put on the coveted New York run. The flights, invariably, went by Shannon and Gander in Newfoundland due to the limited range of the DC4. Passengers were rare: sometimes we went with one passenger and returned empty. It was on one such flight that the steward came up front and said, 'We have 144 oysters on board for one passenger and he doesn't like them.' 'Bring them up here,' said Simon, and we ate the lot.

The system of promotion within Sabena was extremely fair. Providing that you passed the very severe examinations on any new aircraft that you were eligible to fly, the seniority list was faithfully adhered to. You started as a First Officer flying DC3 on freight in Europe. This was very unpopular as one of the chores were the flights carrying hundreds of pigeons all over Europe in the early hours of the morning. The pigeons would be released by the *convoyeurs* that were carried with them and large sums of money would change hands on the result of the ensuing race home. Apart from the unsocial hours of these flights, the smell of pigeons was very hard to get rid of and hung around you for days afterwards. To make matters worse, Sabena secured a contract to fly hundreds of pedigree pigs from Blackbushe, in England, to Belgrade in Yugoslavia. It was on one of these flights, when I was a Freight Captain, that I heard my colleague and friend, Doug Wilson, calling 'Mayday' over Graz in Austria. They had evidently strayed out of the corridor laid down by the Russians and had been fired upon by a Russian MiG, killing the Radio Officer and wounding the other Captain. Doug had made a very creditable landing at Graz without flaps or brakes as the hydraulics had been shot away.

After a spell as First Officer on freighters you would pass to Convair and later, Caravelle, flying the European routes. Once promoted to the long courier sector you would fly DC4 and DC6 also as First Officer. As the aeroplanes improved you would progress to DC7 then, with the advent of the jets to Boeing 707, DC10 and, if you were very lucky and good enough, the coveted Boeing 747. As vacancies for command came up you would go through the whole process again but this time as a Captain. I was fortunate in starting at the very top of the First Officer's ladder because of my extensive experience. I had slightly less than two years of flying as a First Officer on DC4 and DC6 before I was given a command flying DC3 as a Freight Captain.

During July and August Sabena flew a service from Brussels to Le Zoute, on the Belgian coast, and then from there to London via Ostend. This service was called the 'littoral' and was very popular with the Freight Captains as it made a change to fly passengers instead of pigs and pigeons.

It was always pretty full although the DC3 only carried twenty-one passengers. I once found the trim of the aircraft very strange so went back to investigate and found that the sole stewardess had set up a counter on a box in the aisle at the front of the aircraft whilst the passengers queued down to the tail end for their duty-free drinks and cigarettes.

One day, while waiting at London Airport to turn around and go back to Ostend, I walked into the Sabena office. One of the staff said to me, 'You are Captain Levy, aren't you?' When I replied 'Yes,' she said, 'Do you remember getting a letter when you applied for the job, telling you to come for an interview, and you replied that you were working during the week and would not ask your employer for time off to apply for another job?' 'Yes' I said. 'Well, we had over 1,200 applicants and our manager said, "That's one less," and threw your letter in the waste paper basket. When he had gone home I thought that it was a shameful way to treat you after your honest reply so I retrieved it, phoned you myself and arranged the interview for Saturday morning.'

I have often thought how that changed so many lives. It is impossible to imagine how our children and grandchildren would be affected by that simple action, so I just put it down to fate and am content that it happened that way.

CHAPTER FIFTEEN

We had by now purchased a car. It was a second-hand Studebaker in beautiful condition and was a constant source of enjoyment to our small family. We bought a big tent and enjoyed the lovely sands of the Belgian coast. One of our most memorable holidays was at De Panne where we actually went to a pension and had one of the loveliest summer holidays that still remains in our memory. The sun shone, the children were still small enough to only have little problems and Dora was released from the kitchen for the first time ever. We were very happy. I was now a fully fledged Captain flying the finest propeller airliner that I ever flew, the Convair 240. The cockpit was the nearest to a fighter pilot's dream and the aircraft handled superbly. I was flying on the European routes with very few nights away from home and it was no surprise when Dora told me, in the early autumn of 1955, that she was pregnant.

In June 1956 Dora went into a very nice nursing home in Schaerbeek, a nearby district, and we were all thrilled when she brought a little girl into the world on 8 June. I met our three other children from school that afternoon. 'Has it come?' they all shouted. I took them to the nursing home where the little Flemish nurse brought the baby in to show them. *Voilà votre Filleke* she said, giving the usual Flemish diminutive of '*ke*' as in *Madameke*. We decided to call the baby Helen, and I was actually at the counter of the Registry Office completing the form, when the clerk gave me the phone and said, 'Your wife wants a word with you.' Dora had changed her mind and wanted the name 'Susan', so Susan it was. Not that she was ever called that. No. The name 'Filleke' stuck and, although we anglicised the spelling to Feeka, she is still called Feeka to this day. There was a brief spell, much later, when meeting her at school, she would whisper to us, 'Call me Suzanne' but that did not last very long.

The house in Evere was by now much too small so we moved to the leafy district of Woluwe-St-Pierre. We had found a fairly old, but big house in the Avenue de l'Escrime. It had four bedrooms and a nice, small garden. We were very near a good school for the three children, and the little village of Stockel with its shops and weekly market was only a ten-minute walk away. The Studebaker had done its job well but we were more affluent and bought our very first brand new car, a gleaming Opel, appropriately named 'Kapitan'.

Our new house stood on the corner and the house on the opposite corner belonged to one of the directors of Sabena. One night there was a ring at our doorbell and the director stood there. Could he please phone home to his house as he had forgotten his keys? His wife was deaf and had not heard the doorbell. She did not hear the phone either. Eventually our son, Peter, came down and said, 'I can let you in.' He crossed the road, shinned up a drainpipe, went in through a half-open window and let the flabbergasted director in through the front door. 'The maid's room,' said Peter conversationally.

Brussels was preparing for the World Exhibition to be held there in 1958. The city was torn apart and fine ring roads with underpasses were being built. It was chaotic for a long period but left the capital with a very fine road system. Even the trams went underground and one could drive from one end of the city to the other without encountering a traffic light. The exhibition grounds at the Heysel were rapidly taking shape. The Atomium was built and the medieval village called 'Joyeuse Belgique' became an integral part of Brussels' night life. This replica village with dozens of cafés and restaurants was open until dawn and was the favourite spot to go to after work. One of the British architects responsible for the building of the British pavilion had left a convenient secret entry into the fairgrounds and it was hilarious to see a group of fashionably dressed British residents sneaking in there after a cocktail at the embassy. Private citizens were encouraged to let out spare bedrooms to relieve the acute shortage of accommodation and we had a stream of Brits for bed and breakfast. We made many firm friends. Unfortunately restaurant and food prices soared, never to return to pre-expo levels.

As time went on I rose up the promotion ladder. We were still being paid a bonus on actual flying hours and also being paid according to the size of the aircraft that we flew. At one time I was flying two marks of Convair and also DC4. This was very bad for the emergency procedures as you had, first of all, to remember which type of aeroplane you were flying. Once, in a Convair, I was just about to land at London Heathrow when an Air Canada Constellation taxied on to the runway just in front of me. I had already cut my power and was too low to go round again so I dived the Convair the remaining few feet and literally bounced it over the Constellation. There wasn't a lot of runway left and I had to brake and reverse power very hard. A passenger later told me that he had seen the three tails of the 'Connie' pass under his window and, when I braked, his glasses had stood out at the end of his nose and had then gone back again. As it happened I was being 'line checked' by my Chief Pilot. He just sat there, as white as a sheet, and didn't speak for at least five minutes. He later sent me a very nice letter of appreciation. The hapless Air Canada pilot, who had got hopelessly lost in his taxiing, lost his licence for six months.

The British community was quite small but a very good social life was available. I was very active in the Brussels Cricket Club and eventually became their Chairman. Cricket had been played in Brussels before the Battle of Waterloo. There are records of a match being played between Guards' brigades on the eve of the battle in the lovely park in the centre of Brussels, the Bois de la Cambre.

Children's sports day, organised by the British Colony Association, was a well patronised and much anticipated event. One year, the Duke and Duchess of Kent came to celebrate the anniversary of the Battle of Waterloo and presented the prizes.

Royalty was visiting Brussels fairly regularly. We met Princess Margaret and had a long chat with her husband, Lord Snowdon. Our conversation was cut very short by the Princess who pulled him away very abruptly and said, 'Come dear, my throat is very bad.'

Many years later Dora and I were coming back from Johannesburg as passengers and had the pleasure of meeting Group Captain Peter Townsend who was one of the other passengers. I had great discussions with him throughout the long flight and Dora and I were both struck by his charm and courtesy ... the very epitome of the English gentleman.

Without doubt, the big occasion of the 1960s was the State visit by Her Majesty the Queen accompanied by the Duke of Edinburgh. We were invited to a reception on 10 May 1966 at the Canadian Embassy. Dora met the Queen and I met Prince Philip. He spotted my medals and said, 'I see you were a flyer.' 'I still am,' I replied. 'Where do you fly to?' asked the Duke. 'New York and the Belgian Congo,' I replied, giving him my two main routes. 'Oh, from the sublime to the ridiculous,' he said then hastily put his hand to his mouth and moved on to the next chap. 'And what are you doing here?' he fired at the poor man, who was very nervous and probably thought that the Duke was accusing him of gate crashing. 'I'm with the Playing Fields Association,' he said. 'Oh, what's that?' asked the Duke. 'Well, you're the Chairman, Sir,' said the poor little chap. Prince Philip hastily moved on again.

That evening we were privileged to attend the ballet at the Opera House which King Baudouin and Queen Fabiola had specially arranged to be produced by Béjart for the Royal occasion. We were wonderfully seated in the Circle and had a magnificent view of the glittering assembly of kings, queens, princes and princesses together with Heads of State and Ambassadors from over 100 countries all in their regalia and resplendent in full dress and uniforms. The jewellery on display must have been worth many millions of pounds and it was a truly memorable occasion. During the interval we were separated from the Royal Party only by a glass partition and were within speaking distance as they took their refreshments. Sadly the ballet did not live up to the occasion and was one of those stark performances in nondescript costume with no scenery. This was a pity as the occasion cried out for the beauty and scenic splendour of *Swan Lake*.

I had already met King Baudouin when I had flown him from Nice to Brussels. He was very quiet but charming. He questioned me about flying and said, 'I don't think I should like your job. It is very responsible.' I could not resist answering, 'With respect, Sire, I would not change it for yours.' He burst out laughing and agreed with me.

I had flown Prince Albert many times before he became King Albert. I took him to Rome when he announced his engagement to the lovely Italian Princess Paola. On the return flight I had the very highly respected Cardinal Siri as a passenger. I also had a team of Italian sharpshooters, complete with their rifles, on the way to a very big contest in Moscow. When they heard that the Cardinal was on board they asked if he would bless their rifles to which he agreed. It must have been a sight that the other passengers would remember to see them lining up, in the aisle, whilst the Cardinal gravely blessed their rifles.

I resumed a boyhood hobby and carried an autograph book with me on flights. Amongst the personalities that I met was Charlie Chaplin. I met him as he was registering for the flight at London and took him to Brussels for an onward flight to Switzerland. He was very smartly dressed and very quiet. One of the most smartly dressed men I ever saw was the conductor Sir Malcolm Sargent who was on a flight with me to Geneva. Nobody told me that he was on board and I just happened to be standing next to him in the toilet in Geneva when he asked me if I was the pilot who had brought him there. I didn't have my autograph book with me and he signed for me on a handy piece of toilet paper. I took the great singer Paul

Robeson to Moscow and he signed my book in Russian. He was a confirmed Communist and was ostracised in the US because of this. His views were caused by the treatment he received as a black person by many Americans.

On one of my many trips to New York I went into Jack Dempsey's restaurant, just off Times Square. The great heavyweight champion sat every day in a window seat and welcomed all and sundry. He was most courteous to me and, hearing my accent, recalled Tommy Farr as the best British boxer that he had ever seen.

The Aga Khan was my passenger to Kinshasa where he was inaugurating the site for a hotel to be built exclusively for Muslim guests. To my knowledge it never materialised as another of my passengers, Moise Tshombe, appeared on the scene and the country was plunged into bloodshed.

I renewed my boyhood acquaintance with Gracie Fields when I took her to her home in Naples. She was as down to earth as ever and a pleasure to talk to. Another very nice passenger was Richard Todd, the actor, fresh from his characterisation of Guy Gibson in *The Dam Busters*. He stayed in the cockpit for most of the flight to Tel Aviv and was an aviation fanatic despite a very distinguished wartime Army career.

One of the most interesting passengers was Mr Ray Dolby, the American inventor of the Dolby sound system which eliminated all background noise on recordings. He was fascinated with the details of the cockpit and told me that when he invented his system he could not believe that it had not been invented before as it was so simple. He told me that the hardest decision of his life was to turn down a $2 million offer from Sony to buy his patent outright. He was young, married with children and heavily in debt but he said that his father was an inventor who had never made any money out of his inventions and he was determined that he would not make the same mistake. He told me that none of his employees worked on a time pay basis. They came in to work and left when they wanted and he had never had a trade dispute.

Stirling Moss was, as you would expect, in a hurry and was only concerned as to whether the plane would land on time … it did!

In those days of piston-engined aircraft you had time and the passengers were few enough to allow you to go back during the longer flights and talk to them. In later DC10 and 747 days it was more like stepping on to the stage and confronting row after row of faces. Apart from the physical impossibility of speaking to everyone it was unwise to leave the cockpit of a large jet aeroplane to one pilot. Emergencies were few and far between but when they happened they happened quickly and two pilots were an absolute minimum.

My Uncle Stuart had made a very successful film with Tommy Steele, the cockney entertainer, called *The Tommy Steele Story* and Tommy came to Brussels to give a concert at the Beaux Arts Theatre. We took our teenagers, Peter and Linda, together with Anthony to meet Tommy at a rehearsal. Tommy was so nice to them and they thoroughly enjoyed the proceedings.

Our great friend Johnny Kirsch was head of EMI in Belgium. He had two sons and always wanted a daughter so took Linda under his wing and took her to loads of auditions and concerts that he attended in his business capacity. She met the American heart-throb, Bobby Vee, and Sylvie Vartan, amongst others.

One of our best nights out much later when Dora's parents were over, was when we went to see Freddie and the Dreamers, who were under contract to Johnny's firm and were performing in Brussels. Peter's girlfriend, Mary, now his wife, was sharing a flat with two other girls and we all went back with Freddie and his Dreamers and had a terrific party there. It was a real thrill for Dora's parents as they led a very quiet life in industrial St Helens and Freddie had always been one of 'Queen' Nana's favourites. She was always known as 'Queen' Nana because she called Linda 'my little Queen'. It also distinguished her from my mother who was known as 'Blackpool Nana'.

Dora's mother loved the life in Brussels and came to stay long periods with us together with 'Big Dad' as Dora's father was called. 'Queen' was adventurous and loved to experiment with the wonderful variety of dishes available in Belgium. Not so 'Big Dad'. He was a dyed-in-the-wool Northerner who liked his meat well done. 'Burnt to buggery' was how he put it. He had been in the Guards during the First World War volunteering at sixteen, like so many falsely giving his age as eighteen and had survived the horrors of Flanders. His experiences in the cookhouses of those days had put him off restaurants for ever. He preferred to walk around the city whilst we took Nana for a meal in one of the hundreds of small bistros. We caught him once, though, when we persuaded him to come with us and he had frogs' legs. We told him they were 'chicky bits' and he thought they were delicious. 'Queen' mastered every gadget that we had. She loved ironing and when we bought an ironing machine she demurred at first but soon became very skilled and would sit in our 'buanderie', the very nice cellar we used as a utilities room, happily ploughing through the large amount of ironing.

On one of my later trips I was en route to Bombay when the steward asked me to talk to our only First Class passenger, an Indian, who had refused all the food offered to him. When I went back, the passenger, a Mr Ramamruthram, told me that he was fine and there was nothing wrong but he was not hungry as he had come from a company lunch at Eindhoven. When he said 'Eindhoven' I knew that he must be with Philips, the Dutch electronics giant. He confirmed this and I told him that my squadron, 105, had been on the famous low-level daylight raid in 1942 when 2 Group had attacked the factory which had been forced by the Germans to make components for their forces. He told me that he had been talking of that very raid to a retired director at the luncheon, who recalled seeing a Mosquito flash past his window. The window was on the third floor! We became great friends and I visited him and his family in Bombay. One day, several months later, the phone rang in our house in Brussels. It was a secretary from Philips in Eindhoven. 'When are you coming to pick up your video recorder?' she asked. I had, half seriously, expressed my interest in the brand new VCR that Philips had pioneered but the price was astronomical. Well over £1,200 in the 1960s. Mr Ramamruthram had said that he could possibly help but I had completely forgotten all about it. I asked the secretary what the price was and her answer made me tell her that we would be right over to collect it. When I say 'we', 'Queen Nana' was staying with us so we set off for Holland and had lunch in the famous Bali Indonesian restaurant. We had a *rijstaffel* which the menu advertised as having some sixty-odd dishes and Nana enjoyed every one and counted them to make sure.

I had, half-seriously, expressed my interest in the brand new VCR that Philips had pioneered. They were always jamming but, nevertheless, Nana soon mastered the intricacies of it and would beam with pride when we said 'nice picture, Nana' when she had recorded something for us. One of the conditions that Mr Ramamruthram had made was that I would bring him recordings of *It Ain't Half Hot Mum,* the series on the Army concerts in wartime India. He told me that he would play them to his board of directors during a board meeting and that they would all roll around helpless with laughter. He later got me a magnificent TV set at the same low price, which entailed another welcome visit to the Bali with Nana.

CHAPTER SIXTEEN

When Feeka was nearly two we moved to a larger house in nearby Kraainem, Avenue des Hêtres Rouges. It had a lovely big garden, so large that many years later, the landlord, Mr Henneaux, built four houses at the end of it and still left an orchard and large garden. He told us that he and his wife had, several times, hidden Allied airmen from the Germans in the house. His stories were thrilling and the courage that they showed was incredible as they faced execution if they were caught. They were both working and had to warn the hidden airmen not to flush the toilet after use in case they were heard by neighbours who knew that the house should be empty.

We had nine very happy years there but eventually we took the plunge and bought a ten *ares* plot of land (about a quarter of an acre) in nearby Wezembeek and had a large four-bedroomed, two-garaged house built for us. The address was Avenue de la Maison Communale – literally Town Hall Street. One of our friends remarked that it was not a very prepossessing address and I jokingly replied that I was going to have it changed. A couple of weeks later we got a letter from the local authorities that 'due to local demand' the name of the street was being changed to Avenue des Violettes. The friend in question was very impressed with my influence!

The garden at the rear of where the house was to stand sloped down at the back and also across the width so I got one of the Belgian pilots who ran a small building business as a sideline and had a bulldozer to come along and level it out for me. The only day that he could arrange to do this was a Sunday and we had just finished the whole plot when along came the local police in response to the angry neighbours. Hardly an auspicious start but worse was to follow. The department store, A l'Innovation, whose building department was constructing our house, suffered one of the worst fires in Belgian history and was virtually gutted with a horrific loss of life. Sometimes the only clue to the victim's identity was an unclaimed car parked in the area. Many tourists shopping in the store were killed and their identities only presumed when anxious relatives made enquiries after no news came from them. All records of contractors, proposed timetables, estimates, payments received were lost and it speaks volumes for the determination and organisation of A l'Innovation that we only suffered a small delay in the completion of our house.

We moved early in December 1967 and the day could not have been worse. It was bitterly cold and the driveway of our old house was covered with black ice. Although the new house was only a few minutes away, the removal men would not start work until I had warmed them with a few brandies. To complicate matters I had arranged to take most of the family with me on a wonderful trip to Nairobi and Johannesburg, staying in the two cities long enough to go on safari and sightseeing tours.

Sabena had chartered a Boeing 707 to a German tourist firm which required the crew to stay with the aircraft for the whole of the charter, which embraced Christmas, so I arranged places for all the family, except Peter who was married by now and could not get away from his work. Unfortunately, the family had to leave first as I had to meet up with the tour in Nairobi after taking an aeroplane to Johannesburg. So they set off, leaving me in the empty new house and we all met up in Nairobi where we hired two mini-buses to transport us and the crew all around the Kenyan and Tanzanian National Reserves.

What a wonderful experience it all was. We sat outside our hotel on Christmas morning 1967 with Mount Kilimanjaro above us, snow sparkling around the summit whilst we enjoyed the lovely morning sunshine. We saw game by the thousand; zebra, wildebeest, impala, hippo, giraffe, buffalo and gazelle stretching across the plains. At Lake Manyara the flamingos, in their thousands, coloured the surface of the huge lake in clouds of pink.

We stopped our 'combi' under a tree in the Amboseli reserve where a sleeping lion, sprawled high along the branch of a tree, ignored us. Once, our mini-bus got stuck so, foolishly ignoring the strict laws, we got out to push it when a rhinoceros was spotted gravely watching us about 200 yards away. Never did a re-entry to a combi take less time.

One afternoon, we were stopped by a bunch of Maasai warriors, complete with spears. They had visibly been drinking and were very curious. They kept pointing to a soft toy lion which Feeka had been given and obviously wanted it. 'Simba' they kept saying, jabbing their spears menacingly at it and us. Our native driver was scared stiff and had gone a peculiar grey colour. They wanted water but we had none so we operated the windscreen wipers whilst they greedily drank from the jets leaving red ochre stains from their painted faces all over the windscreen. We eventually managed to get away by promising them water from the second combi coming up behind which they also stopped, scaring the rest of the crew and young Anthony, but luckily without further incident.

Before crossing from Kenya into Tanzania we had stayed the night at one of the many lodges. We had arranged for an early start next morning but our driver did not turn up. The other driver volunteered the information that he had gone to visit his 'sister' at a nearby village so we took the other mini-bus and went to find him. We would have gone without him but the local law insisted on a native driver when crossing the frontier. We came to a collection of low mud huts and the other driver went into one of them. A little later one 'sister' emerged followed by several others all clutching their clothes sheepishly about them. There must have been half a dozen of them. Eventually the driver who had taken us there came out and explained that our driver had had his trousers stolen and was searching for them. He eventually staggered out, still blind drunk, clutching a pair of trousers miles too big for him. He slept in the back until we got near the frontier when we propped him up at the wheel and I manoeuvred the combi from his side. We crossed the Tanzanian frontier waved on by the guards as though a driver slumped over the wheel was a normal sight.

One of the nicest places we visited was Arusha where an Austrian couple kept a private game park. We were made very welcome and were allowed to handle many of the smaller animals which were kept almost as pets including chimpanzees and a baby gorilla.

We all loved Nairobi with its beautiful climate and fascinating small shops and markets but we had to press on to Johannesburg where we visited the Snake Park where I was well and truly put in my place. We were given a demonstration of 'milking' a cobra of its venom by one of the South African rangers and I asked him, as he was holding the snake along a stick and withdrawing the venom, had he ever been bitten. 'Yes,' he said 'when some stupid person asked a silly question in the middle of the milking procedure.' I won't go on but my face was very red. We were enthralled by the early Sunday morning spectacle of the 'Mine Dancing', particularly the 'Welly' dancers when off-duty Zulu miners gave a terrific show wearing their impressive feathered outfits clad in their mining wellington boots, which they stamped in the red clay with perfect rhythm and wonderful effect shouting their fearsome war cry and brandishing their spears in perfect unison.

Too soon it was back to cold Europe and the task of getting our brand-new house ready for habitation. The taste of Africa did not disappear and we were fortunate enough to visit Uganda before Idi Amin destroyed the wonderful tourist industry that was just beginning. We went to Murchison Falls where we took the trip down the Nile to the Falls. I will never forget Feeka, who had a talent for imitating the bark of a dog, doing this as we went down a sandbank where enormous crocodiles were basking. Feeka 'barked' and then nearly jumped out of her skin when one monster, at least 18ft long, leaped into the water and came rushing towards the boat.

One night a hippopotamus came up out of the water and placidly ate all the geraniums in front of the wife of the Navigator who was sitting outside her bungalow in her nightdress. An elephant and her calf regularly came along and browsed among the rubbish. The locals called her 'Dustbin Nellie'. Elephants were abundant in the Murchison area and we once had to wait in the car for nearly two hours as herds of them crossed in front of us. A speciality of the region was the enormous Nile Perch, called Le Capitaine by the Belgians and much prized for its delicious flavour. The place to catch them was at Chobe Lodge and specimens of over 100 kilos were not uncommon.

We stayed at the well-known hotel on the shores of Lake Victoria. It was affectionately known as the 'Lake Vic' and was very close to the airport of Entebbe, which was to become the scene of the Israelis' daring raid. Linda had become a stewardess with British United Airways, later to become British Caledonian, and we met up together several times at the Lake Vic where both airlines lodged their crews. I was not there, however, when she had a terrible car accident in a Volkswagen Beetle returning from Kampala. The driver crashed into the stone columns at the entrance of the Lake Vic and she was thrown through the windscreen. She was taken to the hospital in Entebbe, which in fact was just a mud hut with only one bed and they were left lying on the floor. There were no doctors but a Korean dentist arrived and sewed up her knee without anaesthetic. Another ambulance took them to Kampala hospital. There was blood all over the walls and people with gaping wounds lying all over the place. Saturday night in Africa … By a wonderful stroke of luck a professor from the Royal College of Surgeons was visiting the hospital. He so skilfully stitched up her face wounds that there are no scars to be seen to this day. Once again we were lucky in the fact that the Sabena crew staying at the Lake Vic was captained by Charles Waite, one of the original British pilots. The children of all the expatriate British pilots had regarded the parents of other children as the uncles and aunts they had left behind in the UK and Uncle Charles was one of them. He accompanied Linda in the ambulance when he heard the news and saw that she was looked after. It was the middle of the night and the taxi driver refused to take him back to Entebbe when he saw his blood-stained shirt after he had visited Linda as he thought that he had been in a fight. The British Caledonian representative wanted to send Linda back to Gatwick and another 'uncle', Jack Ellis, who was taking the next Sabena plane back to Brussels, made sure that she was on the flight so that she could be looked after by us. The Sabena manager and the airport manager were wonderful and gave her every assistance possible and kept us informed. We were to meet up again later under very different circumstances.

CHAPTER SEVENTEEN

By now I was flying DC7 on the New York route and I was told that Sabena required Captains for the new Boeing 707 for the summer season of 1963.

I studied over six months for the very stiff examination that Sabena gave every prospective 707 pilot. The transition from piston engine to jet aircraft was a big step and Sabena had always, rightly, laid great stress on a very sound theoretical background for its pilots. This standard was the highest that I had ever come across and contrasted greatly with the American practical approach which was, 'If you can't do anything about it there is no need to know about it.'

We were not given any time off for study but had to use the time we had whilst in hotels on trips and at home, much to the dismay of our long-suffering wives. Charles Waite and I decided to do our studying together and spent hours and hours learning such things as the intricacies of the undercarriage system until we could put it together backwards. As our wives took it in turn to put on a gigantic meal we put on many kilos before the final examinations took place. One of the most difficult questions was to elaborate on the formula of thrust. I was determined to master it and learnt the whole formula, which covered a blackboard, by heart.

The long and arduous course eventually came to an end and I was relieved to face the three examiners for the oral examination that would determine my future and was overjoyed when I got the question on thrust!

Both Charles and I passed our examinations and on 19 March 1964 we started our flight training. There was no simulator available at that time and this was our first real view of the 707 cockpit. We were fortunate in having, as our Instructor, one of the finest and well-liked pilots in Sabena, Bobby Laumans. He had escaped to England when Belgium was invaded, had been accepted straightaway in the RAF, had married an English girl and had been shot down and spent the war in captivity. He was a charming man and a wonderful instructor.

I was nearly forty-two years old when I first took off in a jet aeroplane after 14,497 piston-engine hours. On 3 April 1964 I stepped into the cockpit of Sabena 00-SJC and took off for New York with my Instructor and Chief Pilot as my Check Pilots and First Officers. A veritable new era in aviation had dawned and much more was in store for me. What a wonderful feeling that first jet flight was – almost as good as that day back in 1941 when I had first discovered the new dimension in my life.

I flew my first trip as Captain of Boeing 707 to Montreal and then on to Mexico on 28 April 1964. The difference between the jet and the piston-engine aircraft was enormous. For the first time you had more power than you needed. The rate of climb was phenomenal and, especially when the aircraft was lightly loaded, needed a lot of getting used to or else you could easily overshoot your required altitude. The acceleration on take-off was much slower than the piston aeroplane but the acceleration increased all the time instead of stabilising. The very slight lag in reaction to your throttle adjustment was another factor to reckon with, but the main difference was the distance that you were ahead of the landing wheels and also the very high cockpit position at landing altitudes. In the early days there were many cases of 707 landing short of the runway because the pilot had closed the throttles as he came over the runway threshold forgetting that the landing wheels were a long way behind him. Landings had to be more positive than before and quick action with reverse thrust was necessary in order to stop the aircraft before the end of the runway.

One of the more interesting trips was a period of four weeks spent in Anchorage, Alaska. Sabena had obtained a contract to fly 140 thoroughbred race horses from London to Tokyo. A specially converted cargo 707 was used. Once a week the aeroplane would come into Anchorage from London with the horses and a few grooms on board to look after the horses during the flight. I would be there to take it to Tokyo and fly back to Anchorage empty the next day, where the original crew would take it on to Brussels. There were no stewards or catering on board, just sandwiches and hot drinks in thermos flasks so the grooms, mainly Irish, would buy their drinks from the Duty Free shop in London and drink them between there and Anchorage. They would disembark at Anchorage where the temperature was usually between minus 25 and minus 30 degrees and would fall to the tarmac as if pole-axed. We got permission for them to stay aboard whilst the crews were changed and they would sleep it off in the straw and, sometimes the manure. We had no trouble at all with the horses, which were very valuable thoroughbreds and we were well looked after by the charterer, a very wealthy Japanese businessman. The people of Anchorage were most hospitable and we were given the use of a snow mobile by the Alaskan police and invited into the homes of many of the residents.

The years went on and I was fortunate enough to be able to take the family on many of my trips. New York was my favourite. Dora, Linda and young Feeka went there for one New Year. Feeka, who shared a bed-settee with Linda, discovered that television in the US went on all night giving poor Linda a very bad time and square eyes for Feeka. She also discovered hamburgers, which were unknown in Belgium then. On the return to Brussels I bought a big hamburger at Kennedy Airport before boarding and gave it to the steward. The family were in First Class and the steward spread a snowy white napkin in front of Feeka and served her with the hamburger, warmed up and garnished with champagne, which she changed for Coca-Cola, but she thought that Sabena had the finest First Class service of all. Another New Year in New York was terrifying. Once again Linda and Feeka were with us and we were in Times Square just before midnight. It wasn't particularly crowded at first but, suddenly, out of nowhere came thousands of people and we were swept along with them. We had lost Linda and I carried Feeka on my shoulders. We didn't see the traditional ball on the top of the *Times* building but Feeka did, as she had the best view and found it amazing. We eventually met up with Linda but it was a frightening experience.

Another time, I booked for Dora and I to see Mickey Rooney and Ann Miller on Broadway in *Sugar Babies*. Unfortunately we were late arriving and had to wait nearly an hour for a berth at Kennedy Airport. There was no time to go to the hotel to change so we got off the crew bus in mid-Manhattan and dashed to the theatre, me still in my uniform and Dora in the outfit in which she had flown the Atlantic. It was a lovely show and we had arranged to meet good friends afterwards for supper. They insisted on taking us to Chinatown and it was 5 a.m. when we finally got to bed; 11 a.m. Brussels time and we had to leave that afternoon at 5 p.m. from the hotel.

CHAPTER EIGHTEEN

I had flown the 707 mainly on New York, Montreal, Mexico and Congo sectors, when Sabena asked for volunteers to fly on a new European sector that would include London and the main Middle East destinations. It would mean considerably more time at home as the flights were shorter, so I put my name down and was one of the pilots chosen to start the sector in the spring of 1972. One of the more attractive flights was the one to Tel Aviv, in Israel, which left Brussels around midday, stopped at Vienna and then continued to Tel Aviv arriving at 6 p.m. The crew were always well looked after at the Dan Hotel where they gave us a good dinner in the evening. We would leave the next morning around 7.30.

May 6 was a Saturday and it was Cup Final day and I had asked for the day off to watch the match on TV. Dora was not pleased when she heard this. 'You know it is your fiftieth birthday on Monday,' she said, 'and now you are sure to be flying.' Sure enough when the programme came out I saw that I was down to take flight SN571 to Tel Aviv on Monday 8 May. I went to the G2 department that issued personnel with tickets and got her one. I then told her, 'Now we can celebrate my fiftieth birthday together in Tel Aviv.' 'It's silly to go all that way for one night,' she replied but I could see that she was pleased.

Monday 8 May 1972 was a beautiful sunny day. I put Dora on board the plane before the passengers and then went back to the airport to phone Feeka to tell her that Dora was definitively going, as there was always an uncertainty with these free tickets. As I was walking back I passed a very pretty girl who gave me a beautiful smile. I thought, 'Well, I'm fifty today but pretty girls still smile at me.' As the rest of the passengers were embarking I saw two friends from the cricket club getting on board. I told them that Dora was on board and they went and said hello to her. They were only going to Vienna.

The aeroplane was a Boeing 707 00-SJG – Juliet Golf in the phonetic language that we used – and the flight to Vienna was uneventful.

We took off from Vienna at the scheduled time and I climbed the aeroplane to its cruising altitude of 33,000ft. The weather was beautiful and visibility was extremely good. We had just passed over the reporting point of Sarajevo when I heard a scream behind me from the entrance to the cockpit. One of the stewardesses had been pushed out of the doorway and two Middle Eastern looking men burst into the cockpit. One held a pistol to my head and the other pulled the pin out of the grenade he was holding and threw the pin to the floor. They were both in a highly nervous state, the hand holding the pistol to my head was shaking violently. My only thoughts were, how do I calm them down? 'You go to Lod,' they kept shouting. Lod is a small village and was the name for the airport at Tel Aviv, now named after the first Prime Minister of Israel, David Ben-Gurion. 'We *are* going to Lod,' I said and, incongruously, the current joke about the American on a flight to Miami who hijacked the plane to go there because the last few flights he had been on had finished up in Cuba flashed through my mind. They thrust a tattered 'Jeppeson' approach map, showing one of the approaches to Tel Aviv Airport, into my hand. '*Yes, I am* going to Lod,' I kept repeating and this eventually seemed to please them because they tried to find the pin from the grenade which the younger of the two was still holding very firmly. During this time the First Officer managed to get a quick message that we had been hijacked to an Air France aircraft in the vicinity. When the Air France tried to call us up a Swissair plane quickly cut in and said that he had received our message, had understood it and was transmitting it to his base.

I managed to calm the man holding the pistol to my head and pointed out the danger of the grenade to us all. The younger man was obviously complaining, in Arabic, that his hand was very tired of holding the lever against the pressure of the spring. Despite a frantic search it was never found and eventually our Flight Engineer found some strong wire in his toolbox and, under tremendous stress, meticulously bound it around the grenade and the lever, slowly withdrawing the fingers one at a time. I did my utmost, later, to get his bravery and skill recognised but it was a hopeless task. No one seemed to want to even believe it possible.

The two men were very different in appearance and character. The eldest, a man about thirty-five, seemed more moderate and open to reasoning. It was he who had held the pistol to my head. He opened the chamber to show me that it was loaded. The other man was about twenty and very aggressive. They both spoke English very badly but French reasonably well so that was the language that we used. We had in the cockpit the Chief Flight Engineer, who was checking our Flight Engineer. As it happened, he spoke fluent Arabic. He unfortunately let them know this and they promptly bundled him out of the cockpit to the back of the plane. He would have been an invaluable assistance to me had he not said anything.

Soon two young girls came into the cockpit. Sure enough, one of them was the girl who had flashed a smile to me at Brussels Airport. At the command of the eldest terrorist they opened the top of their blouses to show me the two bare wires protruding. In mock display they mimed the result of touching the two wires together and I could see batteries stuck into their brassieres. They opened two Samsonite beauty cases and lifted the tray to show plastic bags taped underneath. We learned later that the bags contained Semtex and that it was the first time that this powerful explosive had been used in a hijack.

I seemed to be seeing the whole scenario as though my mind had detached itself from my body and I was looking at the cockpit from above. I had even said to myself, 'I am responsible for the lives of everyone on board and these people are not going to get away with this so don't do anything foolish. Think, think, think!'

I reasoned to myself that the message would be passed on to Brussels that we had been hijacked and that the longer the flight took, the better prepared the ground authorities in Israel would be. My heart had sunk when I heard the demand to fly to Israel as I knew I was dealing with a suicide mission. The Israelis, I knew, would never submit to terrorist blackmail. Had another country been selected there would have been a chance for negotiation. I therefore throttled back the aeroplane as much as I could and reduced my speed to the bare minimum to make the flight take as long as possible. Luckily I soon realised that neither of the men had any technical knowledge and we were able to switch our transponder transmitter to the international code for an aircraft, 'not under its own control' as the textbook euphemistically put it. Unfortunately most of the flight from there on was over territory not, at that time, controlled by radar so the message would not be picked up until much nearer to Israel.

During the long flight that I had decided on (we took about thirty-five minutes longer than normal) the mood of the terrorists changed every few minutes. For some unknown reason they would suddenly don ski masks and then, just as rapidly, discard them. The older man found my gold braided uniform cap and wore it, announcing, 'I am the commander of this aeroplane.' At times they were friendly and reasonable and then something would trigger off a burst of rhetoric against Israel and the Israelis. They had very little knowledge of aviation and aeroplanes but never left the cockpit unattended. They also told me that they were members of 'Black September'. Although this meant nothing to me at the time,

Black September was the military arm of the Al Fatah movement and had been named after the massacre and removal of the Al Fatah movement from Jordan by King Hussein in September 1970.

During a period whilst there was only one of the men in the cockpit I managed to get a message, quietly spoken in English, to one of the stewards that no one was to let it be known that my wife was one of the passengers. They had allowed me to go to the toilet but I dared not look for her in case I made some inadvertent sign of recognition.

It was now dark and eventually the lights of Israel appeared in front of us. We crossed the coast and communication with the Israeli Control was brief and professional. No mention of the situation was made by either of us. I made as long an approach as I could and landed on the main runway towards the sea. 'Continue to the end of the runway to the right,' were the instructions I was given. The runway in question was well away from the terminal buildings and ran parallel with the Tel Aviv–Jerusalem road on which we could see the lights of many cars.

Right from the beginning I had felt coldly and deeply angry that my command had been threatened. I was concerned for my passengers only and had no wish to be embroiled in the bitter battle that was going on between the state of Israel and the Arabs who were bent on its destruction. I am British and despite my Jewish background, had no connections whatsoever with Israel. My responsibility was to my passengers and to Sabena, my employers. I was, from the start, determined that I was going to do everything within my power to stop the hijackers from succeeding, and even if the positions had been reversed and it had been Israeli hijackers, I would have acted in exactly the same way, whatever the nationality, religion or creed. I knew that however long the ordeal lasted I would be in better shape than they. There were already signs that the two men were taking some sort of stimulant. Their erratic behaviour was a clue to this. Nevertheless the pistol, a Smith & Wesson, never left the hand of the leader and the other one remained an aggressive, dangerous young man.

We were, of course, now on the aircraft's batteries and these would not last long. The Tower asked for permission to connect an external generator for electricity and air conditioning but, fortunately, the terrorists would not allow this. I say fortunately because I knew that the heat of the following day would cause great discomfort and perhaps I would be allowed to open some of the emergency exits and doors. This would serve the twofold purpose of forcing the terrorists to mount a guard over each exit thus splitting them up and also possibly allowing passengers to escape through them if the occasion arose. I must confess that the thought of an armed attack coming from the Israelis had not then crossed my mind.

Unknown to anyone in the plane a squad of Israeli commandos had been in position underneath the plane from the time that it had stopped. There was a moment when the plane shook, which I put down to a tyre bursting and which went unnoticed by the terrorists. Little did I know that the commandos had deflated all the tyres and had cut the hydraulic lines making taxiing impossible.

Occasionally, while speaking to the Tower, the microphone would be grabbed from me by the leader who would speak in Arabic in a very rapid, threatening manner. I had been forced to show him how to use the microphone but when I was speaking I was able to convey one or two things by judicious choice of words and sentences. For instance by stressing and repeating the word 'for' (four) in sentences I was able to indicate how many of the hijackers were on board and received a 'Roger, understood,' from the Tower in reply. The terrorists kept asking the Tower whether the Red Cross representative had been called and were told by the Israelis that he had been notified but that he was coming from Jerusalem and it would take time to get there.

I didn't sleep at all during the night but my First Officer, who had behaved impeccably throughout and was very calm, had a good long sleep and was even snoring at one time. The two terrorists took it in turns to keep their vigil in the cockpit and the two girls made occasional single visits and received terse Arabic instructions from the eldest man. No catering had been permitted to be put on board although the Israelis had been perfectly willing to do so. I was pleased about this as I reasoned that the terrorists themselves would become increasingly hungry and thirsty, which would not improve their physical and mental state. It was very hard on the passengers, of course, as the provisions that had been put on board in Brussels were running very low and drinks had to be rationed. There were ninety-nine passengers on board, the majority of them elderly people. There were some nuns and a Greek Orthodox priest who came in for a prolonged interrogation by the Israelis afterwards. There had been no panic. People seemed benumbed by the situation. I periodically made as many announcements as I was able to, without upsetting the terrorists, telling the passengers to keep calm and assuring them that everything possible was being done to resolve the situation and counselled them to keep calm and not to try to intervene in any way. I did this in as calm a voice as I possibly could but it was very difficult as I was watched like a hawk each time that I spoke. There was only one child, who was travelling accompanied by a Sabena stewardess who had volunteered to look after her but my wife took her under her wing and sat her next to herself.

A very sinister aspect of the situation developed when the men demanded the passports of the passengers and segregated the Jewish names from the others. My wife point blankly refused to surrender hers saying, 'I am British,' and they let her sit on the left-hand side of the aircraft towards the front in row thirteen, just in front of the wing exit door.

As the sun began to warm the plane the heat became unbearable. I decided to take matters into my own hands saying, 'Do you want everyone on board to die?' I strode out of the cockpit and released the emergency wing exits so that they fell out. This did not go down at all well with the terrorists but it was a fait accompli. They now put the girls on guard at the wing exits and, as they kept opening and shutting the main entrance door, one of them had to guard this leaving just one to guard the cockpit. Communication between them was now very difficult as it meant one of them leaving their position to contact the others.

A new problem arose. Hundreds of curious Israelis had parked their cars along the road that ran parallel to the runway to watch the 'goings on' and, especially during the night, their lights and movements had unnerved the hijackers who swore that it was an Israeli ruse to move troops into position. We had to tell the Tower that they would have to be moved and this was eventually done, but it took a deliberately long time.

Despite the terrorists' demand that the airport be closed, the Israelis kept it open. A poignant moment for me was when a Sabena 707 roared overhead. It was captained by Captain Jean Deleu whose wife, Monique, was one of the stewardesses aboard our plane and he had been allowed to pilot the aircraft bringing the Sabena officials and Belgian Government representatives from Brussels.

Up to now no demands had been made by the hijackers despite repeated requests from the Israelis. Suddenly, the leader produced sheets and sheets of paper on which were written over 300 names. They told me to tell the Israelis that these were Palestinian prisoners in Ramla prison and that they – and they named themselves as Black September – demanded the release of all these prisoners and air transport for them all to Cairo. If these demands were not met they would blow up the aircraft with everyone on board including themselves.

The Israelis kept playing for time, saying that there was no one at the airport who could possibly deal with such a demand and that it would take time to find responsible members of the government. The two men in the cockpit became furious and one of them started screaming into the microphone. The younger one rushed out of the cockpit and returned with the two girls. The older one said something to them and I saw their faces go white. They shook their heads but the men were insistent. The girls began to cry and the men embraced them. I knew that they had decided to blow up the aircraft with everyone, including themselves, on board. The younger man left the cockpit and I saw my opportunity. Whilst the other, who was holding the gun in the hand nearest to me, was looking at the girls, I grabbed his hand and bent it back to his body. His finger was on the trigger and I had my fingers pressing over it but he had his thumb over the safety catch and the gun would not fire. All this took seconds and then the younger man came running back, his face contorted with rage, and beat me back into my seat. I was told later, by my wife, that she could hear me crying out to them, 'You promised that no one would get hurt.' They began talking furiously and it was obvious the younger one wanted to kill me there and then but the older one would not let him.

What most probably saved my life was, at that moment, the Control Tower called us up and told us that the Red Cross representative had arrived and wanted to talk to them. This defused the whole taut situation and the relief on the terrorists' faces was plain to see. They had evidently been waiting for some message to be passed to them by the Red Cross – completely unknowingly, I hasten to add – containing a code word passed to the Red Cross by the Black September movement, which would be innocently included in the message. Fortunately, I learned afterwards, Peter Dils, our Operations Manager in Brussels (ex-Battle of Britain fighter pilot, DFC), had thought of such an eventuality and was adamant that only the Israelis should be allowed to speak to us. The Israelis stalled again and told them that the Red Cross representative was standing by but was not permitted to use the R/T. Once again the terrorists were furious. They were arguing amongst themselves when I tried a desperate move. 'Look,' I said, 'it is obvious that the Israelis don't believe that you mean to blow up the plane. Why don't you let me go and persuade them to negotiate with you as it is the lives of my passengers and myself that are at stake.' To my eternal amazement they agreed to this on the condition that the Red Cross would send their representative to collect me and bring me back. I could hear the disbelief in the voice of the ATC when this news was passed to him.

It wasn't very long before a jeep, flying the Red Cross, came out to the aircraft. At the last moment the older of the terrorists handed me a piece of the plastic explosive (it looked exactly like foam rubber) and warned me not to touch my mouth with my fingers after handling it and told me to show it to the Israelis.

I descended to the jeep through a trap in the cockpit floor which led to a door by the nosewheel, in the compartment called the Lower 41. I realised that I had made a mistake in revealing this when I saw the terrorists' eyes open wide. The Red Cross representative was a stolid Swiss who barely spoke during our short journey to the Control Tower.

The Control Tower building was a pandemonium of press photographers, none of whom took photographs of me, obviously acting on instructions from the Israeli authorities. There were soldiers everywhere but no general public. I was taken to a room where there was a long table, at the head of which, instantly recognisable, sat Moshe Dayan, then Minister of Defence. I was angry at once. I went up to him and said, 'You have no intention of releasing those prisoners, have you?' He smiled and said, 'Calm down. Remember you are a Captain and I am a General.' I was furious. 'Alright. If you are a General then you go back to that bloody aeroplane and direct operations and I'll stay here.' Everyone around the table started laughing. Moshe Dayan said something to someone behind him and, miraculously, a glass of whisky appeared at my side.

Amongst the men around the table were David 'Dada' Elazar, General Chief of Staff, Moshe Hod, Chief of the Air Force and General 'Gandhi' Ze'evi, Chief of Central Command in whose province Ben Gurion Airport lay. They asked me many questions and were very interested in the sample of explosive which they examined carefully. They were very interested in the sample of explosive and examined it carefully.

With a heavy heart, I got up and told them that I was going back to the plane and that I held them responsible for the welfare of my family if things went wrong. I saw David Elazar nod firmly when

I said this. Once again there was a throng of jostling photographers and press but the Sabena Station Manager managed to grab my hand and slipped me a note saying that Captain Jack Ellis – Uncle Jack – and his wife Joan, were looking after the family in Brussels. I quickly added a few lines to Dora.

In actual fact Peter, my eldest son, was on business in England. BEA did everything possible for him and kept him informed all the time. Linda, our eldest daughter, was a stewardess with British Caledonian and they told her that they could fly her to wherever it was necessary. Our youngest son, Anthony although a mere AC2 in the RAF at St Athan in Wales, was told by his commanding officer that there was a plane standing by to fly him anywhere in the world, should it be necessary. The world of aviation closed ranks and I was extremely moved when I heard all this much later. This just left our sixteen-year-old daughter, Feeka, alone at home. Sabena had in fact called her and offered her a seat on the next flight to Tel Aviv. She declined the offer saying her place was at home and magnificently dealt with the hordes of reporters, television and radio people as well as the innumerable phone calls which she recorded faithfully, keeping a wonderful log of them all for our return.

I was taken back to the plane by the same Swiss who, once again, said nothing but clearly disapproved of the Red Cross being involved in the affair. This time there was a ladder on the jeep and I climbed it and entered the plane from the rear entrance door and made my way up the cabin and was able to pass the note, which I had concealed in my hand, to Dora but dared not meet her eyes. On entering the cockpit I found that the Israelis had already passed their agreement to the terrorists' demands over the radio and everyone was shouting with joy.

Once again I was handed the list of prisoners and had to read their names, all 300 of them, over the radio. The Israelis kept asking me to repeat and even spell some of the names which gave them at least another hour and a half. I nearly lost my voice shouting the names in the midst of all this euphoria. The Israelis, without permission from the terrorists, connected two external power units, one each side of the cockpit, explaining over the R/T that the cooler conditions would be better for everyone. I reasoned that they had been placed there to provide an escape route for the cockpit crew. It was very difficult for me to hide my emotions, so much so that one of the terrorists looked at me and said, 'Captain, you are thinking too much.'

The terrorists were overjoyed when a voice speaking Arabic came up on the R/T purporting to be one of the prisoners to be released. I was later told by Moshe Dayan that he was a Bedouin officer in the Israeli Army! This gentleman told the terrorists that the prisoners were being assembled but that it would take time to arrange transport and bring them to the airport. He told them that an aircraft would be provided to fly the prisoners to Cairo, as they had demanded. It was then that the Control Tower told us that our aircraft had been damaged on landing and that the tyres would have to be replaced. The terrorists, once again, incredibly, allowed our Flight Engineer to descend through the Lower 41 to confirm this. He was able to do this very quickly as all sixteen main wheel tyres had been deflated.

It should be remembered that, although in 1972 there had been a spate of hijackings, Sabena as the Belgian state airline did not consider themselves likely targets. Belgium had no quarrel with any of the known militant organisations. Relations with its former colony, today's Democratic Republic of the Congo, were always likely to be volatile but the ex-Zaire had never been known to spawn hijackers. As a consequence, security at Brussels Airport was virtually non-existent and, much more importantly in my situation, absolutely no instructions, training or guidelines had been laid down to help crews faced with the predicament that I was now facing. I learned about the so-called 'Stockholm Syndrome' afterwards and recognised that it could have happened in our case had I let it.

In Stockholm, as I remember, hostages were taken in a bank raid and began to form an empathy with the robbers after a certain time.

The oldest of the two terrorists on board was very earnest and I could feel sympathy for the obvious devotion and courage he was showing for his cause. I could feel that, given different circumstances, he and I could become friends and I resolutely put these thoughts out of my mind as I stress, once again, that I had absolutely no political sympathies with either side and only strove to do all I could to get my passengers and crew out of the aeroplane in one piece. There was some talk afterwards that the terrorists targeted my flight because of my name but there was no way that this could have been known to them beforehand: I was only put on the flight at the last minute because I had asked to be free the Saturday preceding and it was total coincidence that I was on board.

There were anguished consultations going on between the two terrorists. It had been most noticeable during the whole affair, which by now was well into the afternoon of the second day, that the two girls had played a very subservient role and were completely under the control of the men. None of the passengers had been badly treated but the majority of them were scared and anxious as to the outcome. The moods of the terrorists were continually changing so that there was no way that you could predict what their reactions would be to anything that might be said or done.

Late in the afternoon a train of small carriages, bearing aircraft wheels, escorted by a team of white overalled men could be seen approaching the aircraft. They stopped before actually reaching the aeroplane and the highly nervous and agitated terrorists told the Flight Engineer to get down and supervise the repairs. He was joined by the Chief Flight Engineer who had mysteriously reappeared. Whilst everyone was occupied I managed to slip down into the Lower 41 and was just in time to follow one of the 'mechanics' up a ladder and on to the port wing near one of the wing emergency exits.

The mechanics, of course, were a squad of crack Israeli commandos, the same squad, in fact that much later carried out the epic rescue of the Air France hostages at Entebbe Airport. They were led this time by a very young major named Ehud Barak who was later to become the General Chief of Staff of the Israeli Defence Force and later, Prime Minister. One of the soldiers was another future Prime Minister, Benjamin Netanyahu.

I went into the plane through the overwing door and found myself in the middle of a battle. Two Israeli soldiers were in a sitting position, back to back, so that they covered the rear and front of the plane and they were shuffling up the aisle with their Uzis at the ready. There were shots being fired but I couldn't tell from where they were being fired or at whom. There were no loud reports but a sort of 'pop'. I was trying to find Dora but, of course, everyone was down on the floor. Everyone that is, except one unfortunate young Danish girl who stood up to see what was going on and got a bullet in her head and later died. I kept calling 'Dora, Dora,' and eventually I saw a small hand waving over the seat where I knew Dora was sitting and found her there protecting the little six-year-old girl. I picked up the child and took her out of the plane and handed her to one of the soldiers then returned to Dora again. The fighting was all over. The two men were shot by the Israelis and one of the girls was wounded. The other girl had been grabbed by one of the passengers and was unharmed. Dora had seen the tall figure of the leader of the Israeli commandos and had heard him saying in a very calm voice, 'Get down. Everything will be alright.' According to other witnesses, the leader of the terrorists had come out of the cockpit, firing his revolver and the leader of the Israeli squad had calmly shot him between the eyes. All this had taken place before I got up to the front of the aircraft again. I saw my cap lying on the floor and picked it up. I quickly dropped it when I saw the state it was in. The terrorist had been wearing it when he had been shot in the head. I got blood on my shirt from this, which gave birth to several false conjectures after the events.

There was a fairly well-organised evacuation of the passengers going on. Those at the rear were helped out of the wing exits by the Israeli soldiers, mattresses had been spread below the wings and the more able of the passengers were sliding down the wings onto these; steps and ladders were soon in position at the front. It was remarkable how many passengers were clutching their bags of Duty Free purchases as they left the plane.

Moshe Dayan was waiting for me as I came off the plane with Dora. 'I told you that everything would be alright,' he said. I introduced him to Dora. 'Mrs Levy,' he said, 'I want you to have dinner with me tonight.' 'But I haven't anything to wear,' she replied!

After a news conference with the media and Shimon Peres, who was Minister of Transport at the time, we collected our personal baggage from the carousel, which was revolving as if nothing had happened. Even my blood-stained cap was going round on it. We arrived at the Dan Hotel to a tumultuous welcome from the crowds that had gathered there. Several of the stewardesses had lost their shoes and were barefoot and most of the women, including Dora, had suffered from the heat of the last two days and their hair was clinging to their heads. Nevertheless, a sympathetic and generous crowd gave us a tremendous cheer as we walked up the steps to the hotel. When Dora and I arrived in our suite we found that it was filled with flowers and bouquets from so many people that we had never met. There was even a lovely bouquet from the cleaning staff of the Dan Hotel.

A small parcel was delivered to the room. In it was the gun that had been held to my head over the last two days with a message from Moshe Dayan.

We were told that we would be picked up later to meet him. Two more small packages arrived. One contained small phials of ancient Phoenician cosmetic glassware excavated by Moshe Dayan himself and beautifully arranged in a presentation case with the inscription 'Phoenician Crystal AD 200'. This was accompanied by his personal card to Dora. For me there was a Canaanite stone dagger blade, similarly presented with the inscription 'BC1500'.

We barely had time to shower and Dora did what she could with her hair, then we were escorted to a waiting car and taken to a very discreet restaurant where a pianist was playing softly. When we entered he broke off what he was playing and started the chords of 'Happy Birthday'. Moshe Dayan and his wife, Rachel, were already seated and we joined them. We had just started the soup when we saw that Dora had great difficulty keeping her eyes open and had actually fallen asleep, so we excused ourselves and returned to the Dan where we had our first good sleep in days.

CHAPTER NINETEEN

Early next morning we were able to speak to the family in Brussels and were assured that they were all well and had rallied round to support each other during the ordeal. There had been scores of telephone calls from well-wishers, friends, relatives, and, of course, the media. The press had even been to both our parents' houses in the UK and our names and photographs were all over the national newspapers. They didn't bother checking facts and I was described as a Battle of Britain hero who flew Spitfires; Dora became Nora and even Deborah (the name published in a book afterwards) and the mother of our four daughters!

The Israelis couldn't do enough for us and we were told that a helicopter would be available in the afternoon to take Dora and I and the First Officer on an aerial tour of Israel. We were waiting for our aircraft to be made airworthy again as, in addition to the damage done to the tyres and the hydraulics by the Israeli commandos, there were several bullet holes in the fuselage. I feel now that we should have been flown back to Brussels immediately afterwards but the Sabena officials who had been sent to Israel to deal with the situation did not even consider this so we were exposed to a great deal of publicity that we could have avoided.

The helicopter trip was wonderful. It was the first time that I had flown in one and the experience was remarkable. I had never realised what a wonderful visibility there was compared with a commercial airliner. We flew over the Dead Sea and I saw that the altimeter was reading more than minus 1,000ft. The heights of Masada were formidable and it was fantastic to see the lines of the Roman battalions still clearly visible when you were high above them. We were actually over the cave where the Dead Sea Scrolls were found when the radio spluttered to life. The pilot answered then turned to me. 'We have to return to Jerusalem,' he said, 'Golda wants you to come and have tea with her.' A black car flying a small flag was waiting for us when we landed. As we got into the car, a taxi from a nearby rank backed out and crunched into the wing of our car. The taxi driver sprang out and started hurling abuse at our driver who sat there calmly with his arms folded then pointed silently at the standard on the front. The tirade stopped immediately. 'Golda?' said the taxi driver. The chauffeur nodded. I do not speak Hebrew but it was easy to understand what the taxi driver said. He put his head in his hands. 'Of all the cars in Israel, I have hit Golda's.'

Golda Meir's house was in a quiet street and had a small path leading to the front door. She came to the door herself, put her arms around Dora and kissed her. She turned to me. 'Would a very brave man kiss an old woman?' she said and then gave me a big kiss. Whilst the tea was being drunk, Golda smoked one cigarette after another. Her son arrived, unexpectedly, from the Negev desert where he was farming and proudly showed the very first peach that had been grown there.

Golda gave Dora a lovely necklet of typically Israeli design and gave me her signed biography. The necklet was, sadly, one of the items stolen from our house in Brussels some time later. Our Boeing 707, 'Juliet Golf', was to be ready for the next day and, although Sabena had sent one of the Chief Pilots to fly it back, I was adamant that I would fly it and my crew backed me up. That evening, though, we were told that we were being taken out to dinner with all the crew and were to meet in the lobby. Dora managed to buy a dress and had her hair done by a hairdresser who told her that she was the only person in Israel that she would stay open late for so that she could have her hair done nicely. We took our time getting ready and then descended to the hotel lobby where, to our astonishment, there were literally hundreds of people gathered there. We were met by the Sabena Manager for Israel. 'You're late,' he hissed at us and to our bewilderment we were whisked through the throng into the Dan Banquet Hall, which was laid out with tables galore and we were seated at the top table as guests of honour. There was a great roar of applause as Golda Meir came in and I rose and escorted her to her seat next to me. Dora was on my left and Shimon Peres was next to her. Moshe Dayan sat on Golda's left with Abba Eban, the Foreign Minister next to him. The speeches that followed the dinner were predictable and broadly defended Israel's stand against terrorism as there were already voices throughout the world condemning Israel's actions in placing passengers in jeopardy. Once again I reiterate that I held no political opinions but I know that if the Israelis had not stormed the plane when they did, then that aircraft and its occupants would have been blown up by the Black September suicide squad aboard. I was called upon to make a brief speech and caused a laugh when I told the guests what, in the aviation world, the acronym 'SABENA' jokingly stood for and how appropriate it was in the present circumstances: 'Such A Bloody Experience Never Again!'

The morning afterwards, 11 May, we climbed into Juliet Golf with very mixed feelings. I looked around the cockpit in which I had spent so many agonising hours and breathed a sigh of relief. 'Let's get back,' I said and we took off towards the Mediterranean, crossed the coast of Israel and pointed the nose westwards to Brussels where our families were waiting for us.

There was a terrific reception awaiting us in Brussels. All the way back, as we crossed various Air Traffic zones, our call sign, Juliet Golf, would be recognised by a Sabena pilot flying in that area and sincere messages of congratulations and good luck would be passed on to us.

It was wonderful to see the children waiting on the tarmac as we taxied in. We were quickly taken to one of the hangars where a press conference was held. The top brass of Sabena were there, of course, and it was a long time before we were able to extricate ourselves from the throng and, eventually, get back to our house in Wezembeek.

We had not been home very long before the phone rang. It was the secretary of the Belgian branch of the Royal Air Force Association. The RAFA were holding their annual general meeting at the *Kursaal* (Casino) in Ostend, that year and would we come and stay in Ostend as their guests? We accepted and were put up in the pleasant Hotel du Parc. We were overwhelmed at the reception that was given to us. The hall was full of ex- and serving RAF personnel who rose and applauded when I was introduced to the assembly by Sir Frederick Pike, the Chairman and a Marshal of the RAF. The highlight was meeting the legendary Sir 'Gus' Walker who had lost a hand whilst saving the crew of a Lancaster which exploded whilst being 'bombed up' on the dispersal of an RAF station where Gus was Station Commander during the war. He had insisted on the ambulance crew retrieving his lost hand because, 'there is a good glove on it'! Anthony, our youngest son, was still only an AC2, the lowest of the low, but Gus and the others were charming and he was chatting away as if he had known them all his life.

The hijack certainly left a mark on us. Dora would fall asleep in the car and at other inappropriate moments. It was as if she were trying to shut the whole thing out of her mind, which she probably was. There was no such thing as counselling in those days and, although Sabena was most helpful, we were left to sort things out very much by ourselves. We were very much aware of the possibility of Arab reprisals for what had been a crushing defeat for Black September. The world had not very long to wait for Black September's answer. Shortly afterwards an Air France plane arrived in Tel Aviv. When the passengers retrieved their luggage from the carousel, three Japanese terrorists who had been passengers on board and trained in the Lebanon by the PLO took machine rifles and grenades from their incoming baggage and opened fire, killing twenty-six civilians in the arrivals hall.

Reg at sixteen years of age taken at Valette Studio, Blackpool, where he worked.

Reg in his football gear.

Reg just after his first solo, only 19 years old, Albany.

In Albany, 'We learned how to fly and we learned the hard way.'.

Reg (in front) and Wally Herbert in AT6 in December 1941. This was taken shortly before Reg graduated to his 200th flying hour.

Pilots 48 course – upward 6 OTU Blenheims – spring 1942. Reg's best friend, Eddy Simon, sits on his right. Eddy sadly died shortly after joining 105 Mossie Squad.

Reg aged 20 in bomber dress in 1942.   Reg in 1944.

Reg in 1943, at 21 years old.   F/Sgt Dora 'Chiefy' Shawcross.

Reg and Dora's wedding 26 June 1943

Left to Right: Reg's mother; sister, Ruth; Jackie (Dora's best friend); Reg (bandaged afetr a crash landing one week before the wedding); Dora, Paddy Graham Warron (W/OP); Harry Shawcross (Dora's dad); Amy (Dora's mum).

Reg and Dora at the Taj Mahal hotel in Mumbai, India, in July, 1948.

Reg in India in 1948.

Reg before a return flight during the Berlin Airlift in 1949.

Dora, Peter, Linda and Anthony arrive in Belgium in August 1952.

Sabena Dinghy Drill, 1953. Reg is seated at the back with the oar.

Reg with a
Douglas–DC3,
Leopoldville (now
Kinshasa) in 1954.

Reg (centre, sporting a dashing moustache) with Sabena crew from a Convair 440 Metropolitan in 1957.

Reg in front of Boeing 707 OO-SJG in 1965 – the same aircraft he was hijacked in.

This series features the hijacked Sabena plane on 8 May 1972. You can make out the Israeli rescue squad who disguised themselves as mechanics. (Courtesy of David Rubinger and Yedioth Ahronoth)

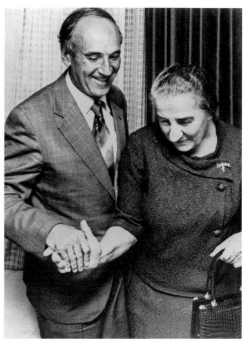

Ehud Barak (on the left holding gun) during the rescue. He autographed the photograph for Reg many years later.

Reg greeting Golda Meir at the dinner in his honour at the Dan Hotel, Tel Aviv, 10 May 1972.

Golda Meir (Israeli Prime Minster 1969–74) addresses the guests at a party held to honour Reg for his part in helping to safely rescue the passengers from his hijacked Sabena jet. Seated left to right: then Defence Minister Moshe Dayan, Golda Meir, Reginald Levy, Dora Levy, then Transport Minister Shimon Peres.

ANNEE / JAAR 1972		AERONEF — LUCHTVAARTUIG		Pilote ou 1er Pilote Bestuurder of 1e bestuurder	2de Pilote Elève ou Passagier Leerling of Passagier	NATURE DU VOL (Remarques éventuelles) AARD VAN DE VLUCHT (Gebeurlijke opmerkingen)		MONO EENM
Mois Maand	Date Datum	Type Type	Immatriculation Inschrijving		2de Bestuurder			Jour — Dag
						Reports - Overdrachten		Double com. Dubbele besturing

MAY	2nd	B.707	OO-SJH			PROF CHECK		
"	5th	" "	OO-SJG	SELF		BXLS-LONDON-BXLS X2 60/8 9/10		
"	7th	" "	SJD			" " " 681		
"	8th	" "	SJG			" VIENNA - TEL AVIV		
		"HI-JACKED" OVER SARAJEVO at 1435						
		LIBERATED BY ISRAELI ACTION MAY 9th						
"	11-	B.707	OO-SJH	SELF		TEL AVIV - BXLS		20 2x
						MAY 1972 B.707		
MAY		DC9	LSEMA			BXLS - MALAGA		
		CARAVELLE	SAFANA			MALAGA - BXLS		
JULY		B.707	OO-SJH	SELF		BXLS/MSTR(LONDON)BXLS		
"		" "	SJA			BXLS - STR - BXLS		
"		" "	SJC			BXLS-LONDON-BXLS (X2) 4/5		
"	15-	" "	SJC	"				
"	18-	" "	SJA	"		" " " (LON)		

| | B/F 20 150 30 Total (col. 1 à 10) 20 185 heures 20 minutes Totaal (Kol. 1 tot 10) uren minuten | | | | | Totaux à reporter Over te dragen totaal | | |

Extracts from Reg's log book which includes his hijacked flight. The simple way in which he notes this incredible event shows the sort of man he was – he was just doing his job.

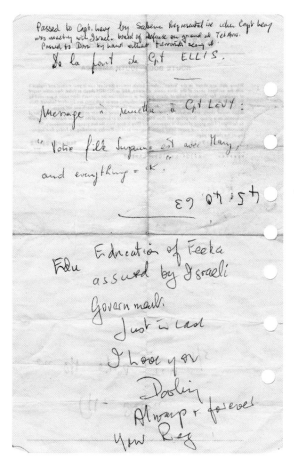

This message from Captain Jack Ellis in Brussels, was passed to Reg by the Sabena representative when he left the aircraft to speak to the Israeli authorities. He quickly scribbled a note to Dora which he managed to pass to her when he returned to the plane. It reads: 'Message from Capt. Ellis to Capt. Levy; "Your daughter Susan is with Mary, and everything ok".' Below is a message written by Reg to Dora, 'Education of Feeka assured by Israeli Government. Just in case. I love you Darling. Always & forever Your Reg.'

Reg with the sixteen-year-old future Crown Prince of Japan, Naruhito. in 1976, on a DC 10 flying from Tokyo to Brussels.

Reg with the famous Belgian cyclist, Eddie Merckx.

Reg with the former sports presenter and Belgian football international, Arsène Vaillant.

Reg with Shimon Peres in 1984. (Photo courtesy of Scoop 80)

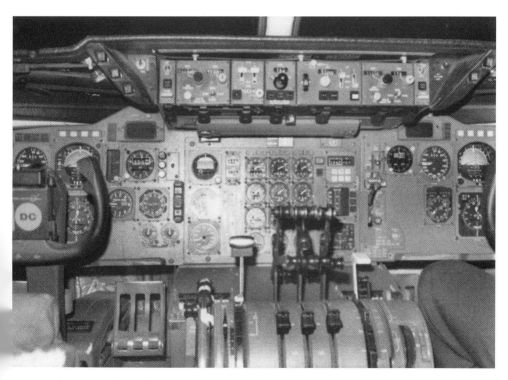

A close-up of the cockpit in a 727.

Reg with a PT-17 Stearman at the Airforce Museum, Beersheba, Israel, in 1992.

Reg with a D.H. Rapide at the Airforce Museum, Beersheba, Israel. He used to take joyriders around London in one of these in 1951. They paid 15*d* per trip, earning Reg 30*s* an hour.

Reg descends the stairs from the cockpit for the final time in September 1981.

Reg at the end of his last flight in September 1981.

Aug 1981		AIRCRAFT		Pilot, or 1st Pilot	2nd Pilot, Pupil or Passenger	DUTY (Including Results and Remarks)	SINGLE-ENGINE AIRCRAFT				
Month	Date	Type	No.				DAY Dual (1)	DAY Pilot (2)	NIGHT Dual (3)	NIGHT Pilot (4)	Dual (5)
						Totals Brought Forward	27:30	208:00	4:35	10:05	210:40
AUGUST	1st	B.747	00-SGB	SELF.	COCK.	SN 541. BXLS - N.Y.					7:3
"	3rd	"	"	"	MARIEN	548. N.Y - BXLS.					
"	6th	"	SGA	"	HUPPI	541. BXLS - N.Y.					7:4
"	8th	"	SGB	"	"	548 N.Y - BXLS. (PETER, MARY, SHARON + ADAM)					
"	14th	"	SGA	"	BAUDOT	567. BXLS - CHICAGO					8:3
"	17th	"	SGB	"	"	568 CHICAGO - BXLS.					
"	21st	"	SGB	"	LEURQUIN	541. BXLS - N.Y.					8:06
"	23rd	"	SGB	"	"	548 N.Y - BXLS					
"	26th	"	SGA	"	BAUDOT	541. BXLS - N.Y.					7:1
"	28th	"	SGB	"	"	548 N.Y - BXLS.					
"	31st	"	SGA	"	DELPLANCKE	541. BXLS - N.Y.					7:1
		TOTAL		AUGUST 1981		B.747	83:20				47:4
SEPT	2nd	B.747	SGA	SELF	DELPLANCKE	548 N.Y - BXLS.					
"	10th	"	SMA	"	MARIEN	541. BXLS - N.Y.					8:3
"	12th	"	SGB	"	"	548 N.Y - BXLS.					
"	15th	"	SGA	"	VAN TORNHOUT	541. BXLS - N.Y. LAST N.Y.					8:2
"	17th	"	SGA	"	"	548 N.Y - BXLS. } N.Y.					
"	24th	"	SGA	"	DELPLANCKE FEINBERG DORA	651. BXLS - MTL - DETROIT} LAST	TOTAL SEPT				8:4
"	27th	"	SGB	"	DE PLANCKE FEINBERG DORA	6 DETROIT- MTL-BXLS. {OFFICIAL FLIGHT SABENA	54:05				25:3
		STARTED	SABENA		MAY 1ST 1952						
		CONVAIR 240 440,			21,222 hrs. in DC.3. DC.4. DC 6 + 6 8. JC 7c	3,875 hrs in 30 mins					
					Boeing 707, DC 10 + B. 747.						
		GRAND TOTAL [Cols. (1) to (10)] 25,097 Hrs. 30 Mins.				Totals Carried Forward	27:30	208:00	4:35	10:05	210:40

Extracts from Reg's log book. It includes his last flight and the sum total of his flying hours – 25,097 hours and 30 minutes.

Reg and his crew relax in a 747 Lounge after landing in Brussels on his final flight in 1981.

Reg appears on the Israeli TV programme *This is your Life* dedicated to Ehud Barak (former Israeli Chief of Staff) in 1993. (Photo courtesy of Nachum Assis)

CHAPTER TWENTY

It was obvious that I could not return directly to flying the normal routes. The company were obviously nervous of further incidents. The Arab stranglehold on the oil industry dictated Belgian policy as in the UK. The director of Sabena suggested that I retire. When I told him that I would do so if he paid me the equivalent of the fifteen years salary that I could expect, plus the customary end of career bonus, he quickly changed his tune. Sabena offered myself and the family a holiday in Spain at the Las Pyramides Hotel in Fuengirola in which Sabena had an interest. We accepted this to try and get together after what we had been through.

Linda and Feeka were the only two members of the family who were able to accompany us to the Costa del Sol. We were really spoiled by the staff at the hotel. We quickly made good friends with the Maître d'Hôtel and his friend who just happened to be the head chef. Lunch was always the big meal and they would strive to provide us with bigger and better meals each day. The maître d' would come to the pool in the morning and 'suggest' the lunchtime meal. The *pièce de résistance* one day was lobster. We were in the *à la carte* section of the dining room, away from the normal set menu section where the majority of hotel guests were seated. Not quite with a fanfare of trumpets, but it seemed as though there were, the maître d' and the chef entered accompanied by two waiters pushing a trolley on which reposed the most enormous lobster that I have ever seen. It was lying amongst the most splendid garniture of asparagus and other exotic vegetables and a huge bowl of sauce was flaming away merrily at the side. It was impossible to finish even half of it. As we went out of the dining room an American diner caught my arm and said, 'Say, are you some kind of lord, or something?'

We had to get away from the enormous lunches that we were being served so when our two friends suggested that we join them on their day off to explore the bars and taverns of nearby Fuengirola, we eagerly accepted. If only we had known that there existed a Spanish ritual of going from bar to bar and taking 'tapas' in each of them! The Spanish hospitality was boundless. We were fuller than we had ever been back at the hotel. 'One last place,' they told us when our stomachs were so full we said that we had to return. We entered this lovely, dimly lit tavern. Our friend, Juan, the maître d' went to the bar where a rapid conversation went on with the patron who kept nodding his head vigorously. We managed to drink yet another sherry at our table when I noticed, in a corner, a young pig turning on a spit over a blazing fire. I groaned inwardly and whispered to Dora, 'I'm sure that's for us.' And it was.

To try and rid ourselves of some of the kilos that we were rapidly acquiring we arranged to play golf at the nearby course at Nueva Andalucia. We had played there several times on previous holidays and the secretary, a charming Spaniard, remembered me and had been following our recent adventures. He asked me if I would let him take a picture of us but explained that he would like me to meet his young son who would be coming a bit later, so suggested that he would meet us when we had played nine holes and stopped for the customary drink. There was an American couple playing ahead of us, rather slowly to tell the truth. My handicap was around twenty at the time but I used to hit a long ball, very rarely straight, but some of my drives ended up rather close to the Americans. When we arrived at the clubhouse we were amazed to find a battery of photographers awaiting us. The secretary explained that they were from the local press so we posed as graciously as we could before continuing on our round. When we got to the tenth tee there was the American couple sitting on a bench waiting for us. 'Please play through,' they said. They were looking at us and you could read their minds. They had seen all the photographers and were trying to place the faces. 'No, not Jack Nicklaus. Gary Player?' I strode to the tee and unleashed a mighty drive which travelled nearly 300 yards into the car park about 200 yards to the right of the fairway. Dora, not to be outdone, topped her tee shot which ran straight as a die at least 40 yards down the fairway. 'Thanks so much,' I said and we left them to their thoughts.

The two girls were thrilled to find that there were stables near the hotel and even more thrilled to have the horses brought to the entrance of the hotel for them to go off on their rides in the beautiful Spanish countryside. We had left them to their riding whilst we played golf one day. When we returned to the hotel we were met by the manager who was terribly upset. The girls had had a riding accident, he explained and the staff were distraught. Our hearts in our mouths we hurried to the room. You have never seen such a sight as the two bedraggled figures that confronted us. They were covered in mud and clay and shaking like leaves – with laughter. Their horses had suddenly bolted, Linda had fallen, cutting her finger and splitting her trousers in the process and Feeka had fallen into a river. The girls had walked back leaving trails of mud and water all over the hotel corridors.

We returned to Brussels towards the end of May and I started flying again but the threatening phone calls kept coming and eventually the company decided that I should be based away from Brussels for a time to try and let things die down. I was given the choice of Luanda in Angola and Johannesburg in South Africa and, not surprisingly, chose South Africa. A few months beforehand we had decided to send Feeka to a boarding school in England but were devastated when the headmistress wrote that she could not guarantee her safety.

We rented the house in Wezembeek to an American family and rented a small *pied à terre* in nearby Woluwe St Lambert for when I would be in Brussels, as it had been decided that I would bring the scheduled flight from Johannesburg to Brussels and then take the next one back the following day. Even renting a small apartment had its hassle as one of the existing tenants went to the Sabena management and local police and complained that we were putting the lives of all the tenants in danger by staying there.

On 27 September 1972, Dora, Feeka and I flew as passengers to Johannesburg. We took Rika, our cocker spaniel with us and went straight to the Quirinale Hotel in Hillbrow where we had stayed before as crew and on our brief holiday in April before the hijack. During this holiday we had flown to Cape Town and made friends with the South African Captain, Blake Flemington. He had invited us to his home if we ever came back to South Africa. Little did we know that we would be back so soon. By a fantastic coincidence he was the victim of the first South African hijack a few weeks later and I sent him a message: 'Welcome to the club!' We met up with him very soon after arriving and became great friends with he and his lovely family.

Unfortunately, in the stress of leaving Belgium, I had parked my car outside the airport whilst I booked everyone in and then boarded the plane completely forgetting to put the car in the garage provided for the crews. The police eventually came and found out that it was mine and suspected that a bomb had been planted and nearly blew it up but, fortunately, did not.

We were made so very welcome in South Africa and especially at the Quirinale, which in those days was a very respectable hotel. We had a suite and Feeka had her own small room. The hotel was now managed by Jack Dante and his wife Sally, and they could not have been more gracious. There was a swimming pool up on the roof and we used to take Rika, our cocker spaniel, there. She loved the water but we were rather concerned as to what the other guests might say. Sally told us, 'If the little darling wants to swim then, of course, she must swim.' So Rika used to dive into the pool with great abandon and enjoyment. Her lunch was served at the pool by a waiter who would bring it on a silver salver covered by a snowy white napkin.

We received a letter from one of the nicest golf clubs in South Africa, Houghton, saying that they had learned that we were in South Africa and would we please consider ourselves honorary members for the duration of our stay? Then one day we were told by reception that there was a car waiting outside. It was from a local Jewish businessman, Benny Wainstein, who owned a big firm, 'Tastic Rice'. He provided the car, a big 'Valiant' for our use whilst in South Africa.

We suspected, but were never able to find out, that the Israeli Government had been behind these and many other acts. In any case, El Al, the Israeli Airline, were often in touch through their local representatives and were always very helpful.

The Quirinale was fine and we made great friends with some of the residents, particularly Selma and Jack Frack. They had a suite and had been living there for years and had furnished it themselves. Selma's brother, Charles, was the oldest member of the Johannesburg Stock Exchange. He was a steward at the prestigious Turffontein racecourse and Dora and I were privileged to be his guests at many meetings. It has completely spoiled us for going to the races any other way as we were treated like royalty, as were all his guests. We viewed the races from a lovely air conditioned box and were served lunch, thirty guests to each steward's table, in the lovely dining room. A bottle of whisky would alternate with a bottle of gin at each guest's place and the champagne would flow. Even though South African champagne is a great wine, only the best French champagne would be served. The stewards and their guests had their own betting windows and we would often be in line with Harry Oppenheimer, who would be placing a very meagre one Rand bet.

Christmas came very swiftly. We had become great friends with the resident band leader, Jerry Collins, and I would often get up and sing with them. New Year's Eve, or as the South Africans call it,

Old Year's Night, was on a Sunday in 1972. The draconian laws of Apartheid South Africa stopped the sale of all liquor after 8 p.m. The Quirinale got around this by allowing all the guests at their News Year's Eve supper to purchase their liquor in advance and put it under the tables and then drink after midnight. You can imagine the scene with the bottles and glasses everywhere and the guests who had been steadily drinking from their stashed bottles making a very merry and Happy New 1973.

It looked as though we were going to have to stay in South Africa for at least a year, so we decided to look for a furnished house. I had just come back from a trip to Brussels and went to an estate agent. The girl took my particulars and when I said that I worked for Sabena she said that a relative of hers was a Flight Engineer and was coming to Johannesburg to attend a wedding in the family. I then told her that it was Roger, and that I had brought him in that morning. She was amazed at the coincidence and told me to go and see a Jewish family called Lipschitz who lived nearby at Athol, had a lovely house, but were trying to let it as some of their children had emigrated to Israel and they were planning to follow them when they had wound up their affairs in South Africa. We went straight round there and a small elderly man answered the ring at the door. We had obviously disturbed their afternoon siesta as he said, 'Look, come and have dinner with us tonight and we will discuss it.' That evening, Sid and Dolly Lipschitz gave us dinner and introduced us to their son, Stan. They explained that he was an accountant and would have to stay in the house – it was big enough – until he could follow them to Israel and that it was up to him whether he liked us enough. He said 'Yes' there and then so we moved into this very glamorous villa. The best part was the garden with a lovely swimming pool with changing rooms, showers and barbecue. The outside living with breakfast set on the patio underneath the thatched awning was wonderful. There was a pair of resident mynah birds who took exception to Rika intruding on their territory and used to, literally, dive bomb the poor dog whenever she went to the pool for her many daily swims. Actually, Rika didn't take a blind bit of notice and went serenely on her own way.

We soon settled in and I would bring the Sabena crews back to the house and we would have some memorable parties. Once I invited an El Al crew back and we gave them a 'Braai' as the barbecue is called in South Africa. You would think that the Israelis had been starved for years. They came into the garden, threw one of their stewards, fully clothed, into the pool and then descended on to the Braai like a horde of locusts. The steward who had taken the involuntary swim hung all his wet money on the trees around the pool with clothes pegs. Years later we were 'dead heading' between Montreal and New York, Dora was a passenger and the same steward from El Al came up to her and said, 'I had the best food that I have ever eaten at your house.'

I came back from a trip to Brussels one day to find Dora and Feeka waiting for me at the Quirinale, where we had left the crew who were staying over. They were in tears and very upset. She and Feeka had been attacked by a swarm of bees at the house. They had dived into the pool and had not been too badly stung, but Rika had been savagely attacked and had swallowed many of the bees who had stung her internally. By a fantastic stroke of luck Millicent Levine had phoned. Millicent's husband Aubrey was the brother of my cousin Audrey's husband, so was the nearest to a relative that we had in South Africa. Dora had answered the phone and had screamed, 'Bees,' and Millicent had grasped the situation. She had phoned her doctor, Bentley Philips. He had immediately phoned a nearby chemist who sent his assistant on a motor scooter round to our house with the requisite antidotes. Our poor dog, however, was in a very bad way and was taken to Bryanston veterinary clinic. I went immediately out there and the vet told me that the treatment involved would be very expensive and he doubted whether he could save her as she had been stung hundreds of times internally and externally. I told him that it didn't matter what it cost, that dog was one of our family. To our, and the vet's, amazement, Rika pulled through.

There is no doubt in my mind that what saved her was the magnificent condition that she was in. We had always taken her with us to the golf course at Keerbergen where she was allowed to run free. She used to dive into the lakes and swim under the water to retrieve the many errant golf balls that I deposited there – and would drop them neatly in the middle of the fairway and look at me as though to say, 'Now hit that one onto the green.' She would never chase after a ball but would flatten herself on the fairway as you made your shot and then go to where the ball had fallen. All this was without any strict training. It just came naturally to her. I had almost lost my life once when she went out onto the ice at Keerbergen to retrieve a ball when we were foolish enough to play in the winter. She fell through when the ice broke. I went in after her and managed to reach her and carry her back to Dora but I was rapidly losing control when Dora managed to hold a golf club out to me and pulled me back out. It was a very near thing.

We had, of course, to find a school for Feeka. She had been very much affected by the whole affair of the hijack. She was sixteen and had been very happy at her school in Brussels. She had to go to school while we were in South Africa so we arranged an interview with the headmaster of nearby Hyde Park High School. When Feeka saw the baggy blue bloomers, wide brimmed straw boater and mini-skirted gym slip which were mandatory wear, she burst into tears. 'I'm not wearing those stupid things,' she cried. Luckily, Hyde Park was a co-educational school and a boyfriend was soon forthcoming. Rainer, the handsome son of an Austrian couple, became her inseparable companion and the boater became a crumpled mass; the socks were worn around her ankles and she soon became a typical South African schoolgirl. Not quite typical because I brought her little 49cc moped back with me on one trip and she became known as 'the girl with the moped' as it was the only one in the school, probably the only one in Johannesburg, and she was very popular.

The doctor who had responded so swiftly to our bee drama became our family doctor and friend. He had heard of the hijack and was fascinated with our story. We would see him every time we returned to South Africa. He never took any payment for any of the many services that he rendered us and some of these have been invaluable.

Our eldest daughter, Linda, was flying as a stewardess with British United Airways and came down for a holiday. It wasn't long before she and Stan Lipschitz, whom Dora had already nicknamed 'Number Three', meaning our number three son, were becoming interested in one another. Stan and Linda came to us on Christmas Eve and told us that they were going to get married.

We were able to get all the family down to us for a holiday, but not necessarily at the same time. Peter, Mary and little Sharon came and we celebrated Sharon's fourth birthday. By now we had moved to another big house in Houghton as the Lipschitzes had sold 'Shane' as their house was called. At Sharon's party we had a puppet show given by Jenny Kirsch. Her husband, Derek, is the son of Johnny and Margaret Kirsch who were our great friends for all the years that we were in Brussels. Our youngest son, Anthony and their youngest son, Barry grew up together, were the same age and were inseparable. Anthony himself came down for a holiday but wasn't really happy as the heat was too much for him. The mynah birds at Shane took a particular dislike to him and used to dive bomb him as he walked around the pool. Derek and Jenny were very much involved with the South African theatre and we went to many plays and after the show parties with them, meeting many of the celebrities including, notably, Rex Garner, by then the Grand Old Man of the South African stage.

Time went by very quickly. We had a very good social life and the outdoor life was wonderful. We enjoyed our golf at Houghton and also at the Wanderers Club which had always extended its membership to the Sabena crews stopping over at Johannesburg. The cost of living was definitively less than that of Europe. We had servants, of course, but found that we were supporting their families as well as the person employed by us.

Earlier, on a never to be forgotten night, our golden cocker spaniel, Rika, had given birth to puppies. We had taken her to be mated to a prize winning cocker spaniel earlier in the year. On the night in question we had a great poker school going on with our lifelong friends, Louie and Tony. Their son and his family were living in Johannesburg and Louie and Tony were visiting them. We had been the greatest of friends from our early days in Belgium where Tony had been living since he was a child and we had established the poker school routine there. Louie's brother, Tom Roper, and his wife, Dorothy, were fellow players; Louie and Tony's daughter and her husband made up the school and we would meet about once a month to have dinner at the house of one of us and then proceed to get down to business. It was a very light-hearted school. Tony was the one that insisted we play 'serious poker' but he was always quickly overruled and 'Roodles', where all kinds of games with various wild cards, became the order of the day and 'Dealer's Choice' made sure that everyone got their favourite game. The stakes were always reasonable but the game would go on until the early hours of the morning and this was the case that night in Houghton. Linda was staying with us and she came in to the room where we were playing and excitedly told us that Rika was performing. From then on during the night, she would burst in with the news that there was 'another one'. There were six interruptions to our game.

We had no intention of keeping any of the puppies and we quickly found homes for them but Feeka persuaded us to keep one, a lovely little black and tan, that she promptly named Tansy.

Our only previous holiday since the hijack had been when I had two weeks leave due to me. I had renewed acquaintanceship with Raymond and Ron who had been so helpful when Linda was injured in Entebbe. Raymond was now Station Manager at Johannesburg and Ron was Sales Director for South Africa. I asked Ron what the chances were of getting me a flight with Dora to Hong Kong. He came up with a trip to Bangkok and then on to Hong Kong for the two of us, taking ten days with hotels and breakfasts included. The trip would be with Luxair, a South African charter company based, for tax purposes, in Luxembourg. We had a lovely flight to Bangkok but, as we had both been there several times, wanted to press on to Hong Kong so, as soon as we arrived, I went to the Sabena office where the representative, an old friend of mine, got us on a flight with China Airlines to Hong Kong via Hanoi. We left a message at the hotel for the charter company representative that we would meet up with them in Hong Kong and were onward bound to Hanoi within a few hours of landing at Bangkok. We had forgotten that there was a war going on in Vietnam and we landed there amidst the most frantic activity.

The security and military presence was very impressive but we were glad to be on our way to Hong Kong where we met up with our very great friends from Brussels, Eric and Ann Proctor. Eric had been with Eurocontrol in Belgium but had taken a very important job with the civil aviation authorities in Hong Kong. In no time at all Ann, who was a teacher, spoke fluent Cantonese and it was a revelation to see the look of wonder and respect on the faces of the various Chinese merchants with whom we were soon haggling when she came out with the juiciest phrases imaginable. We really got some wonderful bargains purely through her linguistic ability. They had a beautiful apartment very high up, overlooking the harbour and we were sitting there one evening admiring the lights of Hong Kong when Eric said, 'Do you notice anything about the neon advertising lights that are everywhere?' I couldn't see anything remarkable and said so. 'Well,' he said, 'if you look closely you will see that not one of them is flashing.' This was true. Eric had seen the danger. The approach to the runway at Hong Kong took you in amongst the skyscrapers and over the town and it would have been very easy to confuse the flashing runway approach lights with the thousands of garish flashing signs that were there when he first came to Hong Kong. Despite furious protests from the local traders he had got the use of flashing neon signs banned.

We were taken out to some of the finest Chinese restaurants that it has ever been our privilege to eat in. Not your usual tourist places but the real thing, with mainly Chinese customers. The rooms would be a babel of noise, shouting and laughter, and the floors would be covered with the discarded shells from lobsters, crabs, shrimp – you name it. The food itself was sublime and we will remember our nights in Hong Kong all our lives.

Eventually it was time to return. Eric and Ann took us to the hotel where the charter tour was staying. We were sitting outside with a drink, when the charter representative spotted us. He came over. 'You've got yourself into a lot of trouble,' he said angrily. 'When you left the charter at Bangkok you cut yourselves off from it as we are only allowed to take out the same number of passengers from Hong Kong as we brought in so you will have to find your own way back to Johannesburg at your own expense unless you can get permission from the authorities.' Eric spoke to a waiter. 'Get me a piece of writing paper,' he said. He wrote several lines and then produced as if by magic a rubber stamp from his briefcase, stamped the paper, handed it to the spellbound representative and said quietly, 'I think you will find that this will do the trick.' He was the Assistant in Chief to the Director of Civil Aviation in Hong Kong. I had heard the expression 'and his jaw dropped' but this was the first time that I had actually seen it happen when the representative read the paper. From then on it was VIP treatment all the way back to South Africa.

CHAPTER TWENTY-ONE

Early in 1973 we received a personal letter from Golda Meir inviting Dora, myself and any other member of our family to come over and have a holiday in Israel at the Israeli Government's expense. We gratefully accepted saying we would be delighted to come to Israel and very soon afterwards we received a proposed itinerary. It was stressed that the arrangements could be changed to suit our requirements so we replied that we would leave ourselves in the hands of the Israelis. When my leave became due we took Feeka, who was the only one who could accompany us, and we left Johannesburg by El Al as VIP passengers to fly directly to Ben Gurion Airport at Tel Aviv, the scene of our still vividly remembered encounter with terrorism.

We were whisked to the King David Hotel in Jerusalem where we were given the same suite that Henry Kissinger had occupied not very long before we arrived. From then on it was a wonderful experience to be taken around Israel in a stretch limousine with our own personal guide. He was called Eli and took his duties very seriously. Luckily his rather heavy descriptions of the various archaeological digs that were shown to us, 'Now this was level eight ...' was compensated for when we went to Haifa and were met by one of the great characters of Israel – a land of great characters –

Ronnie Lourie. He was a big man, the El Al Manager for the area, a bon viveur who knew everything that was worth knowing of all that had gone on in Israel for the past two thousand years. It was obvious that he had been briefed to show us all the sights but when I said to him that we would much rather see some of the typical bars and restaurants of Haifa and Acre he breathed an obvious sigh of relief and proceeded to give us the time of our lives. We met all his lovely family and were shown behind the scenes in the fascinating historical crusader town of Acre. He knew the old town better than, I daresay, Richard Lionheart, and we were fascinated with his tales of the adventures that had taken place within its walls.

We were taken to the old Roman town of Caesarea and stayed there long enough to play golf on the only golf course in Israel at that time. A great privilege was to be taken to the furthermost northern border and see for ourselves the life on the kibbutz there. We were astonished to find pork on the menu and were served our ration of lunch at one kibbutz by a distinguished looking gentleman who was then introduced to us as the leader of the Israeli Philharmonic Orchestra who was doing his stint behind the serving counter. We were taken to the Central Command Headquarters of the Israeli Defence Force where I met up again with one of the generals who had been behind the storming of my plane. 'Gandhi' Ze'evi showed us around the impressive army site and we were struck by the informality that existed between him and his men. He laughed, when I remarked on this. 'In Israel,' he said, 'every man is a general. After an encounter or even a battle, ordinary private soldiers will come to me and ask why I hadn't done this or that and will, very often, come up with a better plan than the one that I carried out. Their obedience to orders is absolute but that doesn't stop them from arguing about it afterwards.' This love of argument was exemplified when I was told a story by Feeka who had been on a bus going in to Jerusalem. A woman got on with a dog and paid the driver for two seats. The bus became full and a man got on and demanded that the woman remove her dog to let him sit down. She refused, saying that she had paid for the seats. A violent argument broke out in which the passengers all joined. The driver stopped the bus and took a vote. The dog won.

We flew down to Eilat and basked in the heat of the Gulf of Aqaba. We were taken to the citadel of Masada and climbed to the site of the siege and gazed down at the, still visible, lines of the Roman cohorts and tried to imagine the feelings of the besieged Zealots so many centuries ago.

Back at the King David in Jerusalem we were told that Moshe Dayan was coming to have a drink with us and we went to the small bar behind the reception. He was sitting there and we were greeted warmly. He said to Dora, 'You see. You did have something to wear.' Word had quickly spread around the hotel and, although he was surrounded by security guards, he was obviously getting uncomfortable. One unfortunate tourist managed to get near enough to start asking him for his autograph. He never knew what hit him and he was out of the bar so quickly that he didn't have time to finish his sentence. Many years later I was sitting in the cockpit of a Sabena 747 waiting for the passengers to embark for our trip to New York. The Sabena rep in charge of protocol came into the cockpit. 'You will have the wife of Moshe Dayan on board,' he said. 'I will bring her to the cockpit and introduce you.' I saw her coming out to the aircraft so went down the steps to greet her. She put her arms around me and gave me a big kiss. 'I see you know each other already,' said the startled representative. Later she told me that the night we went out to the dinner after the hijack she had been feeling very unwell and had only come because of her desire to meet Dora and me. 'When your wife fell asleep at the table,' she said, 'I was so glad of the excuse to go home. When we arrived home I was sitting at my dressing table and was horrified to find my face coming out in spots.' She had measles and was ill for some time.

Ben Ari, the Chief Executive of El Al, came for a drink at the King David and we talked of the future of aviation in Israel. He was adamant that charters should never be allowed into Israel unless

El Al was running them. He presented me with a magnificent heavy silver medallion in a beautiful sandalwood box. It had been struck to commemorate twenty-five years of the existence of El Al.

We met up with Shimon Peres again. He gave me a set of David Roberts lithographs that had been specially printed in a lovely presentation covering. He was present with Moshe Dayan and Golda Meir when we went to tea with her, once again. There had been big political squabbles between them and when we left they were talking together for the first time in a long while.

Feeka had been a bundle of nerves when she learned that we were going to meet Golda. In the event Golda came to the door, gave Feeka a big hug and perched her on the arm of her chair. 'She was just like Nana,' she beamed later.

We met several men who claimed to be one of the Special Corps that stormed our plane. In fact, if all the ones that I met in later years who said that they were involved in the attack actually took part, it must have been one of the largest forces in history!

I found out later from the actual leader, then General Barak, that there were sixteen of them and they were the ones who carried out the incredible raid on Entebbe in July 1976 to free the hostages held there. One of the soldiers who was there was to become the Prime Minister of Israel, 'Bibi' Netanyahu. He claims that he was accidentally shot in the arm by one of the other soldiers. It was his brother, the much loved 'Yoni' who was the sole Israeli casualty at Entebbe when he was shot from the Control Tower by a sniper from the Idi Amin army.

Our wonderful tour of Israel had been supervised by one of the most charming Israelis that one could meet, David Eylath. He was the chief PA of El Al and had worked very hard to make sure that our holiday went smoothly. We became great friends and were honoured to be invited to his grandson's Bar Mitzvah some years later. His early death from a heart attack was a tragedy.

Sabena informed me early in 1974 that they deemed it safe to return to Belgium and they proposed that we do so in March.

In the throes of preparing our return to Belgium I took Tansy with me on one of my flights to Brussels and left her in the tender care of the lady who had been our cleaning lady in Belgium for years and whose daughter, Marie, was and still is Feeka's friend.

The company were extremely nice about our move back to Belgium and I was able to take back Feeka's beloved 'Maxime', the name she had bestowed on her moped. I was also able to take a magnificent pub-style bar which we had had made for us and we promptly installed it in the room adjoining the kitchen at Avenue des Violettes where we very soon settled down in a more normal existence. We had proper Western-style swing doors as the entrance to the 'pub'. I had collected hundreds of exotic wine and beer labels from various South African sources and we papered the walls with these. The bar had its own posts on it, supporting a proper bar ceiling complete with lights and we had the requisite heavy bar stools to sit on. Many really smashing homecoming parties were held in there and we would retire to the bar after one of the wonderful dinners that Dora gave and 'lineshoot' until the small hours of the morning.

South Africa had been very good for us. We had made lifelong friends and the distance from the turmoil and wars of the Middle East had helped heal the mental scars that the hijack had left. I had even been accused, in an influential Arab newspaper, of personally killing one of the terrorists although nothing could have been further from the truth. There was no 'counselling' in those days and we certainly did not sue the company for 'stress' although one passenger was successful, I believe, in getting some compensation for being injured in the attack on the plane. I think that my wartime experience helped me as I had lived with danger for long periods and, presumably, had learned how to handle extreme stress. Having to leave our beautiful, newly built, home in Brussels was a blow that Dora never got over. The house was never the same to her after we got back in the spring of 1974 and Feeka who, at the age of sixteen, had been uprooted from her school and close circle of friends, suffered mental stress that remains, to some extent, with her to this very day. I think that it was because she had been alone when news of the hijacking came and, although family and friends were soon there to rally round, she had borne the brunt of the ensuing horde of media reporters that had descended on the house. The press had even found Dora's mother and father in St Helens and had quickly found a willing victim in my mother in Blackpool, who had furnished them with photographs.

CHAPTER TWENTY-TWO

I was now faced with the choice of continuing as a captain on the 707 or opting to fly on the new DC10 that Sabena had purchased. I had to guarantee that I would stay on with them for at least three years in order that the company could realise their investment in training me. It had always been my ambition, even my dream, to eventually fly the 747 but I was not quite high enough in the seniority at that time to opt for it. The 'bidding' system in Sabena was, broadly enough, the same as most aviation companies. As vacancies on an aircraft appeared, pilots were asked, in strict order of seniority in the company, whether they would like to bid for that aircraft. In return they had to promise to stay on it for the time laid down by the company and could not bid for another aircraft until that time had elapsed. I had reasoned that I was fifty-four at the time of the bidding for the DC10, could fly on it for the statutory three years and then if – and IF was the operative word – there was a vacancy on the 747 and the coveted New York route, I would still be able to complete the mandatory four years on the 747 before reaching the retiring age of sixty.

It turned out exactly like that.

I was accepted for training on the brand new DC10 and had the enjoyable experience of going to Ostia, near Rome for my simulator training and then to Yuma, in Arizona, for the aircraft training. The simulation technology had now reached the level where you could practically fly the aircraft before you actually stepped in it. The DC10 was a brand new concept in flying but I found no difficulty in adapting, and looked forward to Arizona and the aircraft itself. Flying a new aircraft had never worried me and the DC10 was no exception.

Anytime that I see 'Spaghetti Vongole' on a menu I am immediately transported to Ostia. Our Chief Pilot, Marcel Vanderverren, was training with us. He was in England as a schoolboy during the war and was a great friend and helped me with many problems during the stressful times of the hijack. It was he who found the wonderful restaurant in Ostia where the three crews who were training would repair each evening. Your evening meal was swimming around in enormous tanks as you entered the place. Trouble was that by the time it appeared on your plate you felt that you were eating an old friend. Not that it stopped us. The aforementioned Spaghetti Vongole consisted of the most exquisite mixture of clams, shrimps, prawns, oysters, crab, lobster – you name it, it was there.

After the successful completion of the simulator course, we flew to New York by our own company and crossed America to Los Angeles and finally flew with Howard Hughes' airline to the small town of Yuma in Arizona where Douglas had their own field for training DC10 crews.

There were nine of us. Three Captains, three First Officers and three Flight Engineers. We disembarked from the small DC9 that had brought us from Los Angeles and walked out into the searing Arizona heat. A gentleman with 'Douglas' emblazoned on his bright pink blazer welcomed us. 'Hi there,' he said. 'Welcome to Yuma.' He handed us three sets of car keys. 'These are the keys to your transport. They are waiting outside the gate. Your hotel is the only one; it's three miles down the road.' He gave us three credit cards. 'When you need gas, use these. Have a good day.' With that he disappeared into the sunset and, with the exception of one of our number, we never set eyes upon him again. The three cars were brand new Chevrolets and we got great pleasure out of using them. After several hours of flying the great DC10, we would explore the desert around the small town of Yuma. It was absolutely fantastic and we would drive for hours on end just drinking in the wonderful scenery. Our nameless captain drove a bit too far one day and inadvertently crossed the border into Mexico and finished in a Mexican jail where he languished with his crew until the Douglas representative got him out a few hours later.

Our hotel was a typical American motel complete with swimming pool and really nice steak grill type restaurant. We found time, after our 'circuits and bumps' to do a bit of tourist flying. The wonderful Grand Canyon was not very far away and we would fly, with readily given permission from the local ATC Centre, at the authorised low altitude over the magnificent spectacle and wonder at the magnitude of its beauty. My Flight Engineer, Felix, was a very keen geologist and our excursions into the desert were a constant source of wonderful new specimens for him. We visited Phoenix and we revelled in the wonderful dry climate where the searing heat was so supportable.

All too soon it was time to get back to Brussels and down to the real business of flying the DC10 on the routes. Our DC10 were destined to fly the Far East network but Sabena had scheduled a virtual round the world trip for its DC10 crews. Starting at Brussels you would fly to Alaska, over the North Pole, slip (the term used to describe getting off an aircraft, handing it over to another waiting crew then, after taking your rest, continue the flight by taking over the next aircraft to come in) and then carry on to Tokyo, slip again, then take the next flight out but westwards, this time via Manila, Bombay, Athens and so on to Brussels, slipping at Manila and Bombay. Sometimes the flight would go through Dubai or Abu Dhabi but it was a really sapping flight due to the many time zones that you would cross. Alaska was GMT minus ten hours but you would cross the date line en route to Tokyo and land at Tokyo the day after you had taken off from Alaska. One tip that I learned whilst slipping in Bombay, which was six-and-a-half hours ahead of GMT, was to turn my watch face upside down and the hands would then be at the correct place for the time in Bombay if you used your imagination.

My Line Checkout on the DC10 was very nearly the last flight I ever made. One of the Chief Pilots from Douglas was the Checking Pilot. He had been the Captain on the US President's plane, Air Force One, when Nixon was President and was well-known and liked in the aviation world. He apologised to me that regulations made it mandatory that he occupy the First Officer's seat for all take-offs and landings. I had already been passed out as a Pilot on the aircraft and had it on my licence, but this was the check on the actual routes that I would be flying. The first leg was Brussels to Athens and all went smoothly. The next leg was from Athens to Abu Dhabi and I took off from Athens. We were taking off on the sole runway that headed out to sea. As convention required I called for 'undercarriage up' as soon as the Climb and Descent indicator showed positive climb, and this command was followed and the wheels retracted. The next thing I knew the control column started juddering and the stall warning that vibrated the stick was working. In much less time than it takes to write this I saw that the leading edge slats were retracted and I opened up the engines, dived the aircraft (we were about 200-300ft) and was able to regain control just above the surface of the sea. I had yelled for the slats to be put out and this had been done. We climbed away and my Checking Pilot sat there saying nothing. He seemed to be in a state of shock. 'I didn't ask for "slats retract",' I said. 'You sure got them,' were the only words that he said for several hours. The leading edge slats are a device that increases the airflow over the wings at low speeds and are absolutely vital for take-off when the aircraft is at its most vulnerable with its highest weight and lowest speed. There is always a minimum speed for the retraction of the slats and we were below this speed. We were very fortunate in the fact that we were over the sea and had the maximum space available to recover our flying speed but it had been a very near thing. Eventually the Check Pilot spoke to me. 'I don't know what came over me,' he said, 'I have never done a thing like that in my life.' There was little I could say. It only goes to show that we are all human and mistakes are inevitable, but the retraction of slats below flying speed should have been made physically impossible. The anonymous delivery of a case of whisky to my house some time later was the last that I heard of the matter.

Towards the end of October 1974, the hugely publicised boxing match for the World Heavyweight Championship between the reigning champion George Foreman and the challenger, Muhammad Ali was due to take place in the unlikely setting of Kinshasa, the capital of Zaire (now called the Democratic Republic of the Congo).

I was due to take the flight down there that would coincide with the great event and, as it was Dora's birthday on 30 October, the night of the fight, I got her a ticket to accompany me. There are those who would say that, after the events of my own disastrous birthday in 1972, I was foolish but I have always believed in putting things like that behind me and 'pressing on' as we used to say during those exciting times of 1942 and 1943. On the flight down one of the first class passengers happened to be the publicity manager for George Foreman and he promised Dora and myself would receive tickets for the fight. He kept his promise and sent them to our hotel, the Memling, soon after our arrival.

The Memling had improved considerably but could not hold a candle to the only other hotel of any consequence in Kinshasa, the Intercontinental, which boasted a swimming pool. Consequently, the crews who were slipping in Kinshasa used the Intercontinental during their free time and we were no exception.

Sitting around the pool I got into conversation with a very pleasant young man. He told me that he came from South London and that his father was with him. I was introduced to his father and very soon called Dora over as it was evident that they had many common roots. Dora had spent her childhood in and around

Lambeth and very quickly established ties with the father. It turned out that the pleasant young man was John Daly, the entrepreneur and film producer, who was putting on the 'Rumble in the Jungle', as the fight became known.

I don't think either of us will ever forget the days and nights that followed. The atmosphere in Kinshasa was electric. Nothing as big as the forthcoming fight had ever happened in what was little more than a provincial town in this far-flung, little known, republic of darkest Africa. Hundreds of reporters from the various media descended on the town; the few bars and nightspots previously frequented by the locals rich enough to be able to afford their prices, suddenly became invaded by hordes of sensation-seeking journalists, television technicians and their counterparts from all the countries that had suddenly realised that the sporting event of the century was about to take place in the former Belgian Congo.

In the days that followed we became great friends with John Daly and his father and John told us to forget about our own tickets as he would provide us with special tickets that were being issued for the promoters. We accordingly gave away the tickets that we had already received; one to an accommodating taxi driver and the other to the room boy at our hotel. Both of them were overcome as the price of the tickets represented more than their annual wage.

We spent the days that preceded the fight around the swimming pool at the Intercontinental and I played table tennis every day with the fabulous ex-Light Heavyweight World Champion, Archie Moore, who was one of George Foreman's entourage. George would be there with his Alsatian dog. He was always very quietly spoken and meticulously polite. This was in violent contrast with the various characters that we met such as Angelo Dundee, Ali's trainer, and the flamboyant Don King. On the eve of the fight, that was due to take place in the small hours of the morning in order to fall-in with the demands of worldwide television – prime time in the US, we were invited to dinner by John Daly. At a long table by the swimming pool in the grounds of the Intercontinental, we sat with John and his girlfriend.

David Frost had arrived with his then girlfriend, Caroline. At the table was another South Londoner, Terry Mills, later to become a well-known racing owner, whilst the great ex-World Heavyweight Champion, Joe Frazier was hovering around during the evening. It was a sultry, tropical night and thunderclouds were ominously drifting in the sky. The fight was to take place several miles outside the town in the sports stadium where a boxing ring had been erected. John asked Dora and me to accompany him to the fight in their stretched limousine but had not mentioned tickets. There had been a huge black market of stolen and forged tickets and I hesitated to mention the fact that we were still without tickets. David Frost and Caroline were in the limousine with us and we neared the stadium. There were hundreds of soldiers on duty, all with bayonets bared. David Frost said, 'This is the only place in the whole wide world to be tonight,' and I agreed with him with all my heart.

We neared the stadium but the crowds all chanting 'Arlee, Arlee' – the population had taken Ali as their champion – made further progress impossible. 'Let's just show our tickets,' said David Frost. 'We don't have any tickets,' I said. 'Do you mean to say that you don't have tickets?' said David. 'Then there's only one thing to do and that is to put our heads down and run,' and that is exactly what we did. The millionaire promoter of the fight; one of the best-known television personalities; their two girlfriends; Dora and I ran the gauntlet of the astounded soldiers and we found ourselves in the huge stadium in a small room literally bursting at the seams with hundreds of television sets, some of them on their sides. They were the countless monitors for the companies who were beaming the fight to the millions of viewers all over the world. 'Go and find yourselves seats.' John said to us 'and we will see you after the fight'. 'I'm going with Dora and Reg,' said Caroline. 'My mother told me to be careful. She didn't like me coming but she would be happy if she knew I was with you two.'

I now know what a footballer must feel like when he runs out of the tunnel on to the turf of a stadium such as Wembley for an important game. We came out of the darkness of the television room and a long tunnel into the stadium where thousands and thousands of citizens had been waiting for hours. Conscious that every eye in Kinshasa and, probably the rest of the world was on us, we walked down the aisles and eventually found some seats only two rows from the ring that was under the glare of specially erected floodlights. We sat there and Caroline shared Dora's seat. 'What a story I shall have to tell my two boys,' she said, 'I hope that they will do mad things like this.' We were so near the ring that we had to crane our necks to look up to it. Several times people came and looked at us but there had been such a scare with the thousands of forged tickets that had been circulating they must have thought that we were the rightful occupants of the seats and they had been left with forgeries. At any rate we were left unchallenged and very soon the exciting preliminaries started with the introduction of various ex-champions such as Joe Frazier, my table tennis friend Archie Moore, and other well-known fighters.

The fight itself is history and was thrilling. We sat at the edge of our wonderful seats and had the most fantastic view of every aspect of the enthralling contest. At the end of each round we could hear the inter-round commentary going out to the world from David Frost. We could hear every word spoken by Ali who was absorbing every punch that Foreman threw. 'You're not hurting me,' he kept saying, 'You can do better than that.' The heat from the overhead lamps was almost unbearable to us spectators and it was apparent that it was having its effect on the fighters, particularly Foreman. We were so close that the sweat from the fighters was falling on us. Ali kept on taking punch after punch until, suddenly in the ninth round, he unleashed a lethal blow that knocked out Foreman and brought the Heavyweight Championship of the World back to him.

The whole of the stadium seemed to be in the ring afterwards. A beaming Don King, Angelo Dundee, Ali's father and the whole entourage surrounded Ali who was very concerned as to Foreman's condition and insisted on staying with him as he recovered.

Eventually, we fought our way back to the car with David and John and began what turned out to be a triumphal entry to Kinshasa.

It was about 4 a.m. yet the many miles back to the Intercontinental Hotel were lined with thousands of cheering people. 'Arlee, Arlee,' was the chant; the first syllable being heavily accented. The always threatening thunderstorm now broke. It seemed to accentuate the drama of the night and we heard when we eventually reached the hotel that the storm had brought the lights over the ring crashing down half an hour after the fight had ended.

The champagne flowed for hours at the hotel. I was at the bar with some of the most interesting people that I have ever met. We had met some of them in the days preceding the fight. I found Jim Brown, the black All-American football star turned film star (of *The Dirty Dozen*), a very fine conversationalist and one of the nicest possible people. Another drinking companion was Norman Mailer, the celebrated author who wrote a fascinating study of the fight. He had a reputation as a hard drinker and a hell raiser but I found him a charming and intelligent man with whom it was a pleasure to have a few drinks. George Plimpton was another acquaintance who turned out to be so very interesting. He was a very good all round sportsman and a very fine writer. He took the unusual step of playing professional football and then writing an 'inside story' on all the things that went on. Not to be outdone he joined the professional golf tour and then did the same. His ensuing book is one of the best and most humorous books on golf that I have ever read.

Dora had found real pals in Muhammad Ali's mother and father. As happened frequently with my wife, they both took a shine to her. Ali's father had really gone to town on the champagne and was leaning on her shoulder singing his own version of 'My Way' to her. Mrs Clay really opened her heart to Dora and I am sure that newspaper reporters would have given thousands to have had the exclusive interview that Dora got. Mrs Clay had nothing but praise for the Foreman camp. 'Don't take any notice of all that you have seen and heard in the press,' she said. 'The first people to come to me after the fight were the Foreman camp. They congratulated me and told me what a great champion my son is.' She poured her heart out to Dora later, and I have some lovely photographs to prove it, telling her that Cassius, as she called him, was a very mild-mannered boy who first started fighting when someone stole his brother's tricycle and Cassius went and fought this bigger boy to get it back. She told Dora that Cassius was always known as 'Gee Gee' because he won the 'Golden Gloves', which is the highest honour an amateur boxer can win in the United States.

Even though the sun had risen I didn't want the night to end. We looked around and I said to Dora, 'Do you realise that we are the only white people here?' It was true. The black American wives and girlfriends of the two entourages and the hundreds of media were amongst the most beautiful, elegant and superbly dressed women that I have ever seen. Their way of intertwining and braiding their hair was spectacularly beautiful. If ever there was a night to remember, this was the one.

The departure from Kinshasa was quite an event in itself. Unknown to me, until just before the departure there was a law in that every departing foreign passenger had to prove that they had spent at least $100 a day during their stay. As Dora had shared my room, paid for by Sabena, she could not possibly come anywhere near this amount. The Sabena representative was most unhelpful. 'I can't help you,' he said. 'They are being very awkward and you'll have to try and explain.' They *were* being awkward, as I believe they delayed the departure of John Daly and Muhammad Ali for various reasons. In the end I resorted to what had now become second nature. I was of course in uniform so just walked past the emigration officials when they were busy arguing with passengers, with Dora by my side, and put her on the plane.

One of the longer trips on the DC10 was the flight to Tokyo via Anchorage, Alaska which took us over the North Pole. We slipped crews in Anchorage and continued to Tokyo the next day where we stayed for twenty-four hours then took the plane back to Anchorage, stayed on board as passengers from there whilst another crew flew the aircraft back to Brussels.

Navigation was a far cry from the days of carrying a Navigator. There was no Navigator now. The two Pilots operated the new inertia navigation system which was accurate to a hundred yards. This is a gyro-based system which interprets any change of direction of the aeroplane and translates it into an instant reading of the plane's position in degrees, minutes and seconds. It was completely dependent upon the actual position of the aircraft being set into the system before the engines were started. At the beginning of the flight, the Flight Engineer would go out of the aircraft which would be on its stand ready to embark the passengers. He would have a record of the actual position of the stand number and would enter these coordinates into the three independent systems with which the DC10 was equipped. There would then follow a twenty-minute period of 'self-testing' by the equipment. At the end of this period, if all was correct, a green light would come on and the readout would declare, 'ready to navigate'. As part of his pre-flight checks the engineer would then check that the initial coordinates were the correct ones. When the Captain and the First Officer arrived in the cockpit they would each, individually, check the pre-set coordinates from their own personal handbooks of coordinates for the aerodromes and stand numbers that they were likely to encounter on that particular flight.

I had brought the aircraft in from Tokyo and was returning as a passenger to Brussels. We took off and I was a little surprised when the aircraft turned left, as the usual route to Fairbanks and Point Barrow on the Beaufort Sea coast necessitated a right-hand turn. We flew along for several minutes and then I saw vapour streaming out of the nozzles at the trailing edge tip of each wing. The maximum landing weight an aeroplane is allowed is always considerably less than its maximum allowed take-off weight. This is to avoid overstrain on the wing roots as the aircraft lands and ceases to have the support of the air that was taking the load on the wings. The difference in allowed weights is considerable and means that an aircraft that has to land before the requisite amount of fuel has been consumed must dump that fuel in order to be within safe limits. Obviously long haul trips will nearly always mean a take-off with above the maximum allowed landing weight in order to provide enough fuel to reach the destination.

I make this explanation because the vapour streaming from the nozzles was the fuel being dumped so it meant we were going back to Anchorage. The majority of the passengers were Japanese and they were panicking as the vapour looked like smoke and they thought that we were on fire. I did not like to interfere as I was not the Captain but I went up to the cockpit and asked if I could help. The Captain was very busy. 'Yes, Reg, please tell the passengers that we are returning to Anchorage for technical reasons.' This I did and then returned to my seat as the atmosphere in the cockpit was decidedly chilly.

Anchorage's position is slightly less than 150 degrees west of Greenwich. The Flight Engineer had entered east and had not noticed the error. The Captain and the First Officer had then made their individual checks and had both failed to notice the error. The navigation system is linked to the automatic pilot and this had responded to the false position to turn the correct way, according to its initial incorrect starting point. From then on, all navigation would have been impossible and there was no way, then, of correcting the mistake in the air. The aircraft had to return to have the correct starting point inserted, be refuelled and then take off again. A very costly mistake but proof that if any human errors can occur then they will. One of Parkinson's Laws, I believe. Or is it Murphy's? Later, a method of aerial updating or correcting was evolved but was dependent on an absolute, certainly identified navigational point, which took time and was not to be used for polar navigation which was tricky at the best of times. All directions are south from the North Pole!

Anchorage had only one long runway with a narrow taxi track running parallel to it and one of our Captains distinguished himself by landing on the taxiway instead of the runway. Once again the First Officer and the Flight Engineer allowed the approach and landing to take place without comment. Luckily there was no damage done to anyone or anything but the Captain was demoted to First Officer for a period. He flew with me to Tokyo not long afterwards. As we taxied in I noticed that there was an aeroplane that the Japanese had put on the roof of the Terminal building for children to play in. 'Ah,' I said to him, 'I see you have been here.' Luckily he had a good sense of humour. 'You like to twist the knife in my wounds,' he said. As a matter of fact I was landing at Anchorage a few months later and had my Chief Pilot as First Officer. A Lebanese 707 had been taxiing out on the parallel taxiway and had been literally blown off it by a gust of wind. The taxiway had been covered in ice. As we passed it I said to my Chief Pilot, 'I would have given our unfortunate Captain a medal for a wonderful piece of airmanship instead of demoting him.' He laughed but had to agree.

I landed at Tokyo on one of the polar trips to be met by the Sabena representative as usual. He was very agitated. 'Everything must be absolutely correct when you leave tomorrow night,' he said. 'You have the Emperor's grandson on board. He has been invited to Brussels as the guest of King Baudouin. It is the first time that any member of the Japanese Royal Family has travelled with a foreign airline and, as he is the Crown Prince's eldest son, he is the future Emperor.' At that time, the Emperor was still Hirohito, so it was Crown Prince Naruhito whom I was due to take to Brussels the next evening.

On arrival at the Hilton Hotel I endeavoured to send my uniform and a couple of shirts for cleaning and was told that they could not promise them for the next day. I got one of our Japanese stewardesses to explain the situation. The next day, at about 6 a.m., there was a knock at the door and my uniform and shirts were delivered all pristine. There was a large sheet of paper attached to them. It was covered with Japanese writing. I eventually got the same stewardess to translate it for me. She burst out laughing and explained that it was a note from the hotel to the cleaning firm threatening severe punishment, even prison, if the uniform and shirts were not returned immediately in mint condition.

Everything went smoothly the following night. The aircraft arrived on time from Anchorage and I went aboard by way of the red carpet that had been put down. The Crown Prince and Princess came to the cockpit. He spoke good English and wished me a pleasant journey and asked me to take good care of his son, now the Crown Prince himself. They then left and the steps were immediately pulled away. Normal start-up clearance and permission to taxi out could take a very long time but this was immediately given. The normal period to await air traffic clearance and take-off could be any time up to an hour at this, one of the busiest airports in the world, but we were airborne and climbing to our preferred cruising altitude within minutes of starting the engines. When the Prince came to the cockpit I told him that he could fly with me anytime. His English was not good then but he understood and laughed. He was about sixteen at the time but I learned that he went on to Oxford and now speaks English fluently. I later received a thank you letter from the Japanese Royal Palace with some photos taken on the flight deck by one of the security guards accompanying the Prince, and some cigarettes bearing the Royal Chrysanthemum emblem.

CHAPTER TWENTY-THREE

I flew the DC10 for four years and was then given the opportunity of doing what I had always wanted. Some years before, I was a passenger on one of the first Sabena flights from New York on the recently acquired Boeing 747, or the 'Jumbo' as it was quickly and affectionately named. I sat in the first class marvelling at the spaciousness and comfort and told myself that I would fly this marvellous aircraft one day. Due to one of the lucky breaks that seem to run through my life I fell exactly into Sabena's requirements that I complete three years on the aircraft before reaching the then compulsory retirement age of sixty. This was to ensure that the company would recoup their considerable investment in training me. Typical of Sabena, after waiting for years it was decided they needed me in a hurry so I was given all the necessary books to study whilst still flying around the Far East and passed the ground examination in a matter of weeks.

On 16 May 1977 I was sent to Frankfurt with an Instructor and crew to complete thirty-two hours of flight simulator in eight gruelling sessions. Then our Chief Pilot, Raoul Schreiden, came to give me a final run through of every possible emergency scenario – even some impossible ones were thrown at me.

Several kilos lighter I returned to Brussels. On 29 and 30 May I did my circuits and bumps on the aircraft itself. An aircraft that I felt I knew intimately, so realistic was the flight simulator. I was completely at home in the massive aircraft and remembered the age-old adage, 'You don't fly an aeroplane, you fly a cockpit.' Nevertheless, it was very important to remember that, as you came over the threshold of the runway in your very high cockpit, made higher by the nose-up landing attitude, the sixteen wheels of the undercarriage were about the length of a football pitch behind you so you had to make sure that you closed the throttles to touch down a bit later than you normally would have. Taxiing too was strange at first. Once again you had to go a fair distance past the point where you wanted to make a sharp turn, so that your nose was actually over the grass whilst your wheels turned on the concrete. I had no trouble at all coping with the 'circuits and bumps', which were faithfully recorded on film by Peter, my eldest son, stationed at the end of the runway.

On 1 June 1977 I was checked by Raoul Schreiden who accompanied me to New York and back on the 3rd. This was repeated on 6 June returning on the 8th to complete the mandatory two flight checks that satisfied the licensing authority.

I made my first flight as a fully-fledged 747 Captain to Montreal on 11 June 1977.

From the very first moment when I opened the throttles and felt the instant response of the huge plane I knew that the Boeing 747 was the finest aircraft that I had ever flown. Amongst the many military aircraft, the Mosquito and the Lancaster were outstanding. The Convair 240 was the greatest propeller aircraft in my civil career but the Boeing 747 was the 'Queen of the Skies' for me.

The handling qualities of the huge jet were exceptional and its manoeuvrability was an absolute eye opener. It was all too easy to forget the size of the aeroplane and within a very short space of time I was able to land the giant as gently as if it were a Tiger Moth. Sabena, like most airlines, operated a policy of sharing the landings and take-offs between the Captain and the First Officer – a far cry from my first days with them when I, amongst all the other First Officers, never touched controls in my case for nearly two years. The vast majority of the First Officers were excellent pilots but it still hurt me, almost physically, when the odd bumpy landing occurred. I can remember my very first Instructor saying, 'any landing that you can walk away from is a good one' but that philosophy was long outdated and I took great pride in bringing my passengers down as smoothly as possible.

At that time, Sabena only possessed two 747s, 00-SGA and 00-SGB. They made the maximum use of those two aircraft and operated no less than ten round trips to New York and two to Mexico via Montreal per week. I think that the utilisation of nineteen hours per day was the highest of any company at that time.

New York, of course, was now my main destination. The fuel calculation for the trip was always a tricky problem. Every airline in Europe was going to Kennedy Airport and they all wanted to arrive around the same time. In Sabena's case this meant departure at 1 p.m., local time, which allowed the many transit passengers, on whom Sabena depended, to leave their various departure points at a reasonable time and arrive in Brussels before midday. The flight time of around eight hours, together with the six hours' time difference, got them into New York at around 3 p.m., in good time to fly on to other destinations in the States.

The crew operating the flight would 'sign in' one hour before the departure time. The Flight Engineer would go immediately to the aircraft to perform his checks including the vital setting up of the inertia navigation system. The Captain and the First Officer would go to the flight dispatch office where a flight plan with the necessary meteorological forecast would be awaiting them. The fuel needed would be finalised very quickly as the fuel people were standing by the aircraft waiting to hear the final fuel figure decided upon by the Captain. The minimum fuel requirements laid down by the company always had to be respected. This was the fuel required to reach the destination while leaving enough for contingencies: hold overhead at an unfavourable altitude (for fuel consumption) for a laid down period, make an approach, overshoot and climb to an unfavourable cruising altitude, then fly to an alternate airport more than one hour's flying distance (one hour's flying was required in order to pre-suppose different weather conditions at the new destination) and land there.

This fuel, always calculated in weight, was the minimum, but a Captain could, and frequently did, take more if the passenger and freight load allowed. This was because the altitudes that would be assigned to you by the various control zones you overflew were not likely to be the most favourable for fuel consumption due to their own operational requirements. Jet engines love the cold and the higher you fly the colder it gets. Unfortunately the pressure decreases as well and this is a negative factor so there is an altitude where the cold ceases to be an advantage and this is called Optimum Altitude.

When I was flying under standard conditions this was around 40,000ft. Standard conditions suppose a temperature of 15°C at sea level and a drop of 1.98°C per 1,000ft. Pressure is reckoned at sea level at 1013.2 mbs. Unfortunately, a heavy aeroplane cannot reach this altitude so as fuel is burnt off and the aircraft becomes lighter, a higher altitude would be requested. This was rarely forthcoming as there was always another aircraft ahead of you requesting the same altitude and the separation standards are very strict so it was always on the cards that you would be allocated a low, uneconomic altitude and would have to take extra fuel to compensate. A rough rule of thumb, which always came to mind was that you needed 10 metric tonnes (10,000 kilos) of fuel per hour of the trip to cover the taxi (500 kilos), take-off (2,000 kilos), climb and rest of the trip, so 80 tonnes was the rough start for a New York trip of eight hours. This would not include the contingency fuel. The sum of all these figures was your minimum fuel requirement. Coming out of New York was a different matter. Although the trip itself was usually considered shorter due to the prevailing westerly winds it was rare if the taxi time was less than forty-five minutes. I have been number forty-three to take off with a wait of over 1 hour, so 2 tonnes was a fairly standard figure for the taxi fuel.

The perfect trip, which never happened, was where you were allowed to climb out immediately to your optimum altitude for your present weight then step up your altitude as the weight decreased. The standard cruise was always at Mach .80 (later aircraft reached Mach .82) so, as your weight decreased, the throttles would be brought progressively back. The perfect descent would be from your cruising altitude straight into the circuit with the throttles almost closed. This happened to me once or twice on an early morning return to Brussels when the Belgian Controller would allow me to descend from some 34,000ft on picking me up by radar over Dover, enabling a landing at Brussels that could be made virtually without touching the throttles until on the final approach. The saving on fuel was considerable in these cases.

The Mach number is the proportion of the speed of sound, so Mach .80 is eight tenths of the speed of sound, which varies according to the temperature. This, of course, is airspeed. The actual ground speed (speed over the ground) is dependent on the wind. Going to the States an average wind component over the trip could easily be minus 80mph and returning could be plus 100mph. I have seen plus 300mph as the wind factor on my instantaneous ground speed indicator accompanied by the tremendous 'buffeting' that the associated Jet Stream invariably produced. Not very nice for the passengers and it invariably seemed to arrive just as a meal and drink was being served. The route chosen would take these factors into account and you could fly several hundred miles further in distance to avoid severe minus components or to take advantage of plus ones. The routes out could vary by as much as flying out over the north of Scotland and Greenland to as far south as the Azores.

Another important consideration to have in mind when deciding the fuel requirement were the conditions at your destination. Holding a long way from New York was always on the cards due to the enormous congestion of traffic. Even en route holding was not uncommon. When you eventually did arrive over the holding stack, usually over Deer Park or Long Island, you would be progressively brought down from your cruising altitude. It was useless to plead that you were short of fuel. You would be told to leave the stack and divert to your chosen alternate. Only a real emergency got priority and you really had to prove it.

TRANSCRIPT OF TAPE RECORDED BY CAPTAIN REGINALD LEVY AFTER THE HIJACKING OF SABENA FLIGHT TO TEL AVIV ON 8 MAY 1972

This recording was made very soon after the hijacking, and allows greater insight into what happened. The events of May 8 1972 were a cause of tremendous strain and the differences between what Reg recounts years later and but a few hours or days after the hijacking are testament to this. To focus on one or the other narratives misses the point. The hijacking was a life and death situation fraught with stress and irrationality. A precise and straightforward tale of what transpired would not do justice to Reg's very thoughts and actions throughout this trial.

I was due to go to Tel Aviv on 8 May 1972, which was also my birthday. So I talked Dora into coming with me. We normally get into Tel Aviv about half past six in the evening, go to the Dan Hotel where we're usually very well received and have a very nice meal, so I thought it would be a nice treat for both myself and Dora even though we would come back very early the next morning. Anyway she agreed. At the last moment she said to me, 'Oh it's a bit silly going all that way just for an evening,' and I said, 'Oh come on, you know it'll be a change for you.' So she came with me and we set off to the airport together.

When we got to the airport, I saw her down into the waiting room and I noticed that they were searching the passengers when we got there. One of the chiefs of the Sabena security was at the desk where we signed in and I said to him, 'Does my wife have to go through the search?' so he said, 'Oh yes it would be better, just like everybody else.' So we went to the policeman who very perfunctorily searched her handbag and then I took her out to the aircraft first, before any of the other passengers. Incidentally, we'd tried to telephone through to Feeka and there was no reply – this was before we went down to the waiting room. So I put her on board in one of the forward seats, it was an all economy flight, stopping at Vienna first of all.

After I'd put her on, we still had plenty of time, we weren't due to take off until twenty past eleven, I went back to the airport and went upstairs through the waiting room to try to phone Feeka again and this time I succeeded in getting her because she was alone at home and I told her that Mum was on the plane and that everything was OK. She'd actually been having a shower the last time that I'd phoned and hadn't heard and couldn't come out in time for the phone. But whilst I was walking up to the phone, this quite good looking young girl in a white trouser suit and white sweater went past going down the walk towards the waiting room, and she gave me quite a nice smile as she went past. And I thought, 'well I might be fifty, but you know, a young girl can still smile at me.' This later turned out to be one of the hijackers, the girl that was very badly wounded. When I got back to the waiting room, I noticed that two friends of mine from the cricket club were also amongst the passengers, and they were going to Vienna. So I told them that Dora was on board, and I believe later they got to sit next to her and talked to her.

From Brussels to Vienna the trip was uneventful enough, I took off and I landed, made a very nice landing at Vienna, and after a short stop at Vienna of about forty-five minutes, during which time none of the transit passengers left the aircraft and some embarking passengers were put on board, we took off from Vienna – once again I did the take-off – to Tel Aviv. We were a little bit late, and at about

14.35 GMT, this would be somewhere around Sarajevo, I heard a scream from the back, from round about the cockpit door, I looked round and saw one of our hostesses on the floor and this terrorist coming into the cockpit, shaking like a leaf, with a pistol and a grenade in his hand, and he thrust the pistol into my neck and said, 'Keep calm, keep calm. Follow our orders, we are taking over this aircraft.' I can't swear that those were the exact words but they were words to this effect. I looked round and saw that there was another man with him also with a pistol and a grenade. At this time I didn't know but the girls were behind, holding leads to the explosives that were on board.

He then, still with shaking hands, thrust a map in front of me, it was a normal sort of map, the same type of airways charts that we have and said, 'You must go to Lod,' and I said, 'But we *are* going to Lod,' and even at that time this joke flashed through my mind of the man that was so fed up of being hijacked to Cuba that he said, 'Take me to Miami.' And even in this situation I did think that you know, this is somebody who *wants* to go to Lod. So he said, 'Yes and if you follow our orders then everybody will be safe. If not, we will blow the aircraft up.' Gradually things began to calm down a little bit. The Engineer was on check under one of the Chief Engineers who comes from Morocco and speaks Arabic. He was sitting behind me at the Navigator's table and they turned on him and they said, 'you're Jewish.' He said, 'No I'm not Jewish,' and they said, 'Yes you are, you're Jewish, get in the back with the other passengers,' and he was taken out of the cockpit and put in the passenger cabin. They then, I believe, sorted out or tried to sort out the Israeli passengers from the non-Israeli passengers and they asked that anybody with dual passports show them. I made an announcement to the passengers pleading with them to keep calm that if they would all keep calm it would help us and that the situation would be kept under control as long as there was no panic.

We'd told the hijackers that we had to make radio reports and at one time they said that there were ten of them on board, another time they said there were eight of them. The chief, the more elderly of the two, I would place his age around about 35, 36 and certainly the calmer of the two, told me that he knew all about aircraft. As events turned out this was *not* true because we had to explain to him – they were suspicious of anything, anytime we spoke to the ground, they wanted to know what we were doing – we had to explain that we were just reporting our position and if this wasn't so then people on the ground would become worried and would start taking action to see where we were. In the meantime the First Officer, during the flight, had managed to get a message to an Air France plane that we heard in the vicinity – we were still flying over Yugoslavia – that we had been hijacked. I heard a Swissair aircraft call up the Air France and ask if they got the message and I didn't hear Air France reply. In actual fact, I learnt later, it was Swissair who had got through to Zurich and had told the authorities on the ground there that we were being hijacked. In addition, we managed to switch the transponder equipment to the emergency code which would tell the ground that this aircraft was not under the control of the crew. But the only snag was that I don't think the ground stations of the territory over which we were flying at the time had the type of equipment capable of receiving this signal. In the meantime the flight went on normally along airways via the normal route to Tel Aviv.

During the flight, which took some two hours or so from the time we were hijacked, the hijackers began telling us who they were, they told us that they were Palestinians and that they had relatives who were prisoners in Israel, they had relatives who had been tortured and beaten in Israel, and that they were determined to do something about this and they were quite prepared to die, all of them. They were not belligerent to the crew, they were quite courteous. They permitted people to go to the toilets providing they didn't lock the door, but they were very suspicious and very jumpy at the slightest thing. For instance my wife whose identity had managed to be kept secret, I didn't mention to any of them that my wife was on board, had some small spectacles in a case and she dropped it as one of the hijackers was going past and he immediately wanted to know what it was, pointing at it with his pistol.

The coast began to appear and we could see the lights, by this time it was dark, of Tel Aviv. I had realised of course that the very fact that we were going to Tel Aviv which seemed to me incredible, was also putting us in a highly dangerous situation, because I knew right from the start that the Israelis would never *ever* give in to any demands for releases of prisoners and I was by this time quite convinced that the hijackers themselves were extremely dangerous people who wouldn't hesitate to blow the plane and themselves up if these demands were not met. So I realised right from the start that time was going to be one of the essential features of the whole game and that anything I could do to give the Israelis more time to make what plans – I knew there would be plans being made, I was absolutely sure of it – would help. So instead of going straight in and landing, I delayed the actual landing as long as I could, in fact I think it was probably something like half an hour from the time we crossed the coast to the time we touched down. When we landed, we touched down on the runway which was 3.0 which was going away from the main buildings to a deserted part of the airfield. We made a quite normal, quite a nice landing again and the Control Tower called us up and told us to roll to the end of the runway and then turn right onto the north-south runway and go as far as we could down this one. I attempted to do so but as soon as we got off the runway and were turning right, the hijackers, who by now were very, very panicky indeed, told me to stop as soon as I could. I managed to pull as far off the main runway as I could and then stopped. I was thinking of an emergency evacuation of the aircraft even at this time, so instead of doing the normal cockpit check and pulling my flaps up, I left the flaps fully down – the importance of this you will see later.

I kept the engines running for quite a long time because as I explained to the hijackers, the aircraft batteries would not last very long and if I closed down all the motors we would not have communication with the tower, and we would be virtually cut off and eventually we would be without any light at all. So, eventually, I closed the engines down and at this time the Israelis supplied ground power to the aircraft. This was a very, very dangerous operation because the hijackers were terribly, terribly jittery. They had agreed to ground power being supplied with one man, and it was *one* man, but as soon as he got off the ground power, they wanted to know where he'd gone and they were quite prepared at that time to shoot everybody, to shoot the crew because they were so frightened. In the end the ground power was plugged in and the lights came on and then they seemed to calm down, considerably. And it was from then on that the long waiting and the drama really began. Because at this time, the chief of the hijackers gave me a list, a typed list containing 317 names, all Arab names, and he then told me to tell the Control Tower that these were prisoners being held in various prisons around Israel and that their release was being demanded by the terrorists. I then started to read these names, and of course they were Arabic names and I wasn't used to them and also as I know now, the Israelis were playing for time and kept on asking me to repeat various numbers and this must have taken the best part of an hour if not more. But during this time the hijackers became very, *very* angry and lost their temper, they said, 'The Israelis know these people, why do they keep on asking you to repeat them?' and I said, 'Oh probably it's only just a little man in the Control Tower who isn't used to this sort of thing.' So he said, 'Oh they must have the government there by now, if not all the general staff, so I said, 'Well you know what it's like in the middle of the night.' The terrorists kept asking us if any message had been received from the Red Cross. This demand I passed on to the tower and was told that no messages had been received. And this seemed to unsettle them very, very much indeed; they seemed to be at a loss to understand why this message had not been received from the Red Cross. I, on my part, knew that I wasn't going to be told everything that was going on from the Israeli side.

During the middle of all these names being given over the RT, the aircraft suddenly started to shudder and tremble and move and vibrate and this frightened the hijackers. They immediately panicked like mad and said, 'Somebody's trying to get in through the roof.' It was as though somebody was climbing along the roof itself. We, in the crew, didn't quite know what it was until the Engineer suddenly said, 'It's the shock absorbers going down,' and the aircraft was in fact settling. We managed to calm them down by saying it was gusts of wind shaking the aircraft although there was very, very little wind at the time. The next thing, and this was quite a very, very bad moment, was that the red gear light came on showing that one of the undercarriage gears was not locked and the left-hand gear, green light, went off and at the same moment the claxon from the horn warning, which sounds if you have got more than 30 degree of flap down without the undercarriage being locked, made a violent sound and scared the living daylights out of the hijackers who were sure that it was a signal from the Israelis, or to the Israelis, and they panicked like mad. We pulled the horn cut out, of course this didn't have any effect at all and it was only when we realised what had happened that at this minute the Engineer said, 'I have no more hydraulic fluid left,' and we realised that the undercarriage was in fact unlocked and of course I had selected full flap and left the full flap down and left the gear leaver in the full flap position. When I moved the gear leaver into the 30 degree flap position, then the horn stopped. And this was a very, very bad moment indeed but once again when the horn stopped they calmed down and we managed to tell them that in landing we must have had a hydraulic leak and it was absolutely imperative that somebody examine the aircraft.

In the meantime they had spotted car headlights, they must have been half a mile away, and they insisted that it was the Israelis, so we told the tower. They replied that it was a public road and there wasn't very much they could do about it. But of course all these things with the terrorists in the jittery state that they were in didn't help. Anyway, we managed to persuade them that the Engineer should get out of the aircraft and examine it to see what damage had been done because by now they had begun to talk about going to Cairo. I told them that if they wanted us to go to Cairo then we would have to have fuel put on board so they said, 'Well then get it done' and I asked the tower and they said yes, they would send a bowser to put fuel on board. This would take time because normally the refuelling would be done by underground refuelling but as we were so far away, they would have to put fuel into a bowser and then send it out there. This I tried to explain to the terrorists but they weren't very, very technically minded and they mistrusted everybody although we had a *fair* amount of their confidence but of course they were in a very, very dangerous position themselves and they mistrusted everything that the Israelis said or did. In fact they kept saying to us, "You know these Jews, they can't be trusted, they will trick us.' So they agreed to the Engineer getting out and they were amazed when we showed them how he could get out by lifting the seat behind the jump seat and descending into the Lower 41 and going out through the aircraft.

He made a fairly quick check and came back and told me that there were tyres flat and also, he told me confidentially, that there were people around the aircraft. I realised that the aircraft was in such a state that we couldn't possibly get off the ground but I didn't want the terrorists to know this, and when he came in I was hoping that he would leave the door of the Lower 41 open, but unfortunately he didn't do this. I then said to the terrorists, 'The report he has given me, I would prefer to have a look myself to see just whether we *can* get off the ground,' and to my amazement they let both of us get out of the aircraft. In the Lower 41, before we got out, I said to the Engineer, 'If things don't go very well, and if either of us survive this, I shall be amazed, but if you survive it, I want you to tell my wife that I was doing my absolute best for everybody,' and I wasn't very hopeful at that time of the ending of the whole affair. Anyway we got out and I didn't see anybody around the aircraft, I did see that all eight tyres were *completely* flat so there was no question of moving the aircraft under its own power, and of course, the hydraulic fluid was all over the ground. When we got back, this time I was the last in and I made sure that we left the Lower 41 door open. In the meantime, every time I had passed any messages to the Control Tower I had managed to say that the door was open and that the rear of the aircraft was not well guarded. I was able to pass such messages once or twice when the terrorists were out of the cockpit – because they weren't sitting just steadily guarding us, they were having little conferences amongst themselves around the kitchen, watching the cockpit at the time with the door open of course and weren't paying much attention to what was going on over the RT – so I was also able to tell them that the aircraft could be approached from the rear. This, obviously the Israelis knew, but I thought well anything might help coming from the aircraft itself. There were aircraft taking off and at first the terrorists insisted that the tower should ask them for permission before any aircraft took off. They would ask, 'Which company was it?' and if it was El Al they weren't giving permission. However, El Al took off and landed and they didn't seem to do much about it. In fact, they couldn't obviously, but they weren't making any fuss about it.

During all this time, they had been constantly guarding us with pistols, I can always remember seeing even the colour of the cartridges in one of the guns, there were three copper-coloured ones and two metallic ones, and they held also grenades which were wired around. When they originally came into the cockpit, the younger of the terrorists took the pin out of the ring from the grenade and showed us that it was armed. But after that they wired the grenades with some yellow wire to hold them because they were holding them the whole time, and it must have been rather tiring with the pressure. There was also some sort of cap at the top, whether they could be fired electrically or not I didn't know at the time.

The next 'crisis' if you can call it that was the decision to leave Israel and go to Cairo. They were becoming very, very unnerved and they decided that at all costs they must get the aircraft off the ground. I tried to tell them that it was pretty hopeless, I didn't tell them that all eight wheels were flat, they just thought one wheel was flat. I tried to get them to go outside hoping that they would be jumped, but they were determined not to leave the aircraft. I then suggested that it would be quicker for the Israelis to provide us with another aircraft rather than try and take off with this one in the state it was in, a much worse state of course than the terrorists knew. But I also told them that we certainly hadn't got enough fuel to get off the ground and to go to Cairo with the wheels down, because I then explained to them that all our hydraulic fluid had gone, we would have to get off the ground without any nose-wheel steering, without any rudder boost, we could upgrade our flaps electrically but of course we couldn't pull the undercarriage up. Incidentally, I forgot to mention that the reason that they allowed the Engineer off the aircraft in the first place was to place the pins in position in the undercarriage. I had explained to them how dangerous it was *not* to place these pins in with our loss of hydraulic fluid and they allowed him to do this and he placed pins in each of the positions of each gear.

So, then the next thing was this refuelling, and the Israelis kept stalling and stalling and stalling and *eventually* after hours and hours, this bowser appeared and then of course there was immediate panic and they insisted that anything approaching the aircraft should be under the Red Cross, and of course they didn't trust anybody having a walkie-talkie, but on the other hand they wanted us to have contact with the people coming, which didn't make any sense. The first person that came with the ground power came with a walkie-talkie and they made him leave this on the ground. Of course when the bowser appeared with these two men then they panicked like mad, but eventually allowed them to approach the aircraft. The bowser came under the starboard wing and then we waited for the refuelling to take place. We were watching the gauge and of course it wasn't moving at all and they were getting more and more impatient.

They didn't realise this because at no time had we tried to help them with the aircraft's workings, and we didn't tell them that we could see if there was any fuel going into the aircraft, but the Engineer kept, sort of, raising his eyebrows to me and I knew darn well that no fuel was going to come into that aircraft. I suspected at this time that the bowser itself could be empty and possibly had men inside it, I don't think there were in actual fact but I did suspect this at the time.

This went on and on and eventually the men went off and they called us over the tower and said that they were having trouble with the adapters, they couldn't get the fuel into the aircraft because the nozzles didn't fit, and that they were going to go and try and find some adapters, and again this precipitated a new crisis in the aircraft and it was getting very early in the morning and *suddenly* I sensed that a decision had been made. The two men were in the cockpit at this time and the leader turned to the other one and said something rapidly in Arabic and the other one's eyebrows shot up but you could see that he agreed. They then called the girls and the girls came forward and they said this same thing to them and *immediately* the girls' eyes filled with tears and it looked as though they couldn't believe it. But the men nodded their heads and were quite adamant and they began kissing each other and embracing. And I *knew*, I knew without a shadow of a doubt, that they had decided to blow up the aircraft. They'd got tired of waiting, the Israelis were continually stalling, they didn't trust them, they were frightened and I am quite sure that they'd had orders that if they hadn't received their orders from Beirut as they kept asking for and if the Israelis hadn't agreed to their demands then the aircraft should be blown up.

This was the second night and I knew that we hadn't got very long to live. And I did the only thing that I could at that time whilst their attention was diverted. I was sitting in the left-hand seat, and the elder of the two was the one covering me, but he looked to one side to the girl and I jumped him and I managed to get his hand, he was holding the pistol with his right hand and I turned it back onto himself and I got my finger over his finger on the trigger and I pulled it, but he'd got his thumb on the safety catch, pushing it forward, and of course the gun didn't go off. Immediately, the girl, the younger of the two, got between me and him and the other one, the younger terrorist, who was in the passenger cabin. I am told that I shouted, 'But you promised, you promised,' this was referring to the fact that they had promised to be patient and that they had promised not to blow the aircraft up with the crew whilst there was any hope of negotiating with the Israelis. The younger terrorist was trying to get his gun on me but couldn't because the girl and the other one were between him and me and my own Engineer pulled me away from them. I had hoped that the crew, seeing me jump them, would try and jump the other ones but they didn't. It may have been a good thing, it may not have been but as it turned out it seemed to divert their attention completely and they made me sit back in my seat again and then there followed a debate as to whether to kill me or not. I *still* think that this had put completely out of their heads the idea of blowing the aircraft up at that time. I do stress that there was no doubt in my mind, and afterwards when I spoke to the other members of the crew, they were all sure too, and passengers who had seen this little escapade and scuffling going on and seen the girls embracing, that this was *the* moment they had decided to blow up the aircraft.

You have to remember that the Israelis had no intention of letting this aircraft off the ground. The terrorists, once they were there knew that they were never going to get away from the Israelis, so the only thing to do *was* to blow the aircraft up to show that an act of terrorism against Israel on its own soil, an aircraft with Israeli passengers on board could be blown up on Israeli soil and I'm sure that this was their intention. I don't know why they allowed me to live, I can only think that they then thought, well we might go to Çairo. Luckily my First Officer had a very young face and possibly they didn't think he could be experienced enough to get a crippled aircraft off the ground. But the younger of the two turned to me and said, 'I don't kill you now but I kill you tomorrow,' and the menace in his eyes made me believe this threat.

And now comes the strangest part. Up till then they'd allowed me to move freely about the aircraft. I'd managed to warn some of the cabin attendants not to let them know that my wife was one of the passengers and I'd managed to go back to a passenger who'd collapsed from heat and advised giving oxygen and managed to reassure passengers at this time. As I said, I'd had, not the freedom of the aircraft, but I was allowed to move about. Of course all this went by the board.

Now it began to get daylight and it began to get hot. I had deliberately not suggested air-conditioning. I knew that the Israelis would have provided it and I did not want it. At one time the Engineer suggested, 'Why don't you ask for air-conditioning?' and I quickly shut it off before the terrorist could hear the suggestion of it. The reason being I knew it would get hot and knew that the terrorists themselves would get hot and they would have to allow exits and doors to be opened and I hoped that this might help the Israelis in some way if they were going to storm the aircraft. And it worked. Not in the storming of the aircraft but eventually they did agree to the over-wing exits being opened and later on in the day as it got hotter and hotter, at one time it was about 40°C in the cabin, they even allowed the rear door to be opened. I don't know if this helped or not, it may have done because whilst these doors were open they had to station people there and they'd only got four of them and they couldn't be everywhere in the aircraft. I thought all the time that *anything*, every *little* thing, would help and might help and could create some sort of a diversion and might just tip the odds, not in our favour, but lessen them against the terrorists.

About, I can't remember exactly what time, but one of the greater moments, I *think* it was round about 4.35 a.m. local time, the tower suddenly came up and said, 'We have managed to locate the Red Cross, the agent is in Jerusalem and he has to get here, but he is on his way,' and this caused great joy amongst the terrorists. We, in the crew, had been trying to bolster their hopes as much as possible a) to keep our own lives as long as possible and b) to allow the Israelis to make plans. I must admit that I thought if they were going to do anything they would have done it during the night, but I realised they weren't just going to let the aircraft sit there and be blown up, not without doing something about it. What was in their minds, I didn't know. Anyway, as I said this caused great rejoicing and then we sat there and sat there, an hour went by then an hour and a half, and there was still no sign of him and they began to get impatient again. So I called up the tower and asked what had happened and they said, 'We don't know, he's just on his way and that's all.' Eventually, and this was a *long, long* time afterwards we saw the car, they told us that it was on its way and was approaching us from the north, and it came down the runway and it must have been coming at about 2 miles an hour, no more, because *it took hours* to get to us. They couldn't understand, 'Why is he going so slow, why? It's a trick, it's a trap'. He must have stopped the car a good 600 or 700 metres away from the aircraft and then got out and approached the aircraft and waited outside. Then he was told he could enter the aircraft so the Engineer went down and showed him how to get into the aircraft through the Lower 41 and the Swiss Red Cross agent came into the aircraft and sat there and was told the demands which were the release of the 317 prisoners and the aircraft to be repaired, and then allowed to proceed to Cairo where our own passengers would be released and the aircraft would be allowed to fly back once the 317 prisoners were flown to Cairo by any company other than El Al. These were the demands of the terrorists. So, he said that he would do his best and that he would go back and give these demands to the Israeli authorities.

The terrorists were very anxious to find out who was there and the Red Cross agent didn't say anything. He said he didn't know yet who was going to be at the conference.

By this time, of course, it was daylight and planes were landing which caused a great furor in the aircraft. Suddenly we saw a Sabena plane land although we knew there was no service that day. We had been trying to tell the terrorists that the Israeli government would accede to their demands and we pointed to the fact that they had done nothing during the night. I said to them, 'Look, if the Israelis were going to do anything, they would have done it at night and they have done nothing.'

As day broke, tourists and people who were curious were lining the road outside the aerodrome and this disquieted the terrorists terribly. We called up the tower again and they said that they would do what they could. I later learned that one of the cars in fact did have General Dayan inside who was watching the whole operation from fairly near the aircraft and also had a set in his car so he could hear our communications with the tower. Every now and then because we were using a normal frequency, an aircraft who hadn't been warned about this frequency came up on the RT, called the tower and was told to go to another frequency but this also upset the terrorists who couldn't understand why people were talking on the same frequency and they were absolutely sure that something was being hatched, which made it *very, very* difficult indeed in the cockpit. By now, so long after this business of me jumping the hijacker, once again they seemed to be regaining confidence in me, particularly with the crew, and everything we told them. We said, 'You *see*, the Israelis are doing everything that you've asked them to do. They've sent for the Red Cross agent, he's here and he's negotiating, Sabena have come in,' and we even told them that the whole of the Belgian government would be on this plane to put pressure onto the Israelis to release the prisoners.

After a long, long time, the Red Cross agent came back, came into the plane, sat down and I could tell by the very fact that he didn't say straightaway that the Israelis had agreed, that obviously they hadn't. But he came out with something. He said, 'Would you agree to a safe passage? That if you release the prisoners, the Israelis will guarantee you a safe passage, just yourselves, in an aircraft to anywhere you would want,' and of course they said no straightaway and began to get very angry. Then he said, 'The Israelis will agree to a release of some of your prisoners, will you tell me which ones you would give priority to?' this incidentally, had previously been requested by the tower. And he said 'all the prisoners' so then the Red Cross man said he would go back again and negotiate but they got very angry once more over this and said, 'What do they think they are?' But anyway he persuaded them to let him go.

This time, he had driven the car a little bit faster, he had been told he could approach, so off he went again. And while he was away, an idea began to form in my mind that I *might* even be able to get out of the plane myself to get to the Israeli authorities. So I turned to them and I said, 'Look, this man' – and I must apologise, I was trying to do my best to persuade them you must remember – I said, 'Look he's a typical Swiss, he's slow and he doesn't *realise* the position in the plane. *I* know and *we all* know that you *are* completely determined to blow up this plane. But he doesn't believe it and I don't think the Israeli people believe it,' and I said, 'You know what these Jews are, they're going to trick you.' I said, '*You* know and *I* know exactly the situation in the plane, why don't you allow *me* to go back with the Red Cross agent and I will tell them the *exact* situation in the plane,' and I *never* for *one* moment believed that they would agree to this. To my amazement, they began to consider it, then the elder of the two turned around and he said, 'Yes, I think it would be a good idea,' and I still couldn't believe it, all I wanted then was for that Red Cross agent to get back as quickly as possible so that they wouldn't change their mind.

Eventually the Red Cross man came back into the aircraft and this time he said, 'The Israelis will agree to a release of certain prisoners and they will *also* agree to the release of certain Egyptian and Syrian prisoners that they hold, if you will release the passengers on the plane.' This once again got the elder of the two terrorists *very, very* angry and he turned around and he said, 'If the *Egyptians* want to get their prisoners released, let them hijack their own planes. If the *Syrians* want to get their prisoners released, let the Syrians hijack their own planes,' and I think this actually turned it because then he turned to me and he said, 'You go back and tell them,' and the Red Cross man, I've never seen a man more amazed in his life, didn't say anything, he got down quickly. And just as I was getting down after him, one of the terrorists came to me and handed me a small piece of this explosive, a little bit of plastic and he even warned me not to put my hand in my mouth after I'd touched it, he said because it could cause some bad stomach aches. He said, 'Take this and show them that we mean business.'

I got out of that plane and I still didn't believe it and I sat in the car with the Red Cross agent and he drove off, and he couldn't believe it, he said, 'I just couldn't believe my ears when I heard them say you, "go with him".' When I got over, there was an escort car waiting at the end of the runway from the Air Traffic Control and I think they thought that I was one of the terrorists because they looked very, very alarmed and the Red Cross man waved over to them and said, 'It's alright, this is the Captain of the aircraft,' and I could see the disbelief on their faces. We got over to the Control Tower where there were hundreds and hundreds of people waiting and of course they didn't realise as, incidentally, I didn't have my jacket on, I only had my shirt without epaulettes and it was open at the neck and my tie was halfway down because it was very, very hot on the aircraft and of course nobody realised, but word quickly got round and it was more than I could do to get into the building itself, people were thrusting microphones, taking pictures and I was whisked upstairs quickly, and I'd lost the Red Cross man. He didn't, I stress this, he didn't come in with me to the room, where General Dayan and all his staff were waiting for me. I went in there and I sat down on General Dayan's left. I was told by him later, because I don't remember saying this at all, but much later, we dined – my wife and I with General Dayan that evening – and he told me that I came into the Command Headquarters which had been set up at the airport and before he could speak, I turned to him and I said, 'I know that you are never going to release these prisoners' and before I could say any more, he then cut in and he said, 'Captain, would you please remember that *you* are a Captain and *I* am the General,' and I then turned to him and said, 'Very well, if you are the General, then *you* can go back on the plane and take command of the situation there and I'll sit here in your place,' and he started laughing and he said, 'Alright, now let's get down to details,' and of course I was able to tell him exactly what was happening in the plane, exactly where the main guards were stationed: a terrorist in the cockpit, the other one who was more or less roaming around but anytime an exit was opened would station himself at the exit, one of the girls at the back and one of the girls forward and I even drew a plan to this effect and gave it to General Elazar who was there.

I was told at that time that an attack was going to be mounted, that they would be sent out in the disguise of mechanics and that the whole thing, if it was going to be done successfully, was dependent upon this Israeli special squad who would mount this attack as soon as they could. I asked when and they said, 'Oh, probably within the next hour and a half.' I then told them that my wife was on board – I don't know whether they knew it or not then – and I also said, 'Gentlemen, if my wife and I don't come out of this alive, could I have your word that my youngest daughter's education will be guaranteed?', and this they promised to do and of course they reassured me that everything *would* be alright, but I frankly did not believe it.

I then went to the Control Tower and told the hijackers, following my instructions from General Dayan, that the Israelis had agreed to their demands, that they would release the 317 prisoners, that they would be flown to Cairo by some other company, that they were trying to find a company willing to do this, that food and drink would be sent to the aircraft, and that repairs would be done as speedily as possible.

To facilitate these repairs I then said, would they be willing to allow more than the original five men which they had specified, because

I told them that the repairs would take them much longer this way and that if they would agree to ten or fifteen men being sent out, then these repairs would be done quickly. To my amazement, once again they said yes, to get them done as quickly as possible. They also agreed to another ground power being put in, because we had been told that the ground power that they had plugged in, which was running on petrol would be running down, and we would need another one otherwise we would be without communication and they agreed to this.

The reason for this was that the ground power that was plugged in, I noticed, was on the right-hand side of the aircraft and was fairly near the First Officer's cockpit window which was open of course to allow some air in. I reasoned that if they could put another one on the left-hand side, a) it could provide a means of entry but b) more important to us, I was quite determined when this battle started and if explosives went off, just to throw myself out of the window and to warn the crew to do the same, even if it meant some broken bones, at least we *might* get away with broken bones rather than staying in the cockpit and being killed with the grenade or pistols, and the ground power placed underneath the cockpit window might break our fall, and they agreed to this being done.

So then I had to go back to the aircraft and I must say that I looked around and thought, 'Well I don't think I'll see anything of the outside world again' and I got back into the aircraft. I was told by the crew that when I had spoken to them over the RT from the Control Tower and had told them that the Israelis had agreed to their demands, it was just like Mafeking night in the cockpit: the terrorists had shouted with joy and had kissed everybody, including the crew, and they just thought it was wonderful. And I must say that at this time, the crew themselves believed this. Whilst I'd been going out in the car with the Red Cross man I had thought to myself, 'Can I tell anybody?' and I realised that I could not. I did *not* tell the Red Cross man, he was not aware of this and I dared not tell the crew in case by their behaviour they gave away something or they made the terrorists suspicious. So I was the only man who knew that an attack was going to be made and that the repairs were not going to be carried out.

So you can imagine my feelings, I sat in that cockpit and I looked out where the ground power had been placed in position and I didn't think very much of anybody's chances, least of all my own, of getting out without some very, very serious injuries and of course my wife was back in that plane too. And the next hour seemed like days and days and days. Eventually the tower came up and they said, 'We've managed to assemble a group of prisoners and we've got some of them, about fifty of them here. Would you like them to talk to you in the terrorists' own language, in Arabic?' So I asked them and they said, 'Oh yes,' and he grabbed the mic. I thought at the time that they actually *had* got one of the prisoners and I was so scared because I wondered if he'd been brought there under duress and I wondered if he was a brave man that might just suddenly blurt out something over the air that would tell the terrorists of what was going to happen. But in actual fact the terrorist, the elder of the two, the captain, grabbed the microphone, incidentally they had taken our Sabena hats by this time and were wearing them all the time – anytime anybody approached the aircraft they put on stocking masks or an ordinary mask across their face – and he grabbed the microphone and was nattering away in Arabic and he hardly gave this other chap a chance to speak at all. When he did speak, he just listened. He asked him his name and then said something else and then he put the microphone down and I said, 'Did you know him?' He said, 'No, no but that's good, it's good, it's good,' and they were very, very pleased. I later learnt that this man in fact was one of the Israeli army staff, I believe a Bedouin Arab, who must have been a very good actor indeed.

Then, the next thing that came up was that a catering van arrived in front of the aircraft and once again they were terribly jittery and they didn't allow them to come near. Another thought came to my mind now and I said, 'Look, why don't you make them put the catering down on the ground and when the mechanics come' – because I had previously persuaded them that it would be much, much quicker if our own mechanics, our own two engineers who were on board could supervise these repairs – so I said to the terrorists 'when the mechanics appear then the engineers can look to see if there's anything on them, because you know these Israelis are going to trick people if they can, they will examine all the catering first to make sure that it's all alright,' and they agreed to this. And the fact that they were agreeing to everything gave me more hope.

I thought that I ought to get *as many* people out of the cockpit as possible without making them suspicious, and the chance came when after a long, long time, they then said that the repairs were ready to be made and that the train with the wheels and ladders would be on its way. We saw them appearing and to my mind they looked exactly what they were: a squad of commandos in white overalls. Incidentally these overalls had *nothing* on them at all, they were just *white* overalls, they *did not*, as was put in some papers, have Sabena on them and they did not come under the Red Cross flag.

They had started approaching the aircraft and stopped, I would say about 400–500 metres in front of the aircraft. At that time I then said, 'Look, you need somebody outside. Let me go and see if they are all OK, and if they haven't got arms' and they agreed to this so at this time there were three of us outside the aircraft and I thought, 'Now's the time to distract people and we'll pass the food up.' So we began passing the food up. While we were passing it up I went over to the mechanics, and *even* at this time our own engineers *did not* know what was going on, but as one of them came over with me to the mechanics, I said, 'If you find anything, don't show it,' and he realised straightaway. We began searching these mechanics and finding torches and pointing them up in the air and our First Officer in the cockpit, who was in liaison with the terrorists, was putting his thumbs up to show that they had seen it and the mechanics went off shrugging their shoulders as if to say what a load of nonsense this is.

Then the train started moving towards the aircraft and I was opening boxes of tools and showing them that there were just tools inside them. Then I helped also with the food going up and I am told that this did work in fact because the girls were actually engaged in passing out drinks and food when the attack came.

From then on things happened very, very quickly indeed. I was standing under the tail of the aircraft and I moved to the front and just at that minute they opened one of the wing exits and started coming straight in. I dashed up the steps onto the wing and when they'd all gone inside I got inside too and there was firing still going on and all I wanted to find, I was coming from the rear up to the front, I was shouting, 'Dora, Dora.' As I went in, I had to step over the dead body of the younger terrorist, which was lying there in the centre position of the aircraft, but there was still firing coming from up front. I got up to the left-hand side forward of the wing which is where my wife was sitting. Actually she was down on the floor of course as was everybody, except I believe one hostess who told me afterwards, that she was at the back and she was standing up just having a good look at everything going on. When I got up to my wife's position this little girl of six was also there. She'd been with my wife and with a young Sabena hostess who was on holiday. I picked up this little girl, ran down again to the wing exit, stepped out, I *believe* I actually took her down the steps and gave her to somebody then I came back into the aircraft again.

By this time of course people were hurling themselves out, they weren't even waiting for the steps. I saw some quite elderly people just jump from the wing. I had left the flaps down so that did help a little bit and then I ran in again and was calling 'Dora,' I said, 'If you can hear me put your arm up,' because they were still down on the floor and she showed me her position. I distinctly remember a bullet whistling past my ear and then I got to her and pushed her down the aisle. By this time the firing then stopped and people were pouring out of the aircraft. I got out of the aircraft again and I was helping people down the steps if I could, in fact one woman jumped out right on top of me and then it was all over.

In no time at all the whole tarmac was swarming with commandos, paratroops, ambulances, passenger buses, and I was looking for my wife in the middle of it all and then somebody took me over to Moshe Dayan and he shook hands and said, 'You *see*, I said it would come out alright,' and I said, 'Yes.' But I wanted my wife and she'd already been put in one of the passenger buses and we got her out of it. It was just ready to move off and we got her out and took her over to see General Dayan who congratulated her and from there on you know the whole story.

It was just – nobody knew where they were going, what they were doing. I hadn't got my jacket, the aircraft was ringed off, because they didn't know if any explosives had still been left with a time device, so we couldn't go back to it, and we were taken over to the airport building where it was just chaos of course.

Incidentally, a point that I hadn't brought up was during the conference with General Dayan whilst I was allowed off the aircraft. I was informed that the following damage had been done to my aircraft by the Israelis:

- The main hydraulic drain plug was removed, so of course we lost all our hydraulic fluid.
- The left-hand number 1 auxiliary pump pressure line was disconnected at the pump as was the right-hand number 2 auxiliary pump.
- The nose gear steering pin had been removed.
- All eight landing gear wheels had been deflated by loosening the Schrader valves.
- Both the main landing gear shock struts were flat.
- The left-hand down lock canon plug had been disconnected as had been the right-hand one.
- The engine number 1 throttle cable was cut.
- The engine number 4 throttle cable was cut.
- The engine number 2 throttle cable was cut.
- And the high pressure cot cables were cut in the strut.

- Both the main wheel doors had been opened.
- 1 and 4 motor main cowlings were opened.
- The high pressure starting bottle cock had been closed.
- And the forward or the reverse thrust cables had all been cut.

So there was *no* chance of that aircraft even being moved, never mind leaving the ground!

I was told that one commando had been *under* the aircraft from fifteen minutes from when we had landed until the liberation. He was in fact the first man to jump on board. My wife said to me, 'He looked 10ft tall,' when she saw him.

In the debriefing that followed in the light of the after-knowledge, I was told that General Dayan had planned this whole thing from the start. They had *originally* intended to attack by night but decided against it and I was told that when my voice came up over the RT he looked round and grinned and said everything is going to be alright, we've got a fighter in the cockpit. And I must say that, I think the whole time, I had *no choice*. I assessed the situation straightaway that the Israelis were never going to release the prisoners so therefore we were never going to leave the ground, so the terrorists were going to blow up the plane. So the only way of saving my own skin and that of the passengers in the plane was by using *whatever* ally I could, just as England made allies with Russia in the war, the only ally that could possibly save us was the Israelis. So any help that I could give them, I *was going* to give them. I also reasoned that *any little thing*, anything would help, might help, I didn't know, but at least it had to be tried. And the main crisis when I jumped the gun, *that* was when the aircraft was going to be blown up, I couldn't believe I was alive, I still can't believe I was allowed out of the aircraft. I *still can't* believe it.

All these things, the waiting that the terrorists had to make under extreme conditions of heat by not allowing air-conditioning, not even suggesting air-conditioning, might have helped because it fatigued the terrorists. It also meant that they weren't in the positions that they would have liked to have been in because they had to guard the exits that were open. The serving of the food at the time of the mechanics coming on board, that worked too because in actual fact the two terrorist girls were actually serving food and drinks to the passengers, well one of them anyway was, as far as I know, serving drinks to the passengers when the actual attack took place.

The point about the Red Cross, and let me make this *quite* clear, the Red Cross representative, when the attack took place, was on the ground, as I was, and he was needed in the cockpit for some reason or other. I think the hijackers were getting rather jittery and wanted him up there and I could see the men getting into position on the wings and around the aircraft and I did *not* want the Red Cross man on board, and he came to me and he said, 'They need me in the cockpit for something.' Now at this time I'm sure that he guessed, I'm sure that he didn't *know*, and he was never told, as I had been, that there was going to be an attack on the plane. He obviously *guessed* but he was completely powerless. He couldn't act. He wanted to get on board that plane and I wouldn't let him. I would *not* let him get on board the plane, I did *not* want to compromise the Red Cross and I stopped him from getting on board just as the attack was going to take place. Within a matter of seconds of him asking me the attack started.

Another point, since this business, there have been many reports that there were two Red Cross representatives. *We* never saw a second one. When the Red Cross representative came into the cockpit the first time, he asked permission for a second one to accompany him and this *was* refused straightaway by the hijackers. From then on, there was no question of a second man being involved, there was only one Red Cross representative present the whole time, and he was *never* given any knowledge of the attack, did not know of it and was a completely innocent bystander in the whole affair.

There were several little side incidents that happened I am told, authentically. One of the passengers sitting in the front offered one of the hijackers money, an unlimited amount of money, if the hijacker would allow *him*, just this person and his wife, to leave the plane and the hijacker was most indignant about this. He said, 'We're not thieves,' and this was a point that they repeated to me several times. I didn't know of this at the time, I was told afterwards by the passengers around this person who overheard this. The hijackers kept stressing the point that they were *not* thieves, they were *not* after money and they were almost insulted over the whole affair. I wondered why at the time, now I know why they were in this sort of mood.

In direct contrast to this was a father of four children who was on the ground in Israel at the airport. He volunteered to get on board the plane if they would allow the only child, a young six-year-old girl who was on the plane to get off. This man said that he would take her place and *this* the hijackers refused as well.

I must say the Red Cross representative did his best, as I had done earlier, to get the hijackers to allow women and this child off the plane, and there was one man who'd had a heart attack during the negotiating period who was desperately ill. Luckily, there was a woman doctor on board and she'd said that the man must get to hospital at once, but the hijackers wouldn't allow him off the plane nor the child, who we'd all the time been trying to get off the plane. The Red Cross man asked would they allow them off and only at the last part of the negotiations, when the Israelis had told the hijackers that they'd agreed to everything, *at that time* the hijackers did say that *when* the aircraft was in front of them and they saw the prisoners being put on board, they would let this child off the aircraft.

Now this was a point I haven't mentioned – the Control Tower came up after the negotiations had been agreed by the Israelis – these were the pseudo-agreements of the Israelis. They came up and said that TWA had agreed to take the prisoners to Cairo and this was cheered by the hijackers, and that a Boeing 707 with TWA colours would be towed along the runway and put in front of our aircraft so that they could actually see the prisoners being put on board. Now this in actual fact, although many newspapers reported the fact that the aircraft *had* been towed, it never actually materialised, but nevertheless, that news was passed to the hijackers.

A small point that my wife tells me, and I don't remember this, but when I saw my wife I kissed her on the plane itself before we even got off, and a woman told us off for getting in the way.

Another point that I'd forgotten to tell is when I was allowed off the aircraft. After I had spoken to General Dayan and I was going to the Control Tower to pass on the message that the Israelis *were* acceding to the terrorists' demands, the Sabena representative passed me a little note that had been sent with the Captain of the plane that had come in, the special plane, flown by Captain Deleu who, incidentally was the husband of one of the hostesses and knew that his wife was on board. He had given me this little note just to say, from Captain Ellis, one of our English friends in Sabena, that our daughter Susan was safe and sound and was with my eldest son and his wife, and I managed to scribble a few words onto this piece of paper telling my wife that if anything happened to both of us the education of our youngest daughter had been guaranteed by the Israeli Government because I knew that from these words she would know what the situation was and also it would give her some degree of comfort.

Just to give an insight of the psychology of these people, the elder of the two hijackers, the 'captain' at one time when he was talking to this pseudo-prisoner, had the microphone in his hand, and he had it in the same hand that held his revolver. He was sitting behind me and talking. He wasn't *very, very* conversant with how to use a microphone, he didn't realise or he was *too* excited about it, that you had to take your finger *off* the button to allow the other person to speak, and he was holding it in, and he had the *one* finger on the trigger of the revolver and *one* finger on the button of the microphone and I was *terribly, terribly* worried that he would, by inadvertence, push the wrong finger and fire his revolver which was pointed at me, instead of pressing the mic! I just quietly and calmly said, 'Why don't you let me hold the revolver while you're talking,' and I held my hand out, and he *nearly* gave it to me, it was as near as that, he *nearly* gave it to me. Then he suddenly looked and smiled a little smile, shook his head and I *think* he handed the revolver to one of the girls while he went on speaking. But it was as near as that, he nearly gave me the gun just so calmly.

After I had jumped this man with the gun and it was *some time* afterwards actually, as I said I was trying to think of all the things that I could do which weren't very many, but anything, any little thing, anything, I was sitting there just looking around. I must have looked around that cockpit a thousand times, measuring distances trying to judge how near, how long it would take me to get across from one side to another or anything. And the younger of the two, who had this dangerous glint in his eye, he looked over to me and said, 'Captain, you are thinking *too* much,' and that was a horrible moment because I am sure that finger was *so* near the trigger there and then.

Another point was that in the Boeing 707, there is a little panel which is placed on the right-hand side of the First Officer's panel which shows us in the cockpit when any door is open. A little red light comes on and tells us exactly where and which door is open. I knew from observance that the hijackers had *no* idea of this and when I left the door open of the Lower 41 – I must give the First Officer credit because he saw this little light come on showing that this door was open – there is a foot bar which stretches across the cockpit where we can put our feet when we're not actually flying the aircraft. He put his foot up on the bar so that it was covered, and then later on I looked across and I noticed that he'd put a glass there with a serviette in it which completely covered this panel but I could just see through from my side, but the hijacker couldn't see or anybody in the centre of the cockpit couldn't see this panel so I was always aware, at all times, which doors, which exits, were open on the aircraft but the hijackers were not.

The First Officer was the only man in the cockpit who had any sleep. I must admit I was amazed because round about just after dawn, perhaps 7 a.m., he was lying back there in his chair and he was fast asleep and one of the hijackers was just behind him with a gun and a grenade, perhaps a foot away, no more and he was just fast asleep and he was completely calm. I couldn't sleep, I didn't *want* to sleep. I didn't want to dim my senses in any way but I take my hat off to him, he slept, and he was the only one in the cockpit that slept for any time at all. He told me afterwards that normally he regarded himself as quite a nervous sort of chap but he said that at no time was he worried. He was quite calm throughout the whole affair.

I later found out, this was a long time afterwards, when we were flying the aircraft back to Brussels, that when the attack took place, he went out through the window with the escape rope, he burnt his hands, but that was about all. But the front windscreen on his side was shattered from a bullet. We traced the trajectory of this bullet and it would have been fired by somebody coming *into* the aircraft, from underneath, because in its path it had brushed against the seat of the Flight Engineer and taken a button off so it was fired upwards. It had obviously been fired by one of the Israeli commandos coming into the aircraft and who must have seen our First Officer trying to get out and probably thought he was one of the hijackers.

We later found that our DME – our Distance Measuring Equipment – wasn't working and we looked up at the circuit brake and saw the reason why. There was a bullet in the circuit power, between the circuit brake and the actual circuit, so that must have been fired upwards also at our First Officer who had just got out of the aircraft.

The hijackers themselves had been quite conversational during the flight and had told us lots of things. They said that they knew me and they knew me well and the captain of the two said to me, 'I might even have flown with you a few times,' meaning that he had – the insinuation was in his voice. He said, 'We know that you're a very good pilot.' They had even shown us how they had taken the stock off the barrel of the pistol and then stuck it down the waist of their trousers to pass the very perfunctory security check, which they obviously thought very little of. Their guns were covered with paraffin and with talcum powder, because they were meticulous in the cleaning of these guns in front of us during the flight, there were still traces of talcum all over these pistols.

They kept stressing – they told us the stories of the atrocities that were carried out against their families, but there were so many loopholes in their stories, they didn't tally as we found out afterwards. One of the girls said that her parents had been in a concentration camp, but were still actually living in Acre, in Israel. Her father disowned her, this was afterwards of course. Her mother said how could they let a young girl like this go on a dangerous mission.

But they were quite courteous, they helped passengers with drinks, but on the other hand they were completely merciless. They would never allow anyone *off* the aircraft, they would not allow even the quite sick people off. They kept saying, 'No, we have our orders, *no one* must leave the aircraft, *no one* must leave the aircraft.' To any sort of attempt to try and transfer everybody to a serviceable aircraft – this was not even questioned, they just said 'No' straight away. At no time would they ever *leave* the aircraft, they would let *us* off the aircraft but *they* would never leave it.

EPILOGUE

By Alex L. Schiphorst

The intimidating, yet exciting undertaking of publishing my grandfather's autobiography has not always been an easy task, both on an emotional level and a practical one. Reading for the first time his manuscript was a revelation since I had only heard of some of the events he had taken part in or witnessed. I came to realise that I knew absolutely nothing of huge sections of my grandfather's life. Despite the little I appeared to know about many of his past deeds, there is a great deal I owe to him, most importantly my personal interest in history, and subsequently my decision to study the latter at university level.

Reading over his story, many memories I had of him resurfaced and I think I better understand him now, and wish so very much that I could once again talk to him and hear his voice recounting the many tales he was a part of. There are countless questions I would ask him, some of which have and perhaps can be answered by those who knew him well, but most will sadly be left unanswered. My grandfather is a piece of history within history, and I like to think that he touched, shaped, saved and made a difference, by chance, unknowingly, and even if to a small extent, to many of the events and the lives of countless people, some of whom he knew and many of whom he did not. His family is the living proof of his mark upon us and history.

In many ways he is correct in stating that the world he lived in has fundamentally changed to the one of today. It is strange to think that at the same age as I am writing this, he was training to become a bomber pilot. Despite a life that he himself describes as being glamorous at times, as well as being scarred by circumstances that are unbelievably hard to imagine, he always came across to me as an unassuming yet charismatic and brave figure, highly learned but never conceited.

Reg was of course human and had his faults and he made mistakes, which he later came to truly regret. He loved his family tremendously and was always loved by them. He was highly appreciated by people who met him and my memories of him are always good ones and I was deeply fond of him. Reg was extremely forgiving, and infinitely proud of every one of us, children, grandchildren and great-grandchildren. He was amiable with everyone, and never said a bad word about anybody. Furthermore, he treated everyone, whatever their rank or position, colour or creed, with the same respect and cordiality. He was extremely open-minded and never judgemental.

I used to love visiting him and Dora – or Nana as we used to call her. He really went out of his way to make things special for his grandchildren. We would be served the very simple, if slightly odd breakfast of sausages and sliced cucumber placed all around the plate. It would seem that unusual breakfasts were not all that uncommon. Other grandchildren recall tinned spaghetti or steak being served! He would then take us up the White Cliffs of Dover where we would visit the castle and walk along the small paths overlooking the Channel. He had such a vivid imagination, something I believe I inherited from him, and we would constantly make up stories wherever we went. I recall convincing him to dress up in different costumes and poses in order for me to complete my handmade Top Trumps cards. I'm quite sure he ended up thoroughly enjoying it!

Reg had a good sense of humour, usually very witty. Feeka recalls him standing by her side at the entrance to the church on her wedding day. He was ready to walk her down the aisle, patiently waiting for the indispensable, 'Here Comes the Bride', which for some reason the organist forgot to play. After a seemingly long and nervous wait, Reg said to her, 'Oh bugger it, let's go,' making her giggle and walk down the aisle with a big grin on her face.

I am of course aware that his children and many grandchildren, as well as friends and other people who met him all have different memories of the man he was but I am equally sure that they would all highlight the same qualities and describe him as I have done.

Reg was a very talented individual. He could sing, was adept at playing musical instruments, even teaching himself to play the ukulele at the age of eighty-six. He was a member of the Royal Brussels Cricket Club and the Brussels English Comedy Club many years ago and would often direct sketches with singing and dancing for their annual parties. He was also a capable sportsman, whether it was water skiing, football, table tennis, cricket, golf or ice skating. As I have already mentioned, he was a highly knowledgeable man and he read extensively, and was interested in everything that he came across.

Dora's death on 29 June 2005 was a huge shock to him. Loneliness hit him hard, having lost his partner of 62 years.

He always spoke of her as a very courageous lady and reading over old love letters he kept from during the war I realised just how much they loved each other. He recalled people ceaselessly repeating how glad they had been to have known Dora. In a short story he wrote to us grandchildren, he said: 'I got a medal but it was Nana and women like Nana who deserved the medals and praise for their courage and the heartbreak they suffered.'

Reg and Dora's relationship wasn't always smooth, but reading through my grandfather's notes, old letters, and looking at photos I know they never ceased to love each other. Every year, without fail, he would buy Dora flowers on 30 May, little Roy's birthday, he was never forgotten. Nana used to constantly invent wonderful expressions, nicknames, and words which Reg tried to make a list of, and which he rapidly dubbed, 'Nanesian'. Amongst them were strange ones such as 'pot on you' (which I still use today), 'see you air crack', and 'shoomps'. 'It's one o'clock in China', meaning someone's zipper is undone is yet another expression whose origin remains unknown.

A great turning point after her death, which certainly helped him overcome his grief to some extent, was buying a computer and becoming computer literate. His decision to finally purchase one was triggered when my mother called him one day and made him listen to his own voice in a live news report of the storming of the plane in 1972 featured on a YouTube video. He realised how interesting it would be to have a computer and access to the Internet, and with the precious help of his good friend Andy Langridge set one up after following a computer course in Dover. Although he took to it like a duck takes to water, Andy would often get a call from Reg saying, 'My icon has disappeared from my desktop,' Andy would say to him, 'Reg if you can land a 747 then this is easy by comparison.' He would then try to help him remotely, when suddenly Reg would say, 'It's come back, bye!'

He made a lot of friends and contacts through professional pilot forums. He also began to play aviation computer games, enjoyed his flight simulator, book Channel Tunnel travel, and shop online. It was a decision that truly changed his life despite already being over eighty-six years old!

On a blog thread dated 16 February 2010, he wrote: 'I am happy that these threads are being of interest to you all and have increased my circle of friends enormously since I started. It seems incredible that I have only been «Computerwise» since just over a year ago and have my beloved family, especially my daughter, Feeka, to thank for wearing me down as I steadily refused to learn until I was over eighty-six. I can thoroughly recommend it as a therapeutic approach to old age.'

In the following pages I will endeavour to continue to tell the story of my grandfather whose memoirs were sadly left unfinished. In order to maintain people's anonymity and privacy, I have in some instances changed the names of individuals mentioned in Reg's manuscript.

The twenty-eight years after he retired from Sabena were far from monotonous, and he continued leading an exciting and interesting life, never steering far astray from the world of aviation. Basing the narrative on my own personal memory, that of other family members and friends, photographs, logbooks, voice recordings, and notes he left behind, I will attempt to finish the story he began. I believe he would have wanted this and that seeing his story published would indeed have made him very happy as it is something he wanted to do and was so close to achieving just before he passed away.

Reg's last flight, with Dora on board, took place on 26–27 September 1981. It took him from Brussels to New York, then on to Detroit via Montreal, returning to Brussels the following day. It was a highly moving one. A celebratory party was organised in the hotel followed by dinner in Ann Arbor. As it was his last flight, custom had it that the Captain choose his own crew. Talking to crew members about Reg's last flight they recall being very honoured and thrilled to have been chosen. They emphasised over and over again how humorous he was, witty, gentlemanly and professional. His crew bought him some aptly renamed special bottles of champagne representing key years of his life. Notably a 'Wings Clicquot' of 1941, the year he received his wings in Georgia; 'Crystal Dora' for his wedding year of 1943; an 'Indian Perrier', a 'Cuvée Speciale Levy' of 1952, the year he joined Sabena; two bottles of a 1972 Israeli vintage for twice going to the Control Tower and back, aptly named 'Lod Perignon' and 'Moët & Dayan'; and finally a 'Royal Reginald' to celebrate the end of his career in 1981. One stewardess recalls Reg having composed a song which he sang for the crew, and at the restaurant, when she admired the tulip-shaped glasses, he asked the restaurant if he could buy some and presented her with six glasses.

On landing in Brussels, family, friends, previous crew members, many of whom had been on board at the time of the hijacking nine years before, watched and applauded him from the tarmac as he brought his 'Queen of the Skies' to a halt.

Feeka recalls the emotional impact of watching him coming down the steps of the last aircraft he would ever fly. Another celebratory reception was organised with his family, crew and friends at the Sabena clubhouse. He kept the dozens of kind retirement messages and cards he received from friends, colleagues and airport staff in different countries he had flown to.

Flying was his whole life and he took great pride in bringing his plane and passengers to their destination with a smooth landing, even in times of great stress. Proof of this passion is the grand total of flying hours he reached – 25,097 hours and thirty minutes logged in his logbooks – and his interest in where he stood in the 'League Tables' of flying hours. His love of flying and aeroplanes was one that stuck his entire life, as doodles found in his childhood books, or the many aircraft models and paintings in his flat in Dover demonstrate. Reg remained fascinated by the best aircraft he had ever flown and time and time again spoke about the 747, the 'Queen of the Skies' and what a wonderful aeroplane it was to fly.

All matters concerning aircraft and the world of flying always drew Reg's attention and he wrote to the *Montreal Star* two years before his retirement concerning the growing confrontational subject of Canada's air traffic language dispute.

Reg and Dora decided, at the end of 1982, to move back to the UK. They returned to Brynn Street in St Helens where they only stayed for about a year, and most of this was in fact spent travelling abroad, especially to South Africa. They would spend two or three months each year there, visiting old friends and playing golf. The following year they returned to Belgium, buying a flat, which they promptly named 'the penthouse suite' in Middelkerke. They had wanted to have easy access to the UK but also be near their grandchildren. They loved to entertain them during school holidays, treating them to rides on the famous coastal 'Cuistax' even though it was sometimes quite difficult to keep up with them as the children would speed off along the promenade leaving Reg yelling his head off to get them to turn back. Dora would then take them to the local tea room for huge Belgian waffles or 'Dame Blanche' ice creams.

In the early 1990s, Reg and Dora, along with family, visited the Coronation Street Theme Park at the Granada Studios in Manchester and, according to photographs, enjoyed every minute of it. Reg and Dora were particularly fond of the television show and made the best of the event before the theme park closed in 2001.

They celebrated their golden wedding anniversary in 1993 at the RAF Club in London. The reunion was highly memorable for all those concerned and saw, as the guest of honour, Dora's best friend Jackie, who had been her bridesmaid fifty years before.

Reg and Dora were once again invited to Israel in September 1993, this time as guests to participate in the famous Israeli television programme, *This Is Your Life*, with Ehud Barak as special guest. It was a very moving moment for them, and Dora took this opportunity to hug Barak to whom she felt especially grateful as she remembered him, as a young man, leading the Israeli Special Forces when they stormed the hijacked plane and liberated the passengers. They would return to Israel on 22 September 2003, when invited, amongst 400 honoured guests, including Heads of State such as President Clinton, F.W. de Klerk, Mikhail Gorbachev, as well as other celebrities, notably Bono, to Shimon Peres' eightieth birthday. Reg recalls Bill Clinton stealing the show by jumping on stage and playing the guitar whilst singing John Lennon's 'Imagine'. I still today possess a small drum that was given to the invitees, passed on to me by Reg.

In 1993, my family moved to Italy and Reg and Dora decided to leave Middelkerke and buy a flat in Dover, just the other side of the Channel. Dora was keen on this change, mentioning that she was looking forward to finally being able to speak to her neighbours as she had never learnt French, let alone Flemish.

They used to enjoy driving down to visit us by Lake Maggiore. They often came for Christmas, joining in the Italian Christmas traditions of the lovely village we lived in. March was a favourite time to visit, due to my older sister's and my birthdays. In March

1994, Reg and Dora drove down to Italy for my birth. After realising that they had forgotten a suitcase in Dover containing presents for my sister and baby items for me, Reg, who was seventy-two, decided to drive all the way back to Dover, slept a couple of hours and was back in Italy by the time I was born!

In 1995 Reg and Dora took part in a Hovercraft excursion to the South Goodwin Sands organised by the Dover Society. The hovercraft company used to run annual trips out to the Goodwin Sands for various clubs and societies, some of the latter would often turn up in various fancy-dress costumes. The excursions used to be planned in June when the tides and daylight time amongst other factors were the most suitable. Reg used to be fascinated by the hovercraft, which he could see around the port from his flat window in Dover.

The fiftieth anniversary of the Berlin Airlift in 1998 saw Reg return to Berlin, invited as one of the many veterans of the huge operation to supply the city with food and fuel. Separate documents, written by Reg but not part of the manuscript, were found, and I think it is only appropriate if this event is retold by him:

There exists a British Berlin Airlift Association, but I had been out of England for over forty years as I flew as Captain with Sabena, the Belgian Airline, until I retired so knew nothing about this. I contacted the German Embassy in London and was pleased to receive two invitations for myself and my wife to join 300 other 'Veterans of the Luftbrücke' for three days in Berlin. The organisation responsible for this was called 'Stiftung Luftbrückendank' or the 'Airlift Gratitude Foundation'. This organisation was founded in 1959 when, in response to an appeal by Mayor Willy Brandt, the people of Berlin donated over DM 16 million. This money was used to set up the Airlift Gratitude Foundation and has helped more than sixty British and American families of the ninety-three victims of the Airlift. In addition, the Foundation gives financial assistance to young people from the US, UK and France who are studying at one of Berlin's universities.

We caught the BA 06.55 flight to Berlin from Heathrow on 26 June. This was our fifty-fifth wedding anniversary. We landed at the same aerodrome, Tegel, where I had landed so many times in 1949 but, of course, it was unrecognisable. A modern terminal greeted us and we were taxied on concrete taxiways instead of the PSP steel mesh of a long time ago. There were two or three other 'veterans' easily recognisable by the big Association badges which they sported but there was some confusion as there was no representative to meet us, only taxi drivers who were employed by the Association and who had been told to take us to our requested destination. We were told that the main body of the guests were arriving on a later, mid-morning flight. I had been told in my invitation that we were booked in at the Forum Hotel so we went directly there. Despite having landed at Tegel during the Airlift well over 200 times and also having 'visited' Berlin, courtesy of Bomber Command, several times in 1943, I had never actually been to Berlin itself and it was a wonderful experience to see the well-known names such as Tiergarten, Unter den Linden and to actually pass by the Brandenburg Gate and see where the infamous Berlin Wall had stood.

The hotel was a most imposing new skyscraper standing in the old Eastern Zone of the city. We were given a very nice room on the thirtieth floor so we changed and then I went down to the lobby to find out what was going on. The receptionist told us that we were the first to check in and that the others would not be checking in until the evening. So I asked her to get through to someone who was with the Airlift Foundation, which she eventually did and we were told to get into a taxi (paid for by the Foundation!) and go immediately to Gatow airport where the ceremonies had already started.

Once again we were lucky in having a knowledgeable taxi driver. It was a long drive to Gatow which took us through Spandau, famous for its machine guns of the First World War and for the notorious prison where Rudolf Hess languished until his death. It has now been demolished.

We arrived at Gatow which was in the British Sector and was an RAF base until recently. The RAF was there in force together with the representatives of the US and French forces. The Luftwaffe and

German Army bands joined that of the RAF and a moving ceremony followed when a memorial stone to the memory of those who gave their lives during the Airlift was unveiled. One of the workhorses of the Airlift, the DC3, or the Dakota as we called it in Britain, was presented to the city of Berlin by the US Air Force. A Dakota had been flying overhead and later flew over Berlin, duplicating the wonderful idea of Lieutenant Halvorsen of the US Air Force who was better known as the 'Candy Bomber'. He begged, borrowed and cajoled US manufacturers to supply him with chocolates and sweets which his crew released under tiny handkerchief parachutes on the approach to Tempelhof Airport. Hundreds of children used to gather there during the long winter of 1948–49 and were heartened by showers of sweets which symbolised hope to them. Colonel Halvorsen was one of the nine people to be presented with the prestigious Eric-M. Warburg Prize at a ceremony, held later that day, in the magnificent Concert Hall of Berlin. At this ceremony, attended by the Chancellor, Helmut Kohl, representatives of the participants in the Airlift were honoured including officers from the US Air Force, the French Armée de l'Air, the Royal Australian Air Force, the Royal New Zealand Air Force, the Royal Air Force, the Royal South African Air Force and the Royal Canadian Air Force, all of whom had sent crews to help out the overburdened RAF.

We had missed the buffet lunch at Gatow, which had been put on for everyone but were there for the speeches by the Mayor of Berlin and Generals of the German Army and Luftwaffe. It was noticeable that the two German military dignitaries switched easily from German to fluent English so we were proud of our Defence Minister, George Robertson, who followed up his excellent reply in English by switching to what sounded, to us at least, like very good German.

It was into the waiting buses again in mid-afternoon and we were taken directly to the magnificent 'Konzerthaus' in the centre of the city. There an audience of over 1,500 people applauded the Airlift Veterans as we took our seats in the centre and front of the wonderful auditorium. The architecture and decor of the interior were staggering. The stage was taken up by the large orchestra of the Luftwaffe and high above them and facing the auditorium were ranged the choirs of the United States Air Force and the Kaiserslautern Children's and Youth community. A nostalgic film of the Airlift followed on a giant screen erected over the orchestra. It was amazing to see the many types of aircraft used on the airlift. The giant Globemaster was used occasionally but the ubiquitous DC3 had been replaced quickly with the C54, or Skymaster, which carried four times the load. Hastings, Yorks, Lancastrians, Halifaxes and Tudors were all used and the RAF Flying boats, the Sunderlands, were used for carrying salt as they were the only aircraft capable of withstanding corrosive action of the main cargo. They landed on the Wannsee on the Havel River and played an important part in the 'Lift'.

The Chancellor of the Federal Republic, Helmut Kohl, was present to enjoy the wonderful concert and the many speeches which followed. The main theme that was constantly brought out was the very real gratitude of the Berliners to the Allies for the magnificent effort in the dark days of 1948-49 that alleviated the hunger, cold and suffering in a bomb and shell devastated city. Although the certain reality of a Third World War was averted, this was the birth of the Cold War.

After the concert we were surprised to find a magnificent champagne reception awaiting us in the ante-rooms of the theatre. This lasted for about an hour and then we were asked to go to the buses again for an open air concert followed by a dinner at the Hilton Hotel. I am afraid that this was too much for many of us. Our average age must have been well into the seventies and most of us had travelled all night or stayed overnight in London to catch the plane out on Friday 26 June so many of us missed what, we were told, was yet another wonderful piece of hospitality.

Whilst talking to many of the German civilians who attended the reception we were amazed to find the ignorance of conditions in England after the war. They assumed that, as victors, we had speedily reverted to the normal conditions of peacetime and were almost disbelieving when we told them that stringent rationing was still in force as late as 1952–53 and that Britain had been virtually bankrupted by the war. We also met the Vice Chairman of the Board of Governors of the United States Postal Service who had chosen, that day, to issue a commemorative stamp to honour the Airlift. We received lovely little replicas of the stamp in the form of a brooch showing a C54 landing at Tempelhof watched by German civilians. He expressed surprise that the British had not done likewise and I told him that one of the chief organisers and participants, Air Vice Marshal Sir Nigel Maynard had actually been writing to the Prime Minister, Tony Blair, on that subject when he had suffered a heart attack and, sadly, died.

After a good night's sleep and a great breakfast in the hotel's lovely buffet restaurant we all gathered in the lobby and walked to the nearby 'Rathaus' or Berlin's Town Hall for yet another reception and lunch hosted by the indefatigable organiser of the visit, Herr Heinz Gerhard Reese. Although I say 'nearby', the walk was a very long and painful one for many of us and the sight of an imposing staircase, red-carpeted, about 20ft wide and with about fifty steps confronting us as we entered the building was the last straw for some very weary and, by now, aptly named 'Veterans'. Eventually a lift was found but too late for a large number of us who just about made it to the top where a very welcome drink was waiting and then a great lunch in the enormous dining room where, we were told, the Queen had dined when she was the only Head of State to visit a part of the Communist Zone after the war.

The big event of the day, Saturday, was the opening of the Allied Airlift Museum and buses were waiting, after the lunch, to take us on our way. Seated across the aisle, in the bus, was Lady Bennett, the widow of Sir Donald Bennett, the Pathfinder Chief and one of Britain's finest airmen. He had started a company, BSAA, and had brought his aircraft, Avro Tudors, to the Airlift. I was amused to hear an American sitting opposite her enquire, 'Was your husband some kind of Pilot?' She answered quite tactfully but I wonder what Don would have said!

Whilst we were waiting in the buses to assemble for the long procession behind the massed bands of the three Allied Forces to the Airlift Museum, at the end of the very long 'Clay Allee', named after the General Lucius Clay, the heavens opened and the poor bandsmen were soaked by the torrential rain. It did not seem to dampen their *spirits nor those of the hundreds of German citizens of Berlin lining the route, applauding us and mouthing 'thank you' as we passed. Happily the rain stopped and we were able to get out of the buses and march behind the RAF band for the last mile or so to the museum. This was, undoubtedly, the most emotional part of the whole three days as we were so near to the spectators that we could see that many of them were in tears and could hear the cries of 'thank you' as we marched, perhaps not in step, but certainly together.*

The opening of the museum was very well organised. We were seated under awnings close to a huge Hastings presented to the museum by the RAF. We were provided with receivers which gave instant translations to the various speeches which followed. An unusual note was the appearance of a well-known German cartoonist who made a sketch of the speechmaker, as he spoke, on a large sheet of paper which could be seen by all the audience. George Robertson, our Defence Minister, aptly remarked that he would bet that if the Airlift had not taken place, a Communist cartoonist would not have been there making public cartoons to the speakers. When he saw his own picture he remarked that perhaps the cartoonist should have been banned anyway!

Champagne duly made its appearance but the heavens opened again so the visit to the museum itself was put off and we made our way back to the hotel where we just had time to dry off.

Reg continued, whilst living in Dover, to attend 'Brussels reunions' which were organised in different parts of the UK, during which people who had previously lived in Brussels would meet up. He also attended Bomber Command reunions, 51 Squadron Association reunions, as well as the Arnold Scheme Association reunions. In 2006, Reg presented an oil painting of a Halifax to the squadron association which is now placed in their collection of Second World War memorabilia. The associations organised various autograph signing events to which Reg participated, notably at the home of the Mosquito at Salisbury Hall near St Albans, and at Hatfield. Reg in a blog thread wrote about his experience during one such event:

I had never attended one of these signing sessions before and was amazed at the enthusiastic numbers that attended. We were about thirty Veterans all looking about the same and most of us in regulation blazer with a loud jangling that accompanied every step from the rows of medals that were hanging from various points on the body.

It was well organised but I was not prepared for the queues that were everlasting. I must say that the vast majority of people that were presenting us with everything from pieces of paper to toilet roll paper that had come from the seat where some famous name had sat – unused, I hasten to add! – were very polite, enthusiastic and very, very grateful to us for coming, and most of them would add, 'And thank you for what you did,' or words to that effect. One chap had brought a piece of the engine that his father had kept after he had crashed in a Mosquito and also a special pen that would write on the metal.

There were, however, some wonderful paintings and drawings that I had never seen before. There was one book that I thumbed through and was quite emotionally touched when I came across the picture, in a group, of the Navigator, Sergeant Les Hogan, from Southport, who had been my Navigator on the ops that I had done at Marham in 1942. He had stayed on Mossies when I went on to heavies and had been killed very soon afterwards. I was amazed to get a confirmation from Amazon when I ordered the book, with a personal note saying that the Amazon employee that had handled the order was a certain lady with a Polish surname whose father had been a member of 105 Squadron, and she would very much like to know my connection. They enclosed an address and I have replied furnishing what details I could and, genuinely, praising the many Polish airmen that I had met and had only the greatest admiration for their bravery in combat, which surpassed anything that we had known. But then we had not been invaded and occupied since 1066. There had been at least one incident where a Pole had rammed a German bomber when his ammunition had been exhausted rather than let it escape.

To go back to the signing. We were taken by coach to a very lovely nearby pub and given a very good meal with one of the best red wines

I have tasted for a long time. It was a shame that a few of us who were driving had to ration ourselves to one glass. Then it was back to the grindstone and, at a rough guess, I reckon that I finished by signing my name about 400 times. Yes, there were one or two obvious dealers who had about five or six identical prints and the same spiel, 'for some friends' but I was agreeably surprised by the amount of really young people in their twenties and thirties who were present. A surprising amount of children too and, wonderfully, very, very polite and grateful. There is hope for us yet. I felt humble when I heard the chap next to me telling one of them that he had been over Berlin twenty-seven times during his tour with Mossies laying target indicators for the main stream to aim upon. Twenty-seven times! I had been six times and once was already enough.

Although I remember my grandfather having retold the story of the hijacking I never fully realised the scars it left, both on him and other family members. I later found out that the 9/11 attacks in 2001 brought back a lot of unpleasant memories of terrorism and the events of 1972. Reg wrote in a blog thread over forty years after the hijacking that the events had 'left an indelible scar upon my life and the life of my family and I pay homage to the people of all faiths who suffered'.

For many of those who had to deal with the hijacking and its consequences, Reg included, the trying event has in some cases often been treated as a taboo subject. Perhaps with the publishing of the story, and for the first time solely in Reg's own words, will scars begin to heal.

Sabena's bankruptcy in November 2001 was a blow to the 10,000 pilots, workers, technicians and other personnel still employed by the airline company as well as those that had left beforehand. Reg wrote a letter shortly after the bankruptcy which he strongly condemned and saw as being 'caused by the shocking financial misbehaviour of Swissair'. The letter was published in several Belgian newspapers, the *Bulletin* (the English weekly magazine published in Belgium), as well as old pilots associations. Below are Reg's published words concerning the insolvency of Sabena:

As a pilot who had the honour of flying with Sabena for thirty years my heart goes out to all the betrayed personnel of this splendid company.

I was one of some thirty British pilots welcomed to Sabena in 1952 when it became apparent that Belgium could not supply enough pilots for the rapidly expanding company. The Belgian pilots agreed to the plan but insisted that the pilots engaged should be British. This was because of the bonds that had been formed by numerous Belgian pilots, who performed magnificently, with the RAF during World War Two.

I used the word 'welcomed' because that is exactly how it was. We felt that we had joined a family and not a commercial concern. We were treated exactly the same as a Belgian national, never asked to change our nationality (and remember that this was years before the 'Common Market'). Promotion was given entirely on seniority irrespective of nationality as long as the qualifications were met. The language was never a problem, in fact it was hard to learn French or Flemish because our attempts were always met with English as a reply.

Sabena took care of us medically and that included our families. In my early days the Medical Service was led by the revered Dr Allard who was greatly valued as a consultant by the American Space Program. It was quite common to encounter him at one of the very fine restaurants in Brussels entertaining all his medical staff. When one of my young daughters came down with appendicitis it was Dr Allard who made all the arrangements, operated on her personally and made sure that she had the very best care.

I had considerable experience in the flying world before joining Sabena yet the high standard of technical knowledge and skill of the flying personnel and maintenance constantly amazed me.

Belgium was fortunate in having one of the finest airlines in the world and it should be mourning its demise as I, and countless others, are doing.

I can only hope that the people responsible for this debacle will be brought to justice but, somehow, I do not think that this will happen.

Thank you, Belgium and Belgians, for thirty wonderful years whilst flying with Sabena.

Thank you, Sabena, for the wonderful comradeship and your support during all those eventful years.

Responses to his letter, many grateful for having expressed their feelings so well at a time when their, 'pride and ideals have been severely damaged' also acknowledged how essential and effective it proved that British pilots were recruited by Sabena. Without them, Sabena could not possibly have been reborn after the Second World War.

The *Jerusalem Post* published in October 2007 news that the pilot's cap that Reg had worn during the 1972 hijacking had been found and returned to his daughter Linda after thirty-five years.

Back in 1999, Reg had been able to meet Louis Blériot's grandson, also named Louis during the ninetieth celebration of Blériot's famous first crossing of the Channel in 1909. In July 2009, Reg was invited to the 100th Anniversary of Louis Blériot's crossing, as well as to the ball held in Dover Castle notably because of his status as an ex-RAF pilot. This was organised by the Dover Council which Reg helped through his fluency in French. He was interviewed in Dover by ITV *Countrywise*, linked to the Blériot celebration, where he expressed the overwhelming feeling of relief he and other pilots felt when returning from low-level daylight raids, seeing the cliffs rise ahead of them and finally being able to pull up and fly over the white cliffs; an indescribable moment he imagined Blériot must also have experienced.

After discovering a pilot's forum online and making many new friends realising, 'what a wonderful comradeship this forum has fostered', he wrote an interesting paragraph concerning the writing of his memoirs, a task he had just begun. He especially had things to say about the war:

I think that there were a few reasons why people didn't put down their post-war careers and experiences. For probably the majority the post-war was a complete anti-climax and to many, a vast disappointment. A lot of them had escaped from a mundane existence and found the war an exciting and wonderful change. I know that my father, who was thirty-nine when the war broke out and was commissioned as an RAF Signals Officer, spent most of his career overseas and had the best time of his life. The other side of it was the terrible trauma experienced by those less fortunate who had been taken prisoner by ruthless enemies and subjected to inhuman treatment. The disfigured, the terribly wounded and the people who were simply traumatised by what was happening to them. None of these could be expected to put their thoughts on paper. Richard Hillary's The Last Enemy *is a difficult read but outstanding exception. As an example of what must have been going on in the minds of thousands was the response to one simple advertisement in* The Aeroplane *or* Flight *magazines by Sabena in the early part of 1952. They wanted thirty pilots and did not require Civil licences. The response was overwhelming and numbered well over 1,200. Of the thirty that were taken on, I was the only one to have a current 'B' Licence as it was called then. Virtually all the others were ex-RAF pilots back in peace time jobs and seeking to get back to a more exciting life. The lack of the need to have the outstanding ticket to a civil airline career was too tempting to many of them 'stuck' in soul-destroying jobs. Another reason, I think, was the difficulty in getting any sort of memoir published as the demand to read about other people's experiences was low. Such a demand would have to wait another twenty years by which time another generation had grown and wanted to know what their fathers had been doing. Now it is the grandchildren's turn and this has brought the further demand of the post-war experiences but the survivors are all around my age, eighty-eight in two months' time, and possibly the main reason: very few of us are interested or well enough to get down to putting it into words by this medium.*

In later years, when in Dover mainly, he became increasingly concerned with his health. On 1 August 2010 Reg passed away; losing the battle against the enemy he had always feared – cancer.

News of his death went round the world with a particularly well-written article by the Aviation Obituaries writer for *The Daily Telegraph*. Passengers who had been on board the hijacked plane called to express their sympathy and gratitude for his heroism and professionalism. Another ex-Sabena Captain wrote that Reg was, 'truly the man for the situation' and that he 'could think of no other Captain being able to deal with such a situation as the hijacking'. When carrying out research for the book, I was privileged to be able to speak to a crew member who was aboard the hijacked plane, and I noted how again she stressed that had Reg not been the pilot of that aircraft at that moment, the outcome would have been a lot worse. Condolence messages highlighted again how much of a gentleman he was, as well as a brave and remarkable man. When researching for the book, my mother was able to get in touch with many of his friends and previous crew members and noted how they all reminisced about the wonderful times they had together but also his absolute professionalism at all times. Many of them mentioned his children and even his grandchildren, clearly showing how often he spoke about them.

His friend Andy arranged to have a Stearman, the first plane Reg had ever flown, fly over the crematorium the day of his funeral. It was an uplifting and very emotional moment that I will never forget. It felt to me, and I believe to most of us gathered together that day, that it was my grandfather flying a final time over us before slowly disappearing into the skies.

Below is a poem which was read out at a Memorial Service dedicated to Reg which was held in Brussels. The service was attended by family and many friends from Brussels as well as many Sabena staff.

Dear Friends,
As some of you already know,
It's almost time for me to go.
I loved my job, I did my best,
But now I'll give my wings a rest.

'Cos since no one forever flies,
To younger men I leave the skies…
To all the boys who stuck by me,
And gave me so much sympathy.
I'll miss you, in all honesty.
To all the girls I met before,
Who never once knocked on my door,
Well, they were right, because I snore…
Forty years, it's not so bad,
But still it makes me kind of sad,
To leave you all and say goodbye,
It seems to make my mouth go dry…
So there is one more thing you can do,
To make me feel we were a crew,
Come have a drink and hold my hand,
On that final day when I shall land.
Courtesy of Johnny Belpamme, Chief Steward, Sabena

Shortly before he passed away, Reg wrote:

> *I make no apologies for dropping names. I found more pleasure from meeting people that I had never dreamed of meeting, some of them boyhood heroes, than dropping bombs. Another side of meeting them was to make me realise that they were, after all, ordinary human beings with good and bad sides to them and they woke me up to the fact that I was as capable as they were in my own sphere of activity. Meeting with certain types boosted my own self confidence.*
>
> *I thank God every day for my good luck in being able to do most of these things and pay homage to all those far worse off and those who are no longer here but who did so much to make it possible.*
> *C'est la vie and I am the last one to moan, having had such a wonderful life,*
>
> *Reg.*

TYPES OF AIRCRAFT AND ACRONYMS

BOEING STEARMAN PT 17
(10 June 1941)
VULTEE BT 13A
N.A. HARVARD (AT6)
AIRSPEED OXFORD
BRISTOL BLENHEIM I
BRISTOL BLENHEIM IV
BRISTOL BISLEY
D.H. MOSQUITO IV
D.H. MOSQUITO II
MILES MASTER
D.H.TIGER MOTH
BOEING B17 (FLYING FORTRESS)
DOUGLAS BOSTON IIIA
JUNKERS 88 (Captured German)
N.A. MITCHELL
HANDLEY PAGE HALIFAX II SERIES 1A
H.P. HALIFAX III
BRISTOL BEAUFIGHTER
AVRO ANSON
VICKERS WELLINGTON
AVRO LANCASTER I
AVRO LANCASTER III
BUCKER
BRISTOL BUCKMASTER
VICKERS MARINE
  SPITFIRE IX
GLOSTER METEOR

PERCIVAL PRENTICE
(prototype)
MILES MARTINET (prototype)
VICKERS VIKING (prototype)
DOUGLAS DC3 (DAKOTA)
AVRO YORK
D.H. RAPIDE (DH89)
CHIPMUNK
PERCIVAL PROCTOR V
LOCKHEED
CONSTELLATION
AVRO LANCASTRIAN
CONVAIR 240
CONVAIR 340
CONVAIR 440
DOUGLAS DC4
DOUGLAS DC6
DOUGLAS DC7C
BOEING 707
DOUGLAS DC10
BOEING 747 SERIES 200
TWO GLIDERS: KIRBY KITE
& KIRBY CADET
BRISTOL BRITANNIA PIPER
J-3 CUB
CARAVELLE
D.H.COMET
CARVAIR
D.H. HERON
VICKERS VC 10

HAWKER SIDDELEY TRIDENT   *VICKERS VISCOUNT*
DOUGLAS D.C. 8   *BEECHCRAFT BARON*
DOUGLAS D.C. 9   *BEECHCRAFT BONANZA*
BOEING 727   *BEECHCRAFT KING AIR*
BAC 1-11   *BOEING 737*

AC2	Aircraftman Second Class
ATC	Air Traffic Controller
AT6	Advanced Trainer aircraft
BAF	British Armed Forces
BAOR	British Army of the Rhine
BCIS	Bomber Command Instructors School
BEA	British European Airways
BOAC	British Overseas Airways Corporation
BSA	The Birmingham Small Arms Company Limited
BSAA	British South American Airways
BA	British Airways
BAOR	British Army of the Rhine
BBC	British Broadcasting Corporation
BF	Belgian Francs
CFI	Certified Flight Instructor
CV	Curriculum Vitae
DFC	Distinguished Flying Cross
DGA	Directorate of General Aviation
DSO	Distinguished Service Order
DM	Deutsche Mark
DME	Distance Measuring Equipment
EFS	Empire Flying School
EMI	Electrical and Musical Industries
ENSA	Entertainments National Service Association
FA	Football Association
FAA	Fleet Air Arm
GCA	Ground Controlled Approach
GMT	Greenwich Mean Time
G2	Holder of a free ticket (Sabena) Gratuit (category 2)

HQ	Headquarters
IFR	Instrument Flight Rules
ITW	Initial Training Wing
LAC	Leading Aircraftsman
MCA	Ministry of Civil Aviation
MT	Motor Transport section of the RAF
NAAFI	Navy, Army and Air Force Institutes
OC	Officer Commanding
OTU	Operational Training Units
Op – ops	Operation(s)
PA system	Public Address system
PA	Personal Assistant
PLO	Palestinian Liberation Organisation
PT 17 Stearman	Primary Training aircraft
PT	Physical Training
PSP	Perforated Steel Planking
RAF	Royal Air Force
RAFA	Royal Air Force Association
RAFVR	Royal Air Force Volunteer Reserve
RCAF	Royal Canadian Air Force
RSM	Regimental Sergeant Major
R/T	Radio transmitter/telephony
SABENA	Société Anonyme Belge d'Exploitation de Navigation Aérienne
UK	United Kingdom
US	United States
USO	United Service Organizations
u/s	unserviceable
u/t	under training
V sign	Victory sign
VC	Victoria Cross
VIP	Very Important Person
V-1	German weapon known as the flying bomb
V-2	German weapon known as the rocket
VCR	Video Cassette Recording
VHF	Very High Frequency
WAAF	Woman's Auxiliary Air Force

ACKNOWLEDGEMENTS

I would like to express my gratitude to the people who helped me edit, read, write and who offered me endless support and comments regarding my grandfather's autobiography and the epilogue to his unfinished story.

I wish to thank above all my mother, Feeka, without whom this book would never have been finished and published. She was truly the backbone to getting the book done and provided me with endless remarks and comments and assisted in the editing and proofreading. My thank you here will never be enough to give her the proper homage she deserves.

A great thank you also goes to my whole family, my auntie Linda and my uncle Peter, who assisted me with information, lent me material, and helped deal with administrative matters.

My most sincere thanks also go out to ex-Sabena crew members for their valuable help in contacting and identifying fellow staff, planes, routes and places, as well as for their many anecdotes which enabled me to complete the Epilogue.

I wish to express my gratitude to the many people who accepted to have their names or names of loved ones mentioned in the book, for their enthusiasm, best wishes and further encouragement for the publication of Reg's memoirs.

Lastly, I would like to thank Shaun Barrington, our publisher, for his enthusiasm and for believing in the book. His words 'read enough, I want to publish' will forever remain engraved in my memory.

Alex L. Schiphorst, 2015

INDEX

Visit our website and discover thousands of other History Press books.

www.thehistorypress.co.uk